I know Monica through her long ass   ⎯l
Randolph, who for many years ran the training course for mediators at
Regent's University London. I was also taught by her when I attended
the course in 2004 and became aware then – as did my fellow students,
as well as those before and since – of her very considerable expertise in
educating and communicating to students of mediation the essential
skills and techniques (which are often counter-intuitive) required.

Monica's book is a welcome mix of the current theoretical background
to the various methodologies of mediation that have evolved in recent
years and the practical application of mediation techniques, which are still
not sufficiently understood or appreciated. As with RUL's mediation
course, which trained so many of us, a psychological insight into conflict
and its causes gives mediators a distinct advantage when called upon to
help resolve disputes, no matter where or how they originate.

Paul was always frustrated that it was taking so long for the benefits of
mediation, as an efficient, effective, and economical conflict resolving tool,
to be properly recognised and understood; Monica's book will help to
rectify this and go a long way to enabling people to understand how and
why it works, in a way which does not require lengthy study of the under-
lying existential philosophical concepts.

– **Karen Randolph**, Community Mediator,
Local Councillor, Mediator

I highly recommend this well-structured book that moves from the different forms of mediation and co-mediation to the process of psychologically informed mediation in practice.

What makes this book stand out is how the case studies have been written. The context of each tale of conflict is different, but they all read like
short stories with realistic endings. These case studies give the reader
a picture of how multi-layered and complex conflict is, and how the psychological existential approach in mediation works in practice.

– **Diana Mitchell**, Mediator, Trainer, Psychotherapist

Monica Hanaway has positioned herself at the forefront of existential
leadership, mediation, and conflict resolution training, cultivating
a wholly unique approach from a psychological perspective. There are
precious few with such breadth of experience, and this radiates through
her latest work. Monica clearly explores the various mediation techniques and styles, before providing distinct examples to wholly understand the novel dynamic of this paradigm. This book is essential for
practitioners wishing to gain insight into dealing with complex situations,
but also managers, advocates, counsellors – anyone who encounters

conflict and finds themselves wondering what they might have done differently to achieve a favourable outcome.

> – **Marni Alexander**, MA, MBACP, UKCP, MPED, Mediator,
> Company Director, Clinical Director at QRDC Ltd.

Everyone experiences conflict at times. Dealing with conflict is an important skill in business. This is a very accessible book which introduces the reader to a psychological approach to resolving disputes, and then shows through case studies exactly how this understanding and the skills described can be used in practical ways to resolve conflicts.

It is of interest to mediators but also to leaders and managers, as well as the general reader, as we all face conflict situations.

> – **Mirjam Buyteweg**, IFRS, the International Financial Reporting
> Standards Foundation, London

No doubt the most thorough and engaging book on mediation on the market. Monica Hanaway offers an engaging deep-dive into best practices in conflict resolution across a range of case studies reminiscent of both Yalom's academic work and his tales of psychotherapy, combined in a single book. A must read for all mediators and trainees, as well as a vital resource for those who find themselves in a dispute eager to resolve it as amicably as possible.

> – **Yannick Jacob**, Mediator, Existential Coach (MA), Positive Psychologist
> (MSc), Coach Trainer and Supervisor (FMR Programme Leader MSc
> Coaching Psychology), Mediator (conflict resolution) and author of
> *An Introduction to Existential Coaching*

Monica Hanaway's latest book brings a refreshingly new approach to the study of mediation and conflict resolution. Drawing on her extensive psychotherapeutic experience, Monica has developed an outstanding series of case studies that bring conflict to life and deftly illustrate the many different facets and nuances that can aid a psychologically informed mediator to navigate the way to a successful resolution.

> – **Spencer Hilliard**, Mediator, Barrister, and Chair of the
> Bar Council ADR Panel

A good story is an extremely effective way to illuminate theoretical principles. In this book, Monica Hanaway offers not just theory but a collection of studies that support and clarify the proposals she outlines for successful mediation and conflict resolution. An enlightening read.

> – **Karen Weixel-Dixon**, Mediator, author of *Interpersonal Conflict: An
> Existential Psychotherapeutic and Practical Model*

And when you think you know almost everything about mediation, you get this book and realise that only now does the real study begin. Monica puts the right accents and perfectly explains complex mediation terms. Those who assumed that mediation is rational, and that psychology doesn't matter, will think twice after reading Monica's book. A terrific, excellent, perfectly structured book on the most important psychology issues in mediation. A book I was waiting for and that I'll recommend to my colleagues, students, and clients.

> **– Dana Rone**, Advocate at law, Acc. Mediator, Member of the
> Disciplinary Commission of Sworn Advocates in Latvia, Member of
> Certification and Attestation Commission of Mediators in Latvia,
> Docent: Turiba University, Riga

Monica's existential psychological approach provides an interesting and valuable new way to approach the challenges of conflict resolution. This new book shows through a theoretical exploration and practical case examples how this philosophical approach can be used effectively in mediation.

> **– Ulla Zumente-Steele**, Erasmus Institutional Coordinator Riga
> School of Law, and Student Counsellor

Monica has run trainings in Bucharest, bringing her existential approach to business, coaching, and conflict resolution. She details this approach in her new book, *Psychologically Informed Mediation: Studies in Conflict and Resolution*. The book introduces the core concepts of the existential psychological approach and uses practical case studies to show how this approach can be used in mediation. It shows that through effective, mindful dialogue, focused on existential concerns, conflicts can be resolved in a way which is meaningful to all participants.

> **– Madalina Calcun**, Mediator, Department for Open Government
> and Civil Society, Bucharest

I have attended a number of advanced trainings Monica Hanaway has delivered in Bucharest, and in this book she encapsulates much of that training, demonstrating how to bring a philosophical approach into resolving conflict. Using her understanding of conflict can help to reduce the number of conflicts, but should conflicts occur, as they inevitably will, she offers existentially informed introductions to conflict coaching and mediation, and backs these with informative case examples.

> **– Mugur Mitroi**, President of Mediation Council of Romania

This book allows others to access Monica's knowledge as she takes the reader through the theory and practice of psychologically informed mediation and then goes on to demonstrate these, in a practical and thorough manner, through the analysed studies which make up the second part of the book.

– **Susan Blum**, Coach, Consultant, and Mediator

Monica Hanaway is one of the country's leading exponents of psychologically informed mediation. In this book, Monica sets out her approach clearly and backs it up with case studies drawn from her own experience. You see how theory and practice fit together. I recommend it to everyone who wants to learn to solve problems in a 21st century manner.

– **Felix Spender**, FInstLM, Former Soldier, International Negotiator, and SME Business Leader

Monica introduces the reader to different styles of mediation and introduces us to her specific existential psychological approach. In the second part of the book she offers several case studies, which use theory to demonstrate in a very practical way how the psychological approach is used. The psychological skills she shows are of value in dealing with all disputes, be they international or domestic, family or corporate.

– **Yossi Mekelberg**, International Relations and Social Sciences Programme Director, Faculty of Humanities, Arts & Social Sciences, Regent's University London

A really good read and so informative and interesting. It gives an excellent introduction to what mediation is and the different styles used. It is full of useful case studies, which use and explain the role of mediation in each case. Well worth reading by anyone who has been or is in a conflict situation and incredibly useful for those who may want to go further in mediation, whether as a client or as a trainee mediator. Thoroughly recommended.

– **Judy Brown**, Director of EDSA (Education for Democracy in South Africa)

This is a wonderful read. In addition to explaining the process of mediation and the styles and theories used, Monica has taken the complexities of multi-dimensional relationships and has written clear narratives on each person's perspective of the dilemma. She then explains her chosen method of mediation based upon solidly researched principles, making sense of why she does what she does, making for very satisfying reading. Anyone who is interested in therapy, mediation, or counselling should read this book. It is also a page turner for the reader who, like myself, is fascinated by people and what makes us tick. I'd rate this as a five star book, and I hope it reaches a wide audience.

– **Hilary Wainer**, Music Therapist, Founder and Director of
TacPac (Communication Through Touch and Music)

Monica's approach demonstrates the extraordinary parallels between existential phenomenology and the African philosophy and tool of ubuntu, lived and promulgated by Desmond Tutu and indeed Nelson Mandela. This book explains in detail what mediation is and gives an insight into Monica's psychological approach. The studies in the second half of the book show in a very real way how this approach is used.

– **Clive Conway**, Chair of the Tutu Foundation UK
(Patron Archbishop Desmond Tutu, Honorary Patron FW de Klerk)

Monica illustrates the powers of the existential psychological approach through brilliant writing and real-life examples. I would encourage anyone to buy this book as a resource and reference to those who are in, or who have a desire to be successful in, a leadership role where they will undoubtedly be faced with conflict situations.

– **Chris Corbin**, Head of Customer Service, First Central
Insurance and Technology Group

Likely one of the most experienced and diverse mediators in the industry, I take delight in posting this endorsement of Monica Hanaway's new book studying the various methods of mediation and conflict resolution, expertly linking these (through meaningful case studies) to impactful and relevant psychological thought.

– **Kelli Wilks**, CMC Accredited Mediator, Founder, Compass
Mediation Group, Negotiation Strategist, and Trainer for
SMEs and start-ups

Psychologically Informed Mediation

Psychologically Informed Mediation explores the understanding of conflict and the use of a psychologically informed mediation approach to help resolve it.

The book has two distinct parts; it starts with looking at our understanding of conflict, and challenges the more negative views, placing conflict as essential for dynamic development. It then describes the process of mediation and looks at several different models. The author draws on existential and phenomenological philosophy and psychology, and shows how they can enable a mediator to facilitate a meaningful resolution of conflict. The second part of the book offers eight dramatised case studies to illustrate the psychological and relational nature of conflict, giving detailed analysis of the mediation process using supportive theoretical material where relevant.

This book offers a unique approach to mediation, and is accessible to a broad audience.

Monica Hanaway is an executive and leadership coach, business consultant, mediator, psychotherapist, and trainer. She has authored *The Existential Leader, An Existential Approach to Leadership Challenges,* and *Handbook of Existential Coaching Practice.* She is passionate in her mission to bring existential thought beyond the academic arena into the business and wider world, believing it has much to offer in these uncertain times.

Psychologically Informed Mediation

Studies in Conflict and Resolution

Monica Hanaway

Routledge
Taylor & Francis Group

LONDON AND NEW YORK

First published 2021
by Routledge
2 Park Square, Milton Park, Abingdon, Oxon OX14 4RN

and by Routledge
52 Vanderbilt Avenue, New York, NY 10017

Routledge is an imprint of the Taylor & Francis Group, an informa business

© 2021 Monica Hanaway

British Library Cataloguing-in-Publication Data
A catalogue record for this book is available from the British Library

Library of Congress Cataloging-in-Publication Data
A catalog record has been requested for this book

ISBN: 978-0-367-52001-4 (hbk)
ISBN: 978-0-367-51999-5 (pbk)
ISBN: 978-1-003-05599-0 (ebk)

Typeset in Baskerville
by Swales & Willis, Exeter, Devon, UK

In memory of
Paul Randolph
1947–2019
Mediator, colleague, and friend

Contents

Acknowledgements   xv
Foreword   xvi

PART I
Understanding conflict and the role of
psychologically informed mediation   **1**

1 What is conflict?   3

2 What is mediation?   9

3 Different mediation styles   12

4 The mediation process   21

5 Co-mediation   27

6 The relevance of psychological, existential, and
   phenomenological thought to mediation practice   40

7 The psychological ebb and flow within the mediation
   process   55

PART II
Studies in conflict and resolution   **63**

8 Introduction to the studies   65

9   Mother and daughters: a family mediation   68

10 Fear and difference: a workplace mediation   89

11 Competition and challenge: a workplace relationship
     mediation   108

12 Disharmony: a musical mediation   131

13 Desires and drives: a marital mediation   148

14 Access: a family mediation   161

15 Love and hate: a workplace relationship mediation   178

16 Hyperventilating: a school based work mediation   190

17 Warring cousins: global family business mediation   206

     Conclusion   220

     Appendix   224
     Glossary   229
     Bibliography   237
     Index   241

Acknowledgements

I wish to thank my husband and my daughters, who remain patient and supportive of me in all my endeavours; my colleagues on the mediation training courses, particularly Diana Mitchell, Karen Weixel-Dixon, and the late Paul Randolph; and all the course students, each of whom taught me something new.

Foreword

I often skip the foreword in books, looking for the meatier content, and then return to it at the end. That probably tells you something about my impatience to move on once my interest has been captured, and also my dislike of structures, and desire to make my own mind up about things.

This book had an earlier incarnation (Hanaway, 2014) in which the studies were the focus. In this text the studies are set within a more detailed description of what mediation is and how to approach it from a psychologically informed direction.

For those of you wanting to read studies of actual conflicts and how they were worked with in mediation, please feel free to move on quickly to the studies of dramatic or more ordinary events in others' lives, where you can journey with the characters as the dramas unfold and see the protagonists move on their way towards some kind of resolution. The studies are based on conflicts I have mediated, but elements have been combined, names and genders changed, and other aspects fictionalised so as not to be recognisable whilst staying true to the essential narrative.

I am starting, not with these unique human dramas, but by giving a short background to conflict and to the use of psychologically informed mediation as a tool to enable those in conflict to move towards a resolution of the dispute which works for them, and is in line with their values. This may be of interest to those of you considering using mediation to resolve a conflict of your own within your workplace or family, or to those of you perhaps considering training as a mediator. I hope it may also be of more general interest and that like me some of you may have found your way to this foreword having first read the studies.

Conflict is the stuff of existence. We cannot go through life without conflicts. For many of us these will be minor conflicts, easily sorted, yet for others conflicts can take up many months, even years, and be life changing – for better or worse. In fiction, authors know conflict creates tension and interest, and encourages the reader to stay with the disputants' narratives, hoping to see the outcome revealed, the nature of which often remains in doubt until the end. Even a non-resolution creates a closure of sorts, with the reader left wondering what happens to the characters after they close the book. In life, conflict is usually experienced as negative and very challenging, and a sense that an event does not have a clear ending is often very uncomfortable. Although it is rare for a conflict to end in a 'happily ever after' situation, the exploration of the conflict marks an end to at least one phase of the journey, and we can learn a lot along the way.

In literature, as in life, conflict can be internal or external, it can occur within the mind of an individual, or between different characters and exterior forces. There may be multiple points of conflict as we may have more than one desire, or may struggle against more than one opposing force. Conflicts may resolve at any point, particularly where more than one conflict exists, but there will always be some instances where the conflict is not resolved. A mediator working psychologically will work with both the external narrative and the internal individually experienced perception of the dispute.

All mediators bring their own experiences, values, and philosophies into their mediation work. The main influence in my own practice is existential and phenomenological thought and practice. Although they may be seen as rather abstract, they provide a very real framework for a mediation practice which is grounded in understanding the worldviews of others and enabling people to identify and own their choices and their decisions.

Part I

Understanding conflict and the role of psychologically informed mediation

1	What is conflict?	3
2	What is mediation?	9
3	Different mediation styles	12
4	The mediation process	21
5	Co-mediation	27
6	The relevance of psychological, existential, and phenomenological thought to mediation practice	40
7	The psychological ebb and flow within the mediation process	55

1 What is conflict?

We all experience conflict, so a good place to start in considering what we understand by conflict is by reflecting on our individual response. Give a minute to consider your immediate reaction to the word 'conflict'. It is likely that you will have an emotional response, for example, you may feel afraid, angry, excited. You may have an embodied reaction e.g. temperature change, 'butterflies in the stomach', etc. Few people have a neutral response to conflict. When reading this chapter, it is worth holding in mind what conflict means to you, what feelings the word evokes and indeed your immediate unreflective reaction to finding yourself in a conflict situation.

Let us start by looking briefly at how some people have written about 'conflict'. In 2009 Encarta defined it as a

> continued struggle or battle ... open warfare between opposing forces; disagreement or clash between ideas, principles, people; a psychological state resulting from the often unconscious opposition between simultaneous but incompatible desires, needs, drives, or impulses; opposition between characters or forces in a literacy work

whilst Wikipedia offers a more political definition, describing it as an 'ongoing state of hostility between two groups of people' and separates this from individual conflict, 'when two or more parties, with perceived incompatible goals, seek to undermine each other's goal-seeking capability'. I am particularly drawn to this definition, as in speaking of '*perceived* incompatible goals' it introduces the understanding that conflicts are not about facts but about perception. I shall write more of that later.

Some writers have drawn a critical distinction between short-term disputes and long-term conflicts. Shantz (1987:285) defined conflicts as, '"time-distributed social episodes" consisting of a series of discrete components that include issues, oppositions, resolutions, and outcomes' and

Burton (1990) distinguishes between conflict and dispute by time and by the issues involved. Interestingly, he characterises conflict and dispute differently, speaking of short-term disputes which he sees as relatively easy to resolve, and long-term conflicts which may contain seemingly resistant non-negotiable issues involving moral or value differences, vulnerability of ego state, and domination of one party, in addition to more concrete material matters.

People often remain in conflict for years. It can even get to the point where the original dispute is forgotten or no longer relevant, and yet the process, with the almost inevitable attacks on each party, fires the dispute further, so the primary objective moves from the original issue of contention of 'facts' and 'rightness' to the need to 'beat' the other person and be declared 'the winner'.

Costantino and Merchant (1996) also agree with the separation of the terms conflict and dispute, defining conflict as fundamental disagreement between two parties, of which conciliation, conflict avoidance, capitulation, or dispute are possible outcomes. This supports Yarn's statement (1999:115) that 'a conflict can exist without a dispute, but a dispute cannot exist without a conflict'. Yarn saw conflict as a state, rather than a process, involving people with opposing values or needs being in a state of conflict, which may be latent or manifest, and may develop into a dispute.

It is this psychological approach, with its emphasis on unearthing the value systems, emotional language, and worldviews of disputants whilst seeking to preserve or enhance self-esteem through working with the fundamental human psychological needs for identity, security, and recognition, which Strasser and Randolph (2004:27) have developed in their approach to mediation. They see these elements as present in both disputes and conflicts: 'One of the most important elements is the exploration of the covert reasons for the dispute, as well as the overt. The parties will have developed rigid belief systems as their overall strategy for survival in an uncertain world'. It is my belief that conflicts become entrenched for psychological reasons. If one believes that this is the case then there is little point in focusing on what each party insists are the 'facts' of the case, as they are only ever the perceptions of one individual.

Totton (2006:30) looks at conflict within a psychotherapeutic context, and suggests that the debate on conflict has focused on questions of aggression, asking, 'Is aggression an innate human trait, or is it the product of specific conditions? Is aggression wholly negative, or does it have positive aspects and expressions? Can therapy contribute either to minimising aggression or to supporting its positive aspects?' I would suggest that conflict is as much about self-defence as it may be about aggression. If we try to minimise aggression, or any emotion in trying to solve a conflict, we are missing the point. Some people will experience or demonstrate 'aggression' where others will define similar feelings as 'passion' and express them from that understanding. There is a danger that these two emotions may become confused, or misunderstood by a third party.

Freud (1930:111) believed aggression to be innate and dangerous:

> men are not gentle creatures who want to be loved ... they are, on the contrary, creatures among whose instinctual endowments are to be reckoned a powerful share of aggressiveness ... In consequence of this primary mutual hostility of human beings, civilized society is perpetually threatened with disintegration

However, Reich (1973:186) disagreed, seeing human beings as essentially possessing 'natural decency, spontaneous honesty, mute and complete feelings of love', and seeing aggression as 'the life expression of the musculature, or the system of movement' (ibid). Suttie (1936) built on Reich's work, claiming that hate and destructiveness were secondary reactions to threatened primal love, and Melanie Klein based her theoretical approach on an innate conflict between love and hate, which was dealt with by projecting one's destructiveness into others and adopting the depressive position to address the task of reparation.

For many therapists, aggression and conflict are essential parts of our internal human nature. Samuels (1993:198) took a political stance, seeing aggression as lying at the heart of a pluralistic approach to politics, 'often masking the deepest need for contact, dialogue, playback, affirmation'. Here we see a more positive approach, in which conflict is accepted as a precursor or even a necessary component to growth and change. This is reflected in the work of scholars such as Mindell (1995:241) with his clarion cry of, 'Value trouble. Accept nature. Make peace with war' and Totton's (2006:36) clarification of therapy's key contributions to this area: 'affirm aggression, support conflict, speak up for competition – while also affirming, supporting and speaking up for the victims of alienated and destructive expressions of these qualities'.

When I initially read these statements, I felt uncomfortable, and had to consider what they were asking of me as a mediator. I came to understand that they called on me to respect an individual's emotional response to their experience of a dispute. If I considered their reaction to be out of proportion in any way, then I was not understanding the client. To try to 'calm things down' or ask for politeness undermined their experience, demonstrated by lack of understanding, and/or my fear of emotional expression, and was therefore fundamentally disrespectful.

Given that we can never be without conflict, it is an essential element to our lives and to the development and survival of the species. If there is no conflict, there is little incentive to move from the status quo; conflict can bring challenge and creativity into the mix.

It is not surprising, therefore, that conflict provides a constant theme through much of literature and film. It is impossible to define the number of basic plots. However, Foster-Harris (1981:30) claims that all plots stem from conflict. He describes this in terms of what the main character feels: 'I have an inner conflict of emotions, feelings … What, in any case, can I do to resolve the inner problems?' This is also true of life. It is vital that a mediator acknowledges that conflict is focused on an internal emotional struggle more than it is on external 'facts'. Foster-Harris argues that there are only three main plots, all based on conflict. These are generally identified as: 'man against man', which is an external conflict in which characters are set against each other, and which may be overt, as in a physical fight, or more subtle, involving the conflicting desires as found in a romance or family epic. There is also 'man against nature', where man is in conflict with the elements, such as the sea or a storm, or against an animal. Finally, there is 'man against self', comprising an internal conflict, in which a character overcomes his own nature or insecurities and self-doubt to make a choice between two or more paths – good and evil; logic and emotion.

As we can see from this, conflict is relational. It may focus on a relation with another person or group of people, on an intra-psychic relationship within a person, or even on our relationship with our environment or objects within it. This dynamic is central in approaching the resolution of conflict from a psychological understanding. The philosopher and writer Ayn Rand (2000) argued that man against nature is not a conflict, because nature has no free will, and thus cannot make choices. There may be truth in this, yet we have a psychological reaction in the way we relate to nature. We are experiencing this very clearly at this point in our history, with Extinction Rebellion and climate change deniers in opposition. The issue of free will and choice is important in any conflict, as we shall see.

It has also been suggested that there is a fourth basic conflict: 'man against society', where man stands against a man-made institution (such as slavery or bullying); 'man against man' conflict may shade into 'man against society'. In such stories characters are forced to make moral choices, or are frustrated by social rules in meeting their own goals. My apologies for the gender based terminology in these lists, which reflects the time in which they were written; needless to say, all genders experience conflict.

We can find these plots in life, as well as in fiction, but it is important to remember that each conflict is unique to those involved in it and is experienced through the individual's filters of context, culture, values, experience, and beliefs, and is always relational. By noting these elements, it immediately becomes clear that the resolution of conflict does not rely on logic. If disputes were logical, there would be no conflict, as there would be only one 'logical' solution, obvious to all. Conflicts become entrenched because they are not logical but emotional. People 'hang on' to a conflict and can become obsessed with it because it threatens something deep within them. It questions their perspective on themselves, life, and the cosmos, and so is deeply unsettling. It is of little use bringing a logic-led approach to resolving conflict if conflict is essentially emotional.

Before we can mediate effectively we need to understand our own intuitive and emotional reaction to conflict. People react differently to conflict situations. Some people enjoy it, liking the adrenaline buzz. Some may even provoke conflict, as it can make them feel powerful. Others fear it, go numb in the face of it, run from it, or try to ignore it. In the face of conflict, we are inclined to try to defend our self-esteem and to hold on to our beliefs without considering why they are not the beliefs of others. These are all psychological responses.

Conflict is always psychological. There would be no conflict if the event hadn't distressed us in some way. If conflicts were logical, people would calmly sit down and agree a rational answer based on what would be considered the only logical outcome. The truth is, conflicts are never logical; they are emotionally driven, and accompanied by a need to protect our dignity and self-esteem. We want to be proved right, and we want our opponents to be told they are wrong. In truth, we all experience events differently, and so being proved 'right' is an idealised goal.

There may be no universal 'right' within the dispute; what we think we saw, heard, and experienced may differ, and so our reactions to shared events will differ too. It is not the event in itself which is conflictual, but our emotional and psychological response to it. Whatever happened happened. The narratives about what happened can never really be 'the facts', but can only ever be about different perceptions of the same event. Each person creates their own set of 'facts', which they are invested in believing are 'the truth'. It does not benefit the mediator to spend a great deal of time trying to establish the 'truth' of the events, as they 'exist' only in the past. The past cannot be changed. All that can be changed are the resulting perceptions and attitudes. Understanding and exploring the nature and meaning of these perceptions is part of the mediation process and will enable the mediator to understand what will be important in any resolution.

In the next chapter I propose that psychologically informed mediation provides a way of incorporating all the above aspects in the conflict resolution process. So, mediation holds a greater chance of arriving at a resolution which is meaningful to each party, taking account of the individuals' need for self-esteem and for potential solutions which remain in tune with their values. If the mediation succeeds in achieving such an agreement, it is more likely to be adhered to than a solution which is offered by a third party, and focuses on an evaluation of facts and logic, rather than on emotions and values. Firstly, we need to consider what mediation is and look at some of the different approaches to mediation that are currently in use.

2 What is mediation?

There are many excellent books which detail the process of mediation, including some which go into great discussion about important, but very detailed, parts of the process, such as how to seat people during the mediation. These aspects of mediation can indeed be important. Participants in mediations may read a lot into who the mediator speaks to first, where each party is invited to sit, whose hand is shaken for the longest time, and who appears to get most time in private sessions. These are all vital psychological factors that a mediator needs to be aware of, but for readers who may not be familiar with the process, and are wanting a more macro introductory view, I shall start be giving a brief, general overview of what mediation is understood to be.

Mediation is regarded as a form of 'alternative dispute resolution' through which a neutral third party assists those in dispute to work towards their own settlement. The process is becoming widely accepted as effective in a variety of disputes such as family, community, commercial, legal, diplomatic, and workplace. The success rate is high, with the CEDR's (Centre of Effective Dispute Resolution) 2018–2019 survey reporting a success rate of 89%, with the majority of mediations completed within one day. It is much cheaper than legal alternatives, and in the workplace CEDR has estimated that mediation saves businesses around £3 billion in wasted management time, damaged relationships, lost productivity, and legal fees. Unlike court proceedings, it offers confidentiality; the only exceptions usually involve child abuse, actual or threatened criminal, violent, or dangerous acts, or concealment of proceeds of crimes. Mediation allows for a bespoke service based on an agreed framework, and encourages creative thinking, working towards a meaningful resolution tailored to the needs of those in dispute.

One of the main reasons people choose mediation over typical litigation is their concern to maintain an important relationship with the person on the other side. The process is more cooperative and collaborative, and so provides an excellent choice for those disputes where people will need to maintain a relationship after the mediation e.g. family, business partners, co-parents, neighbours, work colleagues, etc. It is equally effective in those disputes where the parties may never need to be in touch with each other following the mediation.

When I first trained as a mediator, I was one of only two students on the course who was not a solicitor or a barrister. I came to mediation through my work as a psychotherapist. For many people, mediation is still seen as part of the legal process, and they may expect mediators to also be lawyers.

Lawyers have argued that as mediation settlement agreements are legal documents, mediators do need to be legally trained. This is not the case. Most agreements call on common sense, rather than legal know-ledge, to ensure that they are workable. If there are legal concerns, then a lawyer can look over the agreement and write it up for court if need be. It is understandable that the legal profession may see mediation as competition. However, many disputants in mediation choose to be accompanied by their legal representatives. If a lawyer is able to please a client by introducing them to mediation, and the process is successful, it reflects well on the lawyer. The late Paul Randolph, a well known mediator and barrister, and much missed colleague, would explain jok-ingly how he needed to explain to lawyers that ADR, the alternative name for mediation, stood for Alternative Dispute Resolution and not for an Alarming Drop in Revenue.

It is often the case that lawyers find the transition to becoming medi-ators more difficult than some other professions. Disputes may have legal and logical elements, but they are always emotional. Lawyers are not trained to place emotions in the foreground. Legal training equips lawyers to be adversarial rather than collaborative. They are well trained to ask closed questions, which aim to back the client into a corner with only a yes or no answer possible. Also, lawyers are told never to ask questions to which they don't know the answer; for mediators this nar-rows down the potential for creative resolution. In many ways legal skills are the opposite of mediation skills.

Another challenge for lawyers working as mediators is the require-ment for mediators to be neutral. This is contrary to legal training, in which lawyers are taught to be strong advocates for one side i.e. 'their side'. In most mediation models it is not the role of the mediator to evaluate the strength of one side's agreement against the other. A mediator is not a judge. It is the role of the mediator to follow what they are told by each party, and not to decide what would be the best solution. What might look like a good solution to the mediator may not fit with the values and needs of the parties. It is not unusual for claim-ants to leave court with what their legal team considers to be a good settlement, only to feel very dissatisfied with the result because it does not meet their needs. This should never happen in mediation.

Men, mainly from legal professions, dominated early mediation courses, but there has been a shift, with the genders more equally repre-sented, and the backgrounds of those in training also more varied. One of the most impressive mediation students I taught was a dry cleaner. She had found the details of the course in the pocket of a suit she was cleaning for a barrister. She was experienced in communicating with people from many different backgrounds, and demonstrated her strong interpersonal skills during her training. She is now working very success-fully as a community mediator.

A good mediator needs to understand people's worldviews, and how to work with emotions. They must be able to make all parties feel safe. With diverse groups looking to mediate a wide range of disputes, the time is now ripe to extend diversity within the profession. Without a sense of safety and trust in the mediator, people may not feel able to express them-selves emotionally and fully, gain further understanding of their own think-ing and positions, and understand a little of the other person's view. In arguments, when feeling under pressure, people often get into 'fight, flight, or freeze' mode. They are emotional and can get angry, afraid, or even shut down completely. When people are upset or shut down, no amount of logic or knowledge of law is going to help. A psychological understand-ing of how people react to conflict is more important.

So it is not surprising that in the 20 years since I qualified as a mediator the backgrounds of those training to be mediators has become more diverse. There are still plenty of people with a legal background, but increasingly business people, HR professionals, community workers, psych-ologists, teachers, youth workers, health workers, police, and people with no previous professional background are training as mediators.

3 Different mediation styles

There are different styles and structural frameworks for mediation. All of the main approaches are valid, offering their own unique pros and cons. They can be grouped into two main approaches: facilitative/transformative or evaluative. Facilitative and transformative approaches are often believed to help empower participants to take responsibility for the resolution of the dispute, while evaluative mediation helps parties understand their legal position. In reality, experienced mediators will probably use a combination of these styles depending on their individual approach, as well as the specifics of the case, and parties involved. I follow with a brief overview of the most common approaches.

Facilitative mediation

Facilitative mediation is considered by many people to be the original mediation approach. The approach grew up in America in the era of volunteer dispute resolution centres, in which the volunteer mediators were not required to have substantive expertise concerning the area of the dispute, and where it was usual for there to be no lawyers present. The volunteer mediators came from all backgrounds.

In the 1960s and 1970s it was the most common type of mediation being taught and practiced. In facilitative mediation, rather than making recommendations or imposing a decision, the mediator facilitates a process in which each party's deeper interests are explored, with the aim of assisting the parties in reaching their own voluntary and mutually agreeable resolution. The mediator does not offer their own views or advice, but helps to validate and normalise the parties' points of view, searches for the emotional and other interests which may lie underneath the factual positions taken by parties, and assists the parties in finding and analysing options for resolution. The mediator is in charge of the process, while the parties are in charge of the content and the outcome.

Facilitative mediators seek to ensure that parties come to agreements based on information and understanding. They predominantly hold joint sessions with all parties present so that the parties can hear each other's points of view, but may also hold individual sessions. If lawyers are present a facilitative mediator will want the parties to have the major influence on decisions made, rather than the legal representatives.

Compulsory or court-mandated mediation

The Civil Justice Council (CJC) in England's 2018 report on ADR and Civil Justice recognised that voluntary mediation processes have low uptake, and, therefore, some level of mandatory mediation process was seen to be the best way of increasing people turning to mediation. There are inherent problems with this, as a cornerstone of mediation practice lies in it being a consensual voluntary process and many mediators do not support any change in its voluntary nature. Having said this, many workplace mediations are not entirely voluntary. It would be very hard for an employee to refuse to go to mediation when their employer was paying for it, and was insisting they attend.

Concerns have been raised that mediation prevents parties from gaining access to their right to trial. This is not the case. Paul Randolph (2013) reported Lord Phillips, the former lord chief justice, as refuting these contentions at a Delhi conference in 2008, stating that it merely briefly delays the progress to court and does not remove any right to trial. Indeed, it aims to reduce the considerable expense of litigation and the amount of time it takes to pursue a legal pathway, with all the accompanying emotional upheaval.

Courts are under a duty to actively manage cases to further that objective. Civil Procedure Rule 1.4(2)(e) expressly states that that duty includes 'encouraging the parties to use an alternative dispute resolution procedure if the court considers that appropriate and facilitating the use of such procedure'. Often, the court will be willing to pause proceedings to enable a mediation to take place, and sometimes it may explicitly order the parties to take part in some form of ADR. The CPR pre-action protocols also require the parties to consider ADR, including mediation, or risk an adverse costs order being made against them. The directions questionnaire (a court form which must be filed in most cases) specifically requires legal representatives to confirm that they have explained to their client the need to try to settle, the options available to do so, and the possibility of costs sanctions if they refuse to try to settle.

If the parties are forced to use mediation it is less likely to succeed. The CJC 2018 report strongly advocated the greater promotion of ADR and mediation but did not support the introduction of compulsory ADR or mediation. Any parties to litigation which are not willing to participate in mediation must be prepared to explain to the court why mediation is not suitable for their case in order to justify that decision, particularly when the court considers which party should pay the costs of the litigation.

Evaluative mediation

Evaluative mediation emerged in court-mandated or court-referred mediation and is modelled on settlement conferences as held by judges. Generally lawyers will work with the court to choose the mediator, and are active participants in the mediation.

The approach aims to help parties to reach resolution by pointing out the weaknesses of their cases, predicting what a judge or jury would be likely to do if the dispute went to court. It could be said that evaluative mediators are primarily concerned with the legal rights of the parties rather than needs and interests, and make their evaluation based on legal concepts of fairness.

It stands in contrast to facilitative mediation, as in the evaluative approach the mediator has a much greater part to play in determining the outcome of the mediation and their primary focus is to reach a quick deal rather than to allow much space for the party's narrative. They will usually have little interest in the emotional aspects of the disputant's experience. The evaluative mediator may make formal or informal recommendations and suggestions and express their personal opinions to each party. They will certainly point out what they consider to be the legal merits of their arguments and make fairness determinations.

Evaluative mediators usually employ a series of separate meetings with the parties and their legal representatives, often referred to as 'shuttle diplomacy' or 'shuttle mediation'. During these sessions the mediator helps the parties and any legal representatives to evaluate their legal position and to examine the costs vs. the benefits of pursuing a legal resolution rather than settling in mediation. The parties are present in the mediation, but the mediator may meet with the lawyers alone as well as with the parties and their legal representatives. The evaluative mediator structures the process, and directly influences the outcome of the mediation.

There is an assumption in evaluative mediation that the mediator will have substantive expertise or legal expertise in the area of the dispute. This, and the connection between evaluative mediation and the courts, plus the assumption that mediators from a legal background will be more comfortable with drawing up a settlement, results in most evaluative mediators coming from a legal or subject specific background.

Transformative mediation

Transformative mediation is a relatively new approach based on the concept that the two parties' relationship may be transformed during the mediation process. It was introduced as the newest of three mediation approaches in Baruch, Bush and Folger (1994).

Transformative mediation looks at conflict as a crisis in communication. It focuses on the values of empowerment, and like facilitative mediation also aims to empower the parties to come to their own resolution, based on their increased understanding of each other's needs, interests, values, and points of view. At its most ambitious, the process aims to transform the parties and their relationship through the process of acquiring the skills they need to make constructive change. Sometimes this is couched as helping each side find a way of empathically relating to each other. In this approach the mediator too has to find an empathic way of relating to all parties, even the most difficult.

When speaking of empathy I am not talking about being sympathetic or caring, but about having the ability to connect with the emotional experience of another person. Perhaps a better term than 'empathy' would be 'emotional dwelling'. This carries a greater sense of dynamism in that it is active and emotionally engaged. Emotional dwelling requires a person to cultivate the capacity to enter into another person's reality without losing one's own. Atwood and Stolorow (2016:1) describe 'dwelling' as not merely seeking

> to understand the other's emotional world from the other's perspective. One does that, but much more. In dwelling ... and exploring human nature and human existence, one leans into the other's experience and participates in it, with the aid of one's own analogous experiences.

Freud (1909), in his case study of Little Hans, offers a similar idea in which we approach another's experiences through a kind of floating, open attentiveness, free from assumptions, or goals.

Once the mediator establishes the trusting working alliance by demonstrating empathic listening/emotional dwelling, the transformational focus is more on material and psychological needs than on wants, and importance is placed on safe-guarding the self-esteem of all parties. The aim is to find a 'good enough' solution with both parties feeling they have benefited from the process, not just from the outcome. The mediation should not end with the parties feeling that one is a winner and the other a loser, but that both have moved, both have given something, and both received something.

In the transformative mediation process, mediators usually meet with parties together in the belief that only they can give each other 'recognition' and so believe that it is more effective to keep them together. However, parties may also be encouraged to structure the mediation process, and although the mediator will have a suggested framework from which to work this does not have to be rigidly stuck to if it is not working for the parties. In this approach the parties are always the leaders and the mediator follows in this way making it very different from the evaluative approach.

Med-Arb

Med-Arb is a blend of mediation and arbitration features.

Contrary to traditional mediation practice, parties normally agree at the outset of a Med-Arb process that the outcome will be binding. The parties then attempt to negotiate a resolution through the help of a mediator. The usefulness of having such a written agreement is to assure that if the mediation ends in impasse, the process isn't over, and the parties can be confident that their conflict will be resolved.

Should the mediation not reach a successful conclusion then the parties will immediately move on to arbitration. The mediator will then shift their role to that of arbitrator and formulate a binding decision quickly based on their judgements regarding the case as a whole, or on any unresolved issues.

In the case that a mediator is unqualified to proceed in the role of arbitrator a qualified practitioner may take over the case after consulting with the mediator.

Arb-Med

Arb-Med is essentially the same concept as Med-Arb, except that the process starts with an arbitration proceeding, after which a non-binding arbitration award is issued. Then, the parties work with a mediator to attempt to resolve their conflict.

The mediator hears disputants' evidence and testimony in arbitration then writes an award but keeps it from the parties. The mediator then attempts to mediate the parties' dispute before unsealing and issuing their previously determined binding award if the parties fail to reach agreement

It is thought that the process removes the concern in Med-Arb about the misuse of confidential information whilst keeping the pressure on parties to reach an agreement. It is not acceptable for the arbitrator/mediator to change the award they drew up at the beginning of the process based on any new insights gained during the mediation.

E-mediation

E-mediation, also called online dispute resolution (ODR) is considered to have many benefits for those with busy time schedules. In e-mediation, a mediator provides mediation services to parties who are located at a distance from one another or whose conflict is so strong that they cannot be in the same room.

It can be a completely automated online dispute resolution system with no human intervention. However, more often than not, e-mediation is more likely to resemble facilitative mediation, only delivered from afar. Video-conferencing allows parties to easily and cheaply communicate with one another in real time, while also benefiting from visual and vocal cues.

Although it can be both cost-effective and convenient, it can have its drawbacks. It may not be suitable for those lacking in computer skills. Accessibility to e-mediation may present difficulties in lesser technologically developed countries and it must be taken into account that lack of accessibility to technology is often paired with a distrust of online services. The vulnerability to cyber crime can be a negative factor. Confidential information is less secure. With this in mind, for business disputes in which the parties are concerned about protecting their trade secrets, e-mediation may not be a suitable option.

Skilled mediators need to take into account relevant socioeconomic factors of all the parties that may affect the appropriateness of such techniques and present their clients with alternatives.

Narrative mediation

Narrative mediation is a relatively new style of mediation, developed in the mid-1980s by Michael White and David Epston in Australia and growing out of Narrative Family Therapy. It challenges the problem-solving orientation and its positivist foundation, prevalent in many fields of mediation. People can be said to think in terms of stories and their constituent parts (themes, roles, and plots), which work together to create a system of meaning around particular people and events (Cobb, 1994). The approach aims to enable the parties in conflict to create a new 'story' or 'narrative' to understand and reshape the conflict. It focuses on language as the main tool in constructing who we are or how we engage or behave with others. Our words do not just simply describe our experience but in a sense serve to create it. By naming something we give it meaning.

Through the use of narrative, the approach seeks to help both parties create distance from themselves and the events that provoked their dispute. It is hoped that the parties will then see the causes of their conflict with greater detachment and a fresher perspective. In the mediation, 'narratives are interactively developed, modified, and contested as disputants elaborate portions of their own and each other's conflict stories' (Cobb, 1994:53). Such stories tend to cast the party in the role of victim or protagonist, which contrasts against the other party in the role of the victimiser or the antagonist. For mediation to effectively use the storytelling metaphor and create a cooperative climate among disputants, it becomes necessary to destabilise those assumptions and theories. The aim is to move parties from a closed personal interpretation (i.e. their story) and open them to new possibilities and interpretations. It is hoped that this new climate of openness will lead to the creation of a new account and mutually satisfying interpretations and outcomes.

In line with the existential psychological and phenomenological approach, which I use, and on which this book is based, there is a belief in narrative mediation that conflicts are not about facts, but about perceptions and the emotions those perceptions generate. There is no one 'truth' to discover, merely individual interpretations of what was experienced. All stories are merely emotional representations of events; therefore the narrative approach places the substantive issues as secondary after considering the primary, relational needs of the parties. The people are not the problem; the problem is the problem.

Unlike the existential approach, narrative mediation contains a political aspect stemming from its postmodernist underpinnings, which involves recognising that one cannot be completely neutral and that mediators must take a stand on issues stemming from the dominant societal discourses which create and recreate systems of oppression. This emphasis means the approach is considered to be particularly effective in working with marginalised groups. Narrative mediation is interested in resolutions that go beyond the simple settlement to consider the effects of the mediation on the society at large and, like transformative mediation, considers mediation as a means for conflict parties to achieve a higher moral self (Baruch, Bush & Folger, 1994). Many narrative mediators come from a psychology background.

As this is still a relatively new approach to mediation, for those wanting to have more details I recommend Winslade and Monk (2001).

Restorative justice

This is not strictly mediation but is often confused with it, so I thought it worth a mention here. Restorative justice stems from an ancient idea in which justice is rooted in human dignity, healing, and interconnectedness. Its origins lie in aboriginal teachings, faith traditions, and straightforward common sense.

Like mediation, it is a voluntary process. However, it differs from mediation in that the central parties are not considered as equal, one is seen as a the 'victim' and the other as the 'perpetrator'. This is not to say that it isn't acknowledged that both parties may have suffered greatly. All concerned in an incident are invited to attend. The focus is on the impact of a specific criminal event. 'Restorative Justice is a process whereby parties with a stake in a specific offence collectively resolve how to deal with the aftermath of the offence and its implications for the future' (Marshall, 1999:5). This means it explores the harm that was caused by the offence, in all its forms, and is forward focused.

Trained restorative justice facilitators typically facilitate restorative justice meetings. Often these RJ facilitators use scripts to keep the process focused. A common form of restorative justice is a face-to-face meeting involving the person responsible for the offence and the person harmed. If the people concerned do not wish to meet, the facilitator acts as a 'go-between', facilitating indirect communication ('shuttle dialogue') verbally or in writing. Restorative justice conferences are a form of face-to-face meeting that includes support people, such as friends and family members of either party.

Before a restorative process begins, the facilitator checks that everyone wishes to proceed voluntarily, that the person responsible for the offence accepts the basic facts of the case and takes responsibility for their part, and that it is safe to proceed. The process focuses on three aspects – what happened, who was harmed, and what was the nature of the harm what should happen next.

Morris (2002), saw the aim of RJ as restoring feelings of security, self-respect, and empowerment to the person harmed. For the person responsible for the harm, it is intended to restore responsibility for harmful behaviour and its consequences, facilitate opportunities to make amends, and assist them to take steps to prevent the reoccurrence of harm.

Psychologically informed mediation

This book focuses on a psychologically informed mediation process. Unlike other approaches, psychologically informed mediation is not a separate approach but a philosophical way of working, which could be used in all of the styles previously introduced. The studies of mediation in this book are all examples of psychologically informed mediation in action. Before I explain more about how the psychological elements are used in mediation I wish to give a brief description of what the process of mediation looks like.

4   The mediation process

Having introduced the different styles of mediation I shall now describe the practicalities involved in one of the more common forms of mediation. I shall refer to the mediator as singular whilst describing the process, but it is common practice for there to be two or more mediators, known as co-mediators. While there is no formal standardised mediation process that a mediator is required to follow, mediation will usually follow certain steps. The first part of this chapter takes you through those steps, whilst the latter part of the chapter explores the benefits and challenges of having more than one mediator.

Pre-mediation

Most start with a pre-mediation meeting or phone calls, and the agreement of a pre-mediation contract (see the Appendix for an example). This covers ground rules such as confidentiality, who will attend, fees, etc. Some mediators, including myself, send a short leaflet to those involved explaining the mediation process and introducing the mediator and any co-mediators. In many mediations, this pre-mediation work covers only these practical requirements.

In working from a psychological perspective, I view these pre-mediation communications as being very significant, and I may choose to have quite long meetings or calls, and there may be more than one. All of what is said is held in confidence. These sessions provide the client and mediator with the opportunity to connect for the first time. I have already stressed the importance of relatedness and this is the first opportunity to bring this aspect into play. This phase of the mediation allows the party to discuss any worries they may have about attending the mediation, such as the process, how it may be to be in the same room as someone you may perceive as your enemy, or who you fear, or are angry with. Through listening respectfully the mediator sets the tone for the coming mediation and aims to start building the trusting working alliance which is needed for successful mediation.

The mediation day

Statistically, most mediation cases only last a day or two. This is partly because mediation is less cumbersome than litigation, but also because people typically take smaller disputes to mediation and save larger claims for litigation. Larger business, divorce/custody, and international mediations may last significantly longer, running into weeks or months, but are still much quicker than traditional litigation.

In the different forms of mediation some of the parties never meet, and in others the parties remain together with the mediator throughout the process. The process which I use as a framework and which I describe here is called the Harvard model. This model was developed at Harvard University, initially to deal with large industrial disputes. In this model, having spent time in person or by phone with each of the parties in the mediation, the mediator will facilitate a day in which all parties come together.

The mediation starts with the mediator welcoming the parties, taking care to address them in the way they have agreed during the pre-mediation process. The mediator will sensitively seat the parties in what seems to be the most comfortable way for those involved. Some people will not wish to look the other in the face, or will need considerable physical space between them. Once people are settled the mediator will reiterate the ground rules, the confidential nature of the process, and that everything said is without prejudice and cannot be repeated in court if the mediation proves unsuccessful. The mediator will also check that each party has the authority to settle. These points will have been laid out in a pre-mediation contract (an example of which is given in the Appendix) but are repeated verbally to emphasise their importance and to allow time for all the parties to settle in what can be a very stressful moment. The parties may be coming together in the same room for the first time, or even after many years.

The mediator's role will be explained, making it very clear that the mediator is neutral and not a judge, and is present as a facilitator. The mediator will explain how the day will work using a mixture of joint and individual sessions. Once this is clear for everyone the mediator will start with hearing brief opening statements from all concerned. Again, sensitivity is required in who the mediator chooses to go first. It should not matter to the process that one person is chosen but it will matter to the individuals if they are not given an acceptable reason. This may just be because the mediator always goes alphabetically, or because if the case went to court the claimant would be heard first. Whatever the reason, one needs to be given.

Each party will then be given the opportunity to describe the dispute as they see it. At this stage some mediators ask for no interruption from the other side. More experienced mediators may be comfortable in managing such interruptions, and so allow them to happen, as it gives the mediator the first chance to see how parties react. If the mediator has laid down a rule of no interruptions then they are placed in the position to police that rule. This may alienate one or both sides from the mediator and does not help build trust. However, the mediator must be aware of any power dynamics which are in play, and not allow one party to intimidate the other. The mediator must check that any discomfort they are feeling belongs to the parties and not just to themselves. Often parties are more comfortable with robust language than the mediator is! An experienced mediator may let any mutual discussion which starts between the parties at this joint session to continue if the mediator is confident that both parties are equally comfortable, or indeed equally uncomfortable.

In most cases, after the opening comments have been heard the mediator will not get into a dialogue with either party but merely thank them for their contribution so far and move on to private individual sessions. The reason for not getting into discussion at this stage is because anything which is said will be in front of the other party and open to their interpretation. They will be looking to assess whose side the mediator is on by noting the tone of voice, the amount of time, etc., which the mediator uses with the other party.

The parties adjourn to their own rooms and throughout the day the mediator will meet with each party separately and confidentially. If any party has something which they want the other side to know the mediator will take great care in checking exactly what the content of the message should be and that they have permission to take that across to the other side. Any breach of confidentiality is very serious and could result in the mediator being sued. If there seems to be some common ground the mediator will usually bring the parties together and use this as a starting point for discussion.

Finally, a written agreement will be drawn up and signed by the parties and witnessed by the mediator. Parties' lawyers, if present, may help in drawing up this agreement, and may also sign as witnesses. If an agreement is not reached, the mediator will summarise the issues the parties did agree on, and may advise them of their rights going forward.

The above is just a framework and in some mediations the mediator may intend to have individual sessions but they may not be needed. It is also possible to have a successful mediation without the parties ever being in the same room.

Figures 4.1–4.3 show a flow chart of the Harvard model.

Following on from the joint sessions, it is hoped that each party's positions may have moved and that collectively the parties can formulate a heads of agreement. For this stage the mediator does not need any legal training but must draw on their common sense, checking each aspect of the agreement as to whether it is realistic and deliverable. This includes being alert for anything which has the potential to go wrong, and then facilitating discussion as to how this may be dealt with. Things often arise during in this part of the process which require further individual meetings, and the process may be repeated many times before agreement is reached, written up, signed, and witnessed.

The process is not linear or chronological and the mediator may need to keep returning to the early stage in which the key aim is to build

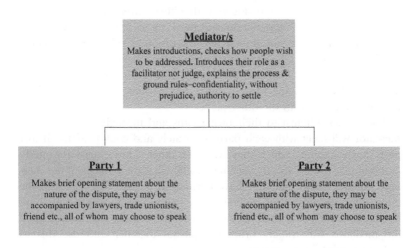

Figure 4.1 The opening

The mediator/s are in control of the process, not the content. At this stage the aim is to make people feel comfortable and allow everyone to hear, perhaps for the first time.

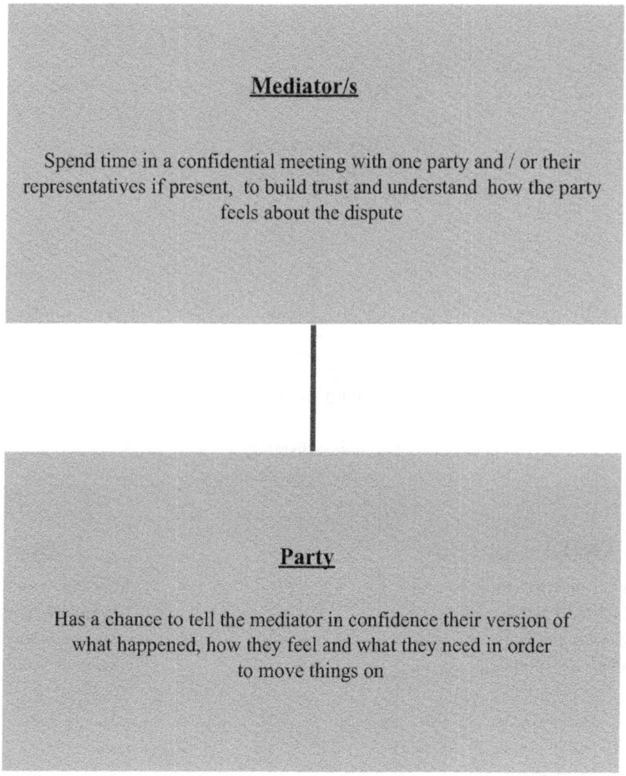

Mediator/s

Spend time in a confidential meeting with one party and / or their representatives if present, to build trust and understand how the party feels about the dispute

Party

Has a chance to tell the mediator in confidence their version of what happened, how they feel and what they need in order to move things on

Figure 4.2 The individual sessions, sometimes referred to as the caucus

Each party has their own room to which the mediator will go for confidential meetings (caucus). The mediator aims to build a working alliance built on trust which will enable the party to tell them fully about the dispute. Having seen one party, the mediator/s will go to the other party and repeat the process. This may happen several times until the mediator/s feel there is common ground which may benefit from bringing the parties back together.

trust between the mediator and the parties. It is important to be aware that things may appear to get worse before they get better, with each party becoming more adamant that they are right and the other wrong. This is often referred to as the diamond of divergence, the mediation time warp, or even more emotively as the diamond of pain.

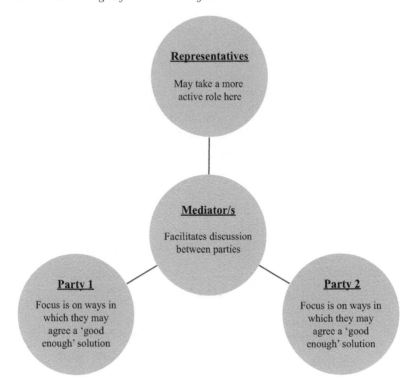

Figure 4.3 Joint session/s

At this stage the mediator/s seek to facilitate a dialogue between all involved and begin working to identify areas they can agree on to form a working document for the future (heads of agreement).

5 Co-mediation

All of the approaches I have outlined can be used by a mediator working alone, or by one or more mediators co-mediating. As co-mediation can seem to be more complex, is less well known, and there is little written on it, I shall spend a little time on it. Co-mediation also provides good examples of the psychological interplay between all those attending a mediation.

It is becoming common for two or more mediators to work together as co-mediators. Richbell defined co-mediation as, 'the harmonious working of two complimentary mediators who offer a diversity of skills, experience and personality' (Newmark & Monaghan, 2005:302).

There are different styles of co-mediation. These are explained fully in *Co-Mediation: Using a Paired Psychological Approach to Resolving Conflict* (Hanaway, 2012). Some mediation partnerships consist of a lead mediator and 'assistant' mediator/s, whereas others may work as an equal partnership. Even where there is a designated lead, the level of autonomy given to the assistant may vary. Some lead mediators may invite the co-mediator to contribute however and whenever they want, others may wish the co-mediator to remain silent unless specifically asked for their opinion, and others may require the assistant to be there simply to take notes and look after practicalities.

I use an equal partnership model in which the co-mediators remain together throughout the process. This means that there may be two or more mediators in a room with one party. In theory it sounds like this could feel overpowering for the individual, but in reality I have not found this to be the case. Other than in special circumstances, the co-mediators do not split up, as I believe that to do so allows for possible collusion between mediator and party, with the danger that a party sees a solo mediator working with them as their advocate and the mediator who is with the other side taking on that role for them.

The mediator's neutrality and ability to form a respectful and trusting relationship with each party is one of the key factors in mediation. If the mediator uses a psychological approach with the parties, then this same awareness should be present in the relationship between mediator and co-mediator. As we have seen, conflict is part of all relationships. The fact that two people are working as co-mediators can lead to hidden and unexpressed conflicts within their working relationship.

When considering the place of relatedness in mediation it was noted that conflicts often ensue when we experience others as different to ourselves. The 'opponent' in a dispute takes on an alien aspect and we struggle to find connection. We can at times experience a co-mediator in that way too. Co-mediators, through their facilitation of a dispute, show how two individuals with differing worldviews can come together using different perspectives on the dispute to create movement and creative change. The co-mediators may well see things differently from each other, they may overtly disagree, but their differences are used to add richness to the resolution.

There are advantages and disadvantages to this way of working.

The advantages of co-mediation

Practical

There are practical aspects involved in setting up and running a mediation. Pre- mediation contracts have to be written up, agreed, and signed with the parties. These will cover agreeing the times, venue, fees, level of confidentiality, etc. Initially the tasks may be mainly administrative such as liaising with a commissioning party, collection and organisation of papers, sending out practical details to the parties, organising transportation, and booking rooms to use for the mediation and accommodation for mediators and parties to stay in if needed. The responsibility for all these elements can be shared when you are co-mediating.

The pre-mediation phase may take up a lot of time over quite a long period, whether it is by phone or in face-to-face meetings. A solo mediator may be able to commit time for a mediation day but find it difficult to do so for the longer period which may be needed in the pre-mediation work. Having a co-mediator means that this pre-work can be done by either co-mediator, and thus free up the other partner for other work.

I believe that it is best if only one of the co-mediation partnership undertakes *all* the pre-work which takes place directly with the parties, as to split the work at this early stage could be confusing. It is usually structured that one mediator concentrates on the practicalities of contracting and arranging the venue while the other makes the contact with the parties and any representatives, friends, family members, union officials, or lawyers who may be attending with the parties.

If the work has been divided in this way and the mediators use an approach where all mediators are equal, then it is essential that the parties do not see the mediator who is speaking to them as the main mediator and the other an administrative assistant. To guard against this assumption it is helpful if the mediator who has so far picked up the more administrative work conducts the opening joint session, explaining the role of the mediator, the process of mediation, checking each party has the necessary authority to settle, and stressing confidentiality.

Mediation can be exhausting, both physically and psychologically, for parties and mediators. Throughout the day, energy levels will peak and drop. If a mediator is working alone there is little recovery time. With a co-mediator a higher level of positive energy can be maintained by the two mediators supporting each other through sharing tasks, noticing when the other is flagging, and taking a more active role while their partner needs some 'recovery time'.

It also allows for a mediator to take comfort breaks when needed, as there is a partner who can remain with the parties. Sometimes such a break can create a change in the dynamics. In one mediation in which I was involved the male co-mediator stepped out briefly leaving me with a party who was being very negative and maintaining a very 'macho'/'I'll show them' stance towards the others in the dispute. During this brief break, the party chose to show me a photograph of his young daughter and talk with some pain about his divorce. During the break between private sessions my co-mediator and I were able to consider the significance of this, noting that at some level the party wanted his caring and vulnerable side acknowledged.

As stated previously, mediations are emotional. It is not unusual for this to get too much for one or more parties, and emotional walkouts can happen. If two or more mediators are working together it allows for the possibility for one to remain with the parties left behind whilst the other goes to speak with the person who has walked out.

The drawing up of the settlement agreement can be conducted and supervised by both mediators, which we also see as a strength. At this stage things can happen very quickly, and it is important that a mediator remain alert to any verbal or non-verbal signs that a person may be feeling unsure or pushed. This is much easier to do with two mediators. Both co-mediators will sign to witness the agreement.

Finally, as well as being tiring, mediations can be thirsty and hungry work. Even having a partner who can pop out for extra coffee or food can be vital to enabling the process to flow without too much interruption!

Emotional support

Mediation can at times be emotionally draining. To have someone to share this with can help both co-mediators to maintain good creative energy levels throughout the mediation. Using two mediators lightens the load emotionally, they can support and 'look out' for each other, noticing and reacting to any signs of tiredness, tension, or frustration, perhaps arranging a break to take stock and 'refuel'.

The Harvard model, which I have described, and other models which use a 'shuttle' approach in which there are a number of individual sessions with the different parties, provides opportunities for co-mediators to emotionally 'offload' between sessions – to share concerns and frustrations or to air questions. It also allows the mediators to help each other remain positive at those points in the mediation where it all feels very stuck, or the intransigence of a party is proving particularly frustrating.

We each have emotional triggers which we carry with us from our own past experiences, both professional and personal. This means we are in danger of being quite suddenly disarmed by the content of a mediation session. It may trigger personal memories of similar situations in our own lives and may take us back to the emotions we felt at the time, leaving us less open for offering a unique response to the party's experience of the situation they are describing. To use a psychotherapeutic term, we may 'project' our experiences onto one of the parties and may experience a response to them which is close to 'transference'. They may remind us of someone who we loved or hated in the past and we may well begin to feel similar emotional reactions towards the party. A finely tuned and sensitive co-mediator will pick this up and a partnership which has established a trusting relationship will be able to openly discuss this between the caucus sessions to ensure that this does not get in the way.

The journey home from the mediation provides an opportunity to offload any emotional aspects of the case with a co-mediator. By sharing any concerns, the mediator can gain a full sense of completion and satisfaction at the end of the day.

Another perspective

We all have different sensitivities, strengths, and weaknesses. The mediator and co-mediator should ideally be confident enough, and trust each other enough, to be open to each other's (possibly different) views and perspectives. If a strong collaborative relationship exists between the co-mediators it is immensely valuable for them to use their different perspectives on the disputants' position, and for this to be expressed and explored during the mediation. Even if both co-mediators are aware of a particular point of principle for a disputant, they might see it differently, and so phrase a question in a different way which the party might be more responsive to. For this to be possible it is essential that co-mediators leave their egos at the door and accept that individual parties may response more positively to one co-mediator than to the other. It is not a competition between the two mediators, but a trusting working alliance aimed at benefiting the parties. If a party is addressing all their comments to one mediator the other must hold back and deal with any need they may feel to 'show their worth' by butting in.

It may be that there is a particular element to a case that might benefit from one working with a particular co-mediator who brings some personal, professional, or cultural experience that may be relevant or reassuring to the parties. However, mediators who feel a professional or personal connection with the parties need to work harder at checking that they are not working from assumptions based on their own experiences and feelings.

There is a debate in the mediation world as to the benefit of having a mediator who shares ethnicity, culture, or language with the parties. Clearly there are many benefits in this (McKimm-Vorderwinkler in Hanaway 2014; 106–177). Believing there is a shared background between the mediator and the party may lead to assumptions by the mediator that the party may have experienced similar events in the same way the mediator has, with similar emotional reactions and meaning. The mediator must guard against this, taking particular care to listen carefully and explore the ways in which their own beliefs and experiences differ from those of the client, in the same way they would if they perceived little commonality with the client. It is essential that all mediators are sensitive to these issues.

Co-mediating does provide the opportunity to offer a male/female partnership and partner mediators from different cultures, races, and backgrounds. This can help guard against perceived 'likeness' and also against a lack of knowledge, experience, or understanding of the parties' background. This can also help to model, in a very overt way, how difference can be used positively and creatively. It provides for on-the-job learning for each mediator as they hear and experience the different ways their co-mediator approaches things due their different experiences and backgrounds.

Exploring human connectedness

A co-mediating team can serve as a pathway to human connectedness in the sense that the relationship between the mediators and the relationship between the mediators and the parties can reveal the uniqueness of each individual whilst simultaneously highlighting the similarities between all individuals. Professor Marcus Feldman of Stanford University (2002) led research which showed that all humans are 99.9% identical and, of that tiny 0.1% difference, 94% of the variation is among individuals from the same populations, and only 6% between individuals from different populations. More recent research suggests the figure is closer to 96%. However, the point is that we are all very alike and share existential givens whatever our background, although the way we live our lives in this world may differ considerably.

In co-mediation these commonalities and areas of uniqueness are explored. Through this exploration the mediators discover what is important to the party and in doing so one mediator may pick up on an important dynamic in the relationship between the parties which may be missed by their co-mediator. Through the co-mediators sharing their insights, greater understanding and collaboration can develop between the parties.

Modelling

Each co-mediator will have their every move watched by the parties. This is one reason why it is important that the mediators have a collaborative relationship which is based on trust and respect for each other's differences. Any sense of a competitive relationship will be clear to the parties. Any collaborative behaviour is also visible to the parties. Indeed, whether we like it or not, the close scrutiny of the parties means that mediators working together are acting as role models.

In a previous book (Hanaway, 2014b) I looked at the 'otherness' of the disputants, and indeed at the otherness of the co-mediator. This otherness is played out, for good or bad, in the co-mediation partnership. The mediation may provide a unique opportunity for the parties to see two people (the mediators) express different perspectives and use that difference respectfully and creatively. For many people, difference is perceived as threatening, and the opportunity to see it modelled as positive by the co-mediators can effectively challenge that assumption.

Co-mediators can demonstrate positive behaviour and respect for difference in simple ways, such as being punctual, reliable, honest, open, and non-judgemental. They can also demonstrate effective communication by using verbal and non-verbal listening techniques such as noticing and responding to cues of discomfort or tension, and also by checking in with each other (and the parties) to ensure that there is a common understanding at all times.

They show respect to their co-mediator by allowing space for them to speak, listening without interruption to what they have to say. If co-mediators do disagree with each other they do not try to take control, put their co-mediator down, or overtly challenge the other's thinking. They may choose to clarify the differences in private during the break between individual sessions when they are away from the parties, or if the trust between the mediators is sufficiently strong they may choose to model how to explore such different views in front of the disputants, thus showing how to make a challenge which respects and validates the other. They may have a brief interaction between themselves which is open for the party to hear e.g.

> *'How interesting, I had never thought of it that way. . .'*
> *'That's an interesting thought, I shall think about that as I was seeing it rather differently. The way I saw it was. . .'*
> *'Oh, tell me a bit more about that way of seeing things, I am very interested. . .'*
> *'That gives us all another useful perspective on things. . .'*
> *'Help me understand that viewpoint. . .'*
> They would then go on to offer the different perspectives to the parties to respond. *'How does that fit with how **you** see things/feel about things/have experienced/understand things. . .'*

Mediators need to be very sensitive to their co-mediator's ego needs. Many mediators could feel very threatened by using this modelling of difference. Co-mediators who work together and have built trust in one another often are less likely to feel uncomfortable working in this way than those coming together to co-mediator for the first time.

Modelling such behaviour allows the parties to experience respectful interaction and a positive approach to challenging and discussing difference. This is more powerful rather than just talking about it. It provides a model for the parties in how to care for each other's self-esteem while exploring their different perspectives. Although the importance of modelling as a technique in effecting behaviour change is well documented in psychology literature (Bandura, 1977; Mischel, 1993), it has not been adequately researched in relation to mediation, although it is briefly discussed with regard to co-mediation in Hanaway, 2014b (75–77).

Value for money for the client

There are considerable benefits to the client in having two mediators. One of the most obvious is financial. As long as the co-mediators have a strong collaborative relationship it is not usual to charge the client more than they would be paying for a sole mediator. This may not be a selling point for mediators but certainly benefits the clients.

The clients have added value in having two points of contact prior and post the mediation. The clients also have access to double the skills, experience, knowledge, energy, and perspective, and also the synergy between the co-mediators which can help to generate more creative solutions.

There is also value to the client in having two styles and views and possibly mediators from different backgrounds.

Supervision and continuing professional development

There is no current legal requirement for a mediator to have supervision. This differs from other psychological professions, where qualified practitioners are required to be in supervision throughout their professional life.

One of the great benefits of co-mediation is that in addition to one's own internal supervisor, mediators have colleagues who can help them reflect on their work throughout the day and with whom they can discuss progress, frustrations, blocks, individual prejudices, and ideas. This helps to maintain a high level of neutrality and authenticity in both mediators, which has a significant impact on the conflict resolution process.

Mitchell (in Hanaway 2014:77) focused on the importance of such a supervisory role in co-mediation, writing that, 'After I have mediated on my own I am left with a burning need to take stock and talk through my experience of the day with another mediator'. Through co-mediation mediators are afforded an opportunity to reflect on how well they are working with aspects of the process such as holding neutrality, maintaining high levels of concentration and energy, sustaining positivity, and maintaining a belief that agreement is possible. The co-mediators can take turns giving space to the other to relax a little, and consider their own responses. This can take place during the breaks between sessions, thus having the potential to compensate for any lapses or shortcomings which may have been identified. This potential for 'in the moment supervision' is extremely useful, particularly during the day of the mediation and in the de-briefing session.

Co-mediation is not necessarily better than external supervision as it is possible that the quality of the co-mediators' relationship can be such that they fear upsetting each other. This can result in it becoming collusive and limiting the learning from the peer-supervision.

An on the spot 'supervisor' can also check for breaches of impartiality, thus reducing the possibility of mediator bias. It is human to be drawn more to one person than the other or to one person's narrative. In the preparation stage, if one mediator is aware and concerned that they may be at risk of taking sides, the other mediator can make sure that they watch out for signs and are ready to step in if the need arises. Both mediators take on this supervisory task on behalf of the other by being on guard to help prevent incidences of partiality occurring in the first place and during the feedback stage of the process they can explore any incidences that have arisen in order to build sensitivity, alertness, and the capacity to remain impartial.

Co-mediation can also provide continuing professional development with each mediator learning from the other: 'we continually learn from one another. We constantly discover and rediscover each other's skills and abilities and are inspired by the insights and energy that both bring to mediation' (O'Kennedy and O'Hehir in Hanaway, 2012:78). Mediation can require a lot of travelling and this presents a good opportunity for mediators to share knowledge of upcoming conferences, training, journals, and books. They can share and disseminate their reading and meet to reflect and share on any CPD opportunities they have undertaken.

Having a co-mediator can also provide elements of quality control by ensuring that standards do not slip. Each partner sees the other's skills and knowledge up close and in a trusting partnership any difficulties encountered can be worked through and used as opportunities for further learning and growth. Co-mediators learn through working with and watching and listening to their co-mediator as much as they do through the shared reflections at the de-briefing.

The tensions and challenges of co-mediating

Trust

Because working with another opens up a mediator to scrutiny, which can result in praise or criticism, co-mediating calls for a high level of trust in one's co-mediator. Co-mediators need to ensure that they feel able to accept both praise and constructive criticism openly.

If a mediator encounters a case where they recognise a potential personal bias, they need to trust their co-mediator enough to be able to share this with them at the outset and call on them to help monitor how effective they are in not bringing the bias to play in the mediation.

Choosing the wrong co-mediator

This need for trust makes the choice of co-mediator very important. Working with a co-mediator one feels unable to trust can be a very uncomfortable experience. Sometimes one has no choice about fellow mediators. If a mediator joins a 'panel of mediators' they will generally be required to carry out three mediations with a more established member of the panel.

The likelihood of tension between co-mediators is increased when there is no clarity about whether there is a lead mediator. This can result in a more competitive approach which gets in the way of trust. A good equal relationship based on trust removes the need for competition or the need to prove oneself which may be present in a lead/assistant model.

Whatever co-mediator model is used, it is good practice for each mediator to be clear about respective values and principles regarding mediation. There are many mediation-training organisations, and not all share the same ethos. Some training focuses most strongly on the psychological aspects of conflict, whereas others focus more on the process and structure. In order to trust one's partner and form a strong working alliance, there needs to be a shared understanding of the reasons why conflict resolution is important to them.

Co-mediators need to agree on the ways in which constructive criticism can be made. When is it appropriate? During the breaks between caucuses? At the end of the mediation? Or at some other agreed time?

A deep understanding of power dynamics is required of partners in co-mediation. Co-mediators have to be aware of how they individually use their power, both in relation to each other and to the parties. A mediator who wishes to take centre stage is unlikely to be a good solo mediator and will certainly make a poor co-mediator.

Co-mediators must be sensitive to their own need for guarding their self-esteem and the same need in their partner. It is necessary to show respect to one's partner at all times, particularly at times of disagreement, as co-mediators model ways of dealing with disagreements. It is essential never to 'put down' one's partner and to know how to pick up cues as to where and when one's input is needed and when it isn't. There is no room for vying for centre stage in a co-mediation partnership. The needs of the parties are the most important thing and may require one mediator to be in the forefront whilst the other takes a more supportive and less obvious role. Any competitive elements between the two co-mediators could prove disastrous to the success of the process.

I have already stressed the importance of human connectedness, and although co-mediation more overtly demonstrates any negative dynamics between the co-mediators it would be wrong to consider that it is absent in the sole mediator model. Indeed, the presence of a second mediator can help prevent this from being played out by the other mediator in relation to their interaction with the parties and the parties' interaction with each other.

Danger of manipulation

Most of us to have a desire to be liked, and so each party in a mediation will want the mediator to see them as being in the right and the other party as being wrong. It is not unknown for a party to try to get a mediator to like them and dislike the other party.

This happens with sole mediators and in co-mediation. One of the dangers of a co-mediating model in which the co-mediators separate is the potential for the parties to attempt to engage in manipulative behaviour with the co-mediators and attempt to set them against each other. A good skilled and experienced mediator will be very aware of this and work to avoid it. However, this can happen from the outset where one mediator may have taken responsibility to undertake all the pre-mediation work. This means that the parties and the mediator will have formed some impression of each other and begun to form some kind of working relationship. At this stage this may be either positive or negative.

Even when the mediator is careful not to agree or disagree with the parties it is possible that one party may try to make a mediator appear impartial e.g. *'Your colleague agreed with me that. . .' 'That's not what your co-mediator has been saying. . .'*, etc. This may still happen even though it is clear that a mediator would not collude with any party in this way. Clearly impartiality in the mediator lies at the heart of the mediation process. For this reason, most mediators working with the Harvard model, in which there may be a large number of private caucuses, believe that the co-mediators should remain together throughout the process. Very conscious of confidentiality and the importance of how easily words can be misinterpreted, they will work hard not to become mere messengers for the parties, but will only take across offers or other communication which has been rigorously checked out with the party and where the party has given explicit permission for it to be shared with the other party. Where there is more than one mediator there is a greater security that mediators have checked and hear exactly what may be shared.

It can be tempting when pushed for time to try to split the mediators, but this increases the danger of things being misinterpreted or manipulated, and mediators must work with this in mind. Some mediation models do not follow the same process and may rarely, if at all, hold private caucuses. The co-mediators will plan in the opening joint meeting which mediator will work with which party in the event of an individual meeting. Following such an individual meeting, the whole group resumes, with the mediators spending a couple of moments agreeing on how they will share what was discussed in the separate meetings to the benefit of the process.

Communication

Some mediators only co-mediate with the same partner all of the time. Others will co-mediate with a number of different partners. Whatever the arrangement, the way the co-mediators communicate together has to be thought about and carefully carried out.

The mode of communication is seen by the parties and provides a model of how to communicate with another person, even when differing views are held. Co-mediators need to have a very respectful way of communicating, particularly when they are in disagreement. They also need to know when to speak and when to leave a silence for their co-mediator.

This does not mean that the co-mediators are clones of each other. In respecting differences they may have very different communication styles. One co-mediator's language and style may be more informal than the other's. One may hold relevant technical knowledge and language which the other does not. These differences allow the party a choice of styles in which they may feel comfortable expressing themselves.

Ego

In co-mediation there is always the danger that the ego of one or both co-mediators can get in the way. Sometimes a co-mediator's personality, experience, or style makes it easier for them to set up a trusting working alliance with one or both parties. Their co-mediator needs to greet this positively and not feel threatened by it. It is not a reflection on them; it is natural that we get on with some people more quickly than we do with others. A mediator who is looking to gain glory or affirmation from being a mediator, or seeks to 'rescue' a situation or 'drive through' a resolution, may not find what they are looking for in a co-mediation approach.

Each co-mediator has to learn to step back when their partner is making progress and to resist the temptation to say something just in order to justify their presence and boost their ego.

Financial

Although there is a financial advantage to the client in co-mediation, there is a financial disadvantage for a mediator who chooses to co-mediate.

Co-mediators who work as equal partners usually split the fee 50/50 and do not charge the client extra for the involvement of two mediators rather than one. Clearly this means they are earning half the fee they would if mediating alone. In other models where there is a lead mediator and an assistant mediator the fee is split differently, with the usual arrangement being that the lead mediator takes most of the fee. In some cases, a lead mediator will take the entire fee and expect an assistant to work pro bono.

Novice mediators looking to co-mediate in order to gain experience may find that not only are they not paid but also that they have to fund their own expenses. It is not unheard of for experienced mediators to charge new mediators for the privilege of being their co-mediator.

The advantages of solo mediation

Most of the advantages of mediating alone are more or less the opposite of those for co-mediating. Financially there is a gain, as the fee does not have to be split two ways.

The extra dynamic of working sensitively with another, in order to model good communication and power dynamics, is not present in solo mediation, and so there is less to take the mediator's attention away from the parties.

A solo mediator is still open to the possibility of parties being manipulative but does not have to worry about being set against another mediator. For some people it may feel better for their ego and less complicated to be the one entirely 'in charge' of the process.

6 The relevance of psychological, existential, and phenomenological thought to mediation practice

The success of mediation does not lie in strict adherence to process. The key task of the mediator is to understand the parties in dispute, what is important to them, and what might enable them to move on. The truth that conflicts are primarily psychological has been understood for a very long time. Sun Tzu (545BC–470BC), in *The Art of War*, wisely informs us that, 'If you know the enemy and know yourself, you need not fear the result of a hundred battles' (2009:11). The importance of knowing oneself is often ignored. We can come to know ourselves by listening to what we say. Hearing ourselves speak out loud and noting the passion with which we do so is an opportunity which mediation offers. However, it is essential to know and understand all parties in any conflict: 'If you know yourself but not the enemy, for every victory gained you will also suffer a defeat. If you know neither the enemy nor yourself, you will succumb in every battle' (ibid).

Conflict is always inter-relational and psychological. We need something, or someone, to be in conflict with. Even if I am struggling with inner conflict, the conflict will be between two or more opposing wants and aspects within myself, and so is still relational. If conflict is about a person's perception and understanding of an event, and not about 'facts' which cannot be changed, then our primary task in mediation is to gain a better understanding of those involved in the dispute. Other people impact on our emotional state, and so all conflicts have relational and emotional elements. Indeed, if we were not emotionally affected by a difference of view there would be no conflict. We would solve conflicts easily if they were logical and open to a purely rational answer, which everyone could see as the only logical outcome. However, conflicts are never logical; they are driven by emotions and a desire to protect our dignity and self-esteem. We want to be proved right and our 'opponent' to be proved wrong.

We all experience events differently. We may be present at the same event, at the same time, and in the same place, and yet perceive it very differently. We may differ in what we believe we saw and heard, and our emotional reactions to the event will differ too. One person can find something funny which another person finds devastating. It is not the event in itself which is conflictual, but our emotional and psychological response to it. A conflict can never really be about 'the facts' as they do not exist as universal truths. It can only ever be about different perceptions of an event, and what each person believes to be 'the facts'. There is little point in spending time trying to explore these 'facts', as they 'exist' only in the past. Whatever happened, it cannot be changed. All that can be changed are the perceptions and attitudes attached to the event, which in turn may alter any desired outcome.

Any such change in understanding of our perceptions calls for a psychological reassessment in which people are called on to examine their motivation, needs, wants, values, and beliefs and to challenge their behaviour. This makes any conflict intervention a psychological encounter and mediation 'a philosophical and psychological process ... [which] stems from a psychological disturbance to the parties' equilibrium, one which is strong enough to prevent a logical working through of the dispute' (Hanaway, 2020:119).

My training and work as an existential phenomenological psychotherapist influences my own approach as a mediator. I do understand that even the word 'philosophy' may be off-putting to some readers. It may be considered to have a place in academic navel gazing, abstract and often unintelligible, but seem to be far removed from daily life and struggles. Yet philosophy is a very concrete tool for practical work in appropriate contexts, including conflict resolution. Philosophical thinking equips us to work with change through questioning the status quo. The status quo can be seen as representing a form of 'stuckness', which mirrors the feelings of those caught up in what feels like a time consuming non-resolvable dispute. It is a mediator's role to understand this and to accompany the parties through the sticky swamp of emotions on the journey to a resolution. The main focus of existential thought can provide a road map through that mire and offer a practical framework for the psychologically informed mediator's approach. Using existential and phenomenological thought in mediation practice may seem a world away from finding a practical resolution to conflict; in the following chapter I offer a brief overview of some core existential concepts which I draw on in my mediation work and which are illustrated in the studies in this book.

There are supporters and detractors of all approaches described above. Those in favour of facilitative and transformative see them as empowering parties, helping them take responsibility for their own disputes and their resolution. However, some people believe these approaches take too long, and too often end without agreement. They worry that outcomes can be contrary to standards of fairness and that mediators in these approaches cannot protect the weaker party. There is a whole area of debate here about individual assumptions as to who the 'weaker party' might be. Unfortunately it isn't within the scope of this book to discuss this.

Supporters of transformative approaches argue that evaluative mediation may be quicker, often a just few hours, but that evaluative mediators put too much pressure on clients to reach a resolution, opening the danger of parties feeling pushed to agree to something which does not suit their needs but appears fair to the outside world and boosts the mediators' self-esteem through reaching a quick agreement.

In reality there is quite a crossover of styles. Imperati (1997), for example, sees evaluative mediation as ranging from soft to hard: from raising options, to playing devil's advocate, to raising legal issues or defences, to offering opinions or advice on outcomes. He therefore believes that it is not appropriate to assume that evaluative mediation is necessarily heavy-handed.

Baruch, Bush and Folger (1994) see more distinct differences in the styles, particularly the difference in 'top-down' vs. 'bottom-up' mediation, and believe that transformative mediation is ultimately flexible and suited to all types of disputes, whereas they believe that evaluative and facilitative mediation may take legal information too seriously, and that resolutions coming from the parties are much more deep, lasting, and valuable.

These styles are often more of a continuum than distinctly different approaches, from least interventionist to most interventionist. Mediators tend to use some facilitative and some evaluative techniques, based on individual skills and predilections and the needs of a particular case. Each has its usefulness and its place in the pantheon of dispute resolution processes. I shall now return to my own belief that conflict, no matter what the presenting issue, is essentially psychological and benefits from an approach which recognises this.

As conflict is driven by psychological and emotional elements it necessitates a psychological understanding in any approach aimed at resolving a dispute. Such an approach emphasises the need to work with core existential elements such as the importance of authenticity, relatedness, values and beliefs, the emotional content of language, both verbal and non-verbal, the pursuit of meaning, the experience of time and temporality, and the exploration of the worldviews of all those involved in the dispute. The approach seeks to explore and challenge aspects which have become unreflected and sedimented, and may not be serving an individual in reaching resolution. At the same time, the mediator will aim to preserve or even enhance the disputants' self-esteem through working with their fundamental human psychological needs for identity, security, and recognition. When we are engaged in a difference of opinion, the other person may be experienced as very different to us. Yet as humans we all share the need to be heard, valued, and respected. We are all emotional and develop ways of behaving which stem from our values and beliefs. We seek to protect our self-concept and look for affirmation. All of these human needs are at play when we are in conflict, and so an understanding of them becomes an important tool for a mediator.

Strasser and Randolph (2004:27) based their model of psychological mediation on an understanding of the importance of these existential elements:

> One of the most important elements of ... mediation ... is the exploration of the covert reasons for the dispute, as well as the overt. The parties will have developed rigid belief systems as their overall strategy for survival in an uncertain world.

This leads to the belief that conflicts occur when existential givens are threatened.

Existentialists are interested in the subject of 'being' (by which we mean all human experience). As humans we are invested in the process of being, and experience it through time, environment, and relationships. When we are in conflict with another person we may struggle to find any commonality with them yet there are many existential givens which we all share; these include death, freedom, responsibility, existential isolation, and meaninglessness. Linked to these are our interaction with relatedness, uncertainty, emotionality, and anxiety. All of these human aspects are present in a dispute, even if on the surface the conflict appears to be about cold facts.

Relatedness in the context of conflict

Existential thinking calls for us to consider ourselves as beings-in-the-world-with-others, and so we must take heed of the fact that we experience ourselves, and everything around us, the world, other people, ourselves included, in the context of a relationship. Even when we are alone we are alone because in that moment we are away (physically or emotionally) from others. If there were not others, then we would not be alone, we would just 'be'. Even when disputes are between organisations or geographical areas they involve human beings, and so they are inter-relational. In all disputes something has happened in the relationship between two or more entities, be they individuals, organisations, or countries.

The importance of understanding these relational aspects of conflict is central to an existential approach to resolving the situation. Weixel-Dixon (2016:20) reminded us that, 'As a given of existence, it is not possible to be totally isolated, nor is it possible to be fused with another person; we stand always in relatedness, in some form'. Conflict is one of the potential outcomes of the inter-relational aspect of our being. Most conflict is concerned with the different ways in which two or more people perceive an event or idea. These differences can be positive and enablers of creative change, or can be experienced as one person refusing to give another what they want, and so lead to animosity.

In conflict situations we can lose sight of any commonalities between us and of the existential givens we all share. Instead, conflict encourages us to experience a separation or 'otherness' in relation to the other people or entities involved in the dispute. Those with whom we are in disagreement can come to be perceived as 'strange', 'alien' or 'other' and experienced as obstacles standing in the way of us getting what we want. This leads to a focus on the perceived differences, making it harder to understand the position the other is taking in the dispute. Once the mediator has shown that they have an understanding of what is important to a party, and how they perceive the other, the task of the mediator is to look for the commonalities which will always be there. The parties may both value honesty, integrity, or loyalty, and place family values high in their priorities, but they may express these in different ways. If the mediator is able to enable the parties to recognise the commonalities, than the mediation can move from being competitive to being collaborative as each party begins seeing the humanity in the other.

Fortunately for a mediator, one of the existential givens is that we all desire to be heard and understood. This is indeed a gift to a mediator. Each party in a dispute will wish to form a relationship with the mediator and be heard by the other side. Firstly, they will look to the mediator to listen to them and to affirm their position. A common cause of conflict stems from a person not feeling listened to, and the mediator's skill in reflective listening is at the core of a successful relationship between the mediator and all parties. If the mediator can listen and show understanding without collusion, it gives the disputant hope that their opponent may also be able to listen, and so come closer to understanding their perspective, even if they don't agree with it.

People will stay in conflict if relational factors are not addressed. Conflicts can be extended purely because one person dislikes the other, even if both suffer as a result. During a psychologically informed mediation the mediator will explore each of the parties' individual worldviews, privately noting the differences in the way the individuals experience the world and how this affects the way they live in the world.

A mediator also needs to be alert to relational power dynamics. These may seem very obvious if working with an employer and their employee or where there may be cultural power issues such as race, gender, language, or culture. However, there may be subtler power dynamics in play. The grandmother who has sat quietly in the corner may be the person who will have the main say in what is an acceptable resolution.

Authenticity in the context of conflict

In existentialism, authenticity is the degree to which an individual's actions remain congruent with their values, beliefs, and desires, despite any external pressures. To lack authenticity is to live inauthentically, or in bad faith, a term used by the philosophers Simone de Beauvoir (1947) and Jean-Paul Sartre (1958). It is not only necessary to know oneself but to be oneself, and in doing so to accept responsibility for one's actions.

Mindell (1995), writing about conflict, stresses the importance of authentic communication. In disputes, communication may be focused on winning the outcome which suits one side, rather than on being authentic. Authentic communication comprises a willingness to take responsibility for communicating in an authentic and compassionate way, resulting in accountability, transparency, and honesty. It requires mutual respect, valuing differences, and developing an ability and willingness to listen openly. This authenticity indicates respect for ourselves and our views, and respect for the views of others. We all wish to be understood, and need to understand the other, or we remain stuck in the dispute. It is important for the mediator to make each side feel safe enough to speak their truth and to encourage the other to do so. This is not an easy task for a mediator, who will be spending time separately with each party and must remain empathic and open to their different authentic 'truths', whilst not colluding with either side. If I try to mediate between colleagues, I am faced with a challenge to my authenticity. I may like or value one more than the other. I may trust the judgement of one and question that of the other. To mediate such a dispute,

I must remain authentically open to the possibility of being wrong, and so listen with equal openness to both sides.

Through authentic communication, self-esteem can be developed and maintained, making it possible to work cooperatively towards a 'good enough' solution to any dispute. Authentic open listening can be a challenge to any mediator who often feels they are meant to present themselves as invincible and all knowing.

Time and temporality in the context of conflict

The way we relate, give meaning, and take responsibility is set in the context of our temporality. We will not go on forever. To live with this knowledge and acceptance of death and uncertainty is to live authentically. Existential thought puts great emphasis on the task of living as authentically as we can.

We may not often be dealing with matters of life and death in mediation but we are always dealing with time. Randolph (2016:19) points out that people in dispute often need reminding of the subjective nature of time, 'that both the past and the future exist only in their perceptions' and so 'The constant and fixed exploration of past events may therefore be futile'. In looking to the future, those in conflict 'may have an overly optimistic or unduly pessimistic perception of future possibilities' (ibid).

The mediation can benefit by bearing in mind the importance of time. Disputes can go on for years and steal precious moments from our temporal existence. A reminder of the importance of this lost time can sometimes help the parties focus and take on a new dynamism in a desire not to waste any more of their lives in pursuing their equally desired, but opposing goals.

Time can also be used manipulatively in mediation. Time means different things to different people. If the parties in mediation have different relationships with time the mediator must handle this sensitively and be aware of possible manipulation. Some people have endless time whilst others are severely pushed for time. Most mediators work to a contract which stipulates an agreed start and end time, and aim to complete in one day. Other mediators will work in an open-ended way, continuing through the night if necessary. I believe the open-ended approach is open to being ethically dangerous and can ignore issues of inequality. It may be easier for one person to continue longer because they have no commitments that they need to attend to or their energy level is higher. I have been offered extra money to extend the time of a mediation because one side knew it was impossible for the other side to continue because they had a plane to catch. The party offering the money wanted to be seen as positive and willing to continue working towards a resolution, yet knew it was impossible for the other person to do so. They wanted it to seem as though the other person had refused to continue the mediation and was therefore the 'bad' party.

When working to unlock a dispute we cannot expect a linear timeline. People need time to build trust in the process, and trust in the mediator. At any point this trust can be lost and the process needs to return to the beginning while trust is rebuilt. Some people, by their nature, take longer to explain things. They may favour narrative and metaphor, whilst another may wish to remain factual and to the point, believing time is money. They may speak more quickly, and not wish to explore anything that they do not believe is directly related to 'the facts of the dispute'. The mediator must respect and work with both approaches. This can mean that a private session with one party may run much longer than that with the other. It is important that this possibility is addressed at the start of a mediation. A mediator is not promising equal time with each party, but is promising equal opportunity for each party to have the time they need to tell the mediator what they need to.

Values and beliefs in the context of conflict

Our behaviour is governed by our beliefs and values. If these are threatened in any way we will experience an emotional reaction which may cause us to flee, fight, or freeze. The attack may come from others, or ourselves (when we find ourselves behaving in ways which go against our beliefs). An attack to our values or beliefs, including what we believe about ourselves, can be the basis for the most painful conflict.

In understanding a dispute, we seek to gain insight into the emotional world of each party and the behaviours which flow from that. At the core of an individual's behaviour lies their values and beliefs. By understanding this we can identify emotional stressors. When our values are threatened we can become fearful, not wish to expose our values, or instead wish to shout them from on high and try to convert others to our ways of thinking. These two ways of attempting to defend values and beliefs will always be present in a dispute.

We can become too rigid (or sedimented) in our adherence to a value to the extent that it becomes problematic; for example, if an individual places 'loyalty' high of their list of values they may feel the need to be loyal to their peer group or organisation and follow their behaviours even when they experience them as destructive or wrong. Schools and workplaces are often made up of cliques, and it takes bravery to stand alone. We can be so used to not questioning our beliefs that we may fail to notice they are no longer relevant, and continue to live as though they are. This may be comforting at some level, but it does not serve us well.

It can take hard work to loosen sedimented beliefs and to change behaviours as they serve to define the self-construct, create a feeling of stability and security, and act as a guard against uncertainty. Challenging them may be essential in mediation, but could be met with fear and resistance.

The task of the mediator is not to challenge the values of the individual but to enable the person to understand how they are being played out within the dispute, to challenge tensions and ambiguities, and to explore whether the values are working for or against the person in this specific dispute. We can hold contradictory values. I may believe that it is disrespectful to act in an authoritarian and directive manner with those working for me and yet I may also believe that providing excellent service to a client is an important value. If an employee can only produce good work by being given strong and detailed direction, I can find myself in a position where I cannot practice both values at the same time. Sometimes the mediator may need to help a party to identify these paradoxes and to decide which is the priority in this instance.

Our values lead us to behave in certain ways. We may value our independence and believe that others should be independent and confident enough to take responsibility for their own actions, or we may believe in the need for collaborative working, or we may like to check everything with someone else. If somebody believes in taking a leadership role, then the mediator must work with that, not against it. Such a person will want to lead the dialogue and the mediation process and if this does not disadvantage the other person then the mediator will not try to stop this. The mediator will take care not to get into competition with a party who seeks leadership. The mediator must be equally sensitive to the person who is constantly seeking reassurance; the most a mediator would do in either case would be to draw attention to this pattern and enquire whether it is playing out to the person's advantage in this dispute. Mediation is not about making value judgements or changing a person outside of the context of the dispute.

In working towards a resolution the mediator will hold in mind the values of the parties in dispute. Ignoring these might risk coming to a 'logical' solution in what is essentially an emotional situation. Such a solution may seem a good one to the mediator but is unlikely to be sustained if it does not address the values and emotions of those in dispute.

Meaning in the context of conflict

Human beings by their nature seek meaning. If we understand or believe in something it gives us meaning, and so lessens our anxiety, and makes sense of the world for us. Meaning provides a framework for understanding from which we can make choices, not just about our values and beliefs, but also about what we want to do with our lives and how we want to behave and define our lives.

Many conflicts are caused because of the meaning an individual invests in a particular action or statement from another person. There are many occasions where we misread or misunderstand even the transactional meaning in a communication. Emails and texts are particularly prone to creating conflict, as they are so easy to misread without any accompanying bodily or verbal cues. When another correctly understands the meaning we place in things they are in a powerful position. They can use that knowledge to hurt us or to engage with us in a positive way.

Understanding the ways in which a particular dispute is threatening meaning for all the individuals concerned increases the mediator's understanding of what is at risk for each person. It can be money, status, challenge to values and beliefs, or other reasons. If our meaning is taken away or challenged we can be left feeling very vulnerable. A clash in worldviews, particularly in relation to values and beliefs, can cause deep conflict and feelings of alienation and existential loneliness. A mediator must listen openly and patiently and encourage the parties to do so if at all possible.

A conflict may paradoxically answer an individual's need for meaning. It can mean they have something important to fight for or against. A mediator needs to identify the meaning which the dispute holds for all concerned. Is it really about a one-off incident, or is there something deeper connected to the meaning, values, and the beliefs of an individual? We become emotional when our sense of meaning is at threat, and may seek to run away, or to fight. To resolve a conflict, any agreement has to hold personal meaning for those involved. If the settlement addressed these meanings it creates a stronger commitment to abide by the agreed outcome.

Uncertainty in the context of conflict

Existential thought requires us to engage with the truth of uncertainty, and any mediation approach which is primarily evaluative or logical rather than psychological does not fit, as it carries an implication that there is a certain right or wrong, or some argument which is better or worse. The challenge in working in a creative existential way is to not to be side-tracked by a fruitless search for what is right, or by pursuing what looks to you to be just or positive outcomes. We may never know what is just or positive for those involved, but are more likely to think about what would suit us if we were in their situation. A mediator must creatively engage with and explore this uncertainty in order to create a new way forward.

We cannot escape uncertainty; life is uncertain in its meaning and its future. There exists no certainty beyond the finite nature of our existence. Existential thought equates uncertainty with the potential for creativity and encourages us to embrace uncertainty and find individual meaning. This anxious state can result in us feeling challenged by difference and lead to conflict. In an argument we often stick with our view because we do not want the uncertainty which flows from considering other views. We may fear that considering alternative viewpoints may change how we see ourselves and leave us feeling uncomfortable, vulnerable, and unsettled. This can lead to us questioning our certainty about other things. Ultimately, if one is capable of changing one's mind about something, how certain can one be about one's beliefs, and if these become uncertain then we are left to question just who we are.

In conflict there is very little we can be certain of, although we may believe that we feel very certain that we are right and the other person is wrong. However, what we choose to see as 'certain' facts are only ever our perceptions stemming from past experiences and beliefs, and despite any 'certainty' we may choose to cling to regarding the outcome of any dispute, it remains uncertain until the end.

Even when a written resolution is agreed, uncertainty remains. How will this agreement be seen by others; will one side be considered to have won? What are the implications of what has been decided, both in the here and now and in the future? How has the resolution changed the relationships for all involved?

Although it is not the role of the mediator to make any party feel unsafe, it is also not the role of the mediator to collude with a party's fear of uncertainty and change. A psychologically informed mediator will make it safe enough to explore potentially uncomfortable areas in the party's understanding of the dispute. These may include existential concerns such as freedom, responsibility, authenticity, purpose, meaning, paradox, uncertainty, anxiety, values, time, and temporality. Existentialism and phenomenology do not prove any 'truths' to fall back on. They require to 'bracket' assumptions and to focus on things as they appear in our experience and the meaning we give them.

Uncertainty may be difficult for parties in dispute but it is also challenging for the mediator. Those from a legal background will have been well trained in searching for certainty, which an existentialist would say does not exist. Whether mediators come from a legal background or not, it remains a challenge to work with the parties towards a resolution when there is no certain truth and no certain route to success, and where the mediator is tasked with bracketing their own sense of certainty, their views, and their suggestions for solution.

Freedom and responsibility in the context of conflict

Existentialists give importance to acknowledging our freedom, and the responsibility that brings with it. It is true that there are circumstances in which we experience little or no freedom. We are thrown into an existence we did not choose. We cannot choose our family or if, where, or when we are born. Existentialists acknowledge these limitations and term them 'thrownness'. We are however free to choose what we make of our lives. The responsibility for choosing often causes anxiety, and can lead to us living authentically or inauthentically.

People arrive at mediation because they feel they have lost the ability to choose and they feel they are stuck in the dispute. However, at the very least, they always hold the freedom to step away from the dispute, or to step further into it. There is no certainty about the outcome of mediation and the parties must exercise their freedom to make or not make an agreement. Whatever the outcome, they must then take responsibility for authentically living with it. Parties are often afraid to use their freedom to agree a settlement because they doubt that they are getting the best possible deal. As there is no certainty as to what the best 'deal' would be, the parties have to ask themselves what really matters on an emotional as well as material level.

Emotions in the context of conflict

We are all emotional. Having acknowledged my own existential/phenomenological approach, it may already be expected that I would consider our emotional way of experiencing and existing in the world to be significant in our understanding of self and other. The experience of existential guilt and anxiety is laden with emotion. Existentialism is often connected in people's minds with what are considered to be *negative* emotions, such as anxiety (worrying), dread (a very strong fear), and mortality (awareness of our own death). As a group willing to express these aspects of being, existentialists are deeply interested in emotions.

Emotions are felt in relation to the values and beliefs we hold. We get upset or happy about something because we value it, we believe in it, and it holds meaning for us. If the mediator understands this, then working with the emotions unlocks the values and beliefs which may have been threatened in the dispute. One cannot be in a dispute without being emotional about it. A disputant can be angry, sad, confused, but never neutral and unemotional. Even when a person is representing an organisation in a dispute they will have an emotional reaction to being in that position and will wish to maintain their self-esteem in the process and the outcome.

How we emotionally react to an event, including a conflict, will be unique, e.g. for one person appearing onstage may induce emotional feelings of exhilaration, happiness, power, freedom, and fun, whilst for another person the emotions may include fear, powerlessness, etc.

Many psychological minded mediators see the expression of emotion as a gift they can work with. Strasser & Randolph (2004:146) stress their importance:

> Every emotion is connected with the givens, and each emotion is a manifestation is an aspect of people's worldview. Indeed, emotions are most useful tools for the mediator and for the parties to gain insight into aspects of their own worldview ... they can highlight some of the ambivalences each party holds.

Scheff and Retzinger (1991) draw our attention particularly to the emotion 'shame', with the 'core sequence' in 'emotional conciliation' requiring that one party express shame or remorse before the other can move towards a position on reconciliation. Although not necessarily agreeing with this, I believe it is important to consider what shame means within the culture of the individual. My belief is that in some cultures it is easier to express shame than in others. If we look to shame one party and elicit forgiveness from the other, then we create an additional 'otherness'. In my view, it is more important to create a sense of commonality between the conflicting parties that opposes and eventually nullifies the alienation, or tendency to see the other disputant as 'THE OTHER'. This returns us to the importance of relatedness and the emotional reaction that too little or too much of another person evokes.

Phenomenologists focus on the nature and meaning of emotions and are interested in the ability of emotions to engage with reality. Emotions are always about something. This is termed 'intentionality'. Emotions tell us about ourselves, and others, and the values and beliefs we hold.

By looking to understand the 'something' which is attached to the emotion the mediator learns what is most important for the person.

We have an emotional reaction about something because we value it and it is meaningful for us. So, emotions help us to be more self-aware. Often we only recognise how important something is to us by the strength of emotions it evokes. Recognising a true emotion can sometimes be difficult, as an emotion can be disguised by another emotion, e.g. we can hide fear behind anger. This is important to the mediator and to the party, who may not realise what the most important element of the dispute is until they connect with the depth and truth of the emotional reaction.

By tuning in to the emotions, a mediator gains access to how the party sees the world and the dispute. Even individuals known for their coolness, or poker face, will be experiencing emotions as they seek not to divulge their thoughts and feelings. The desire to hide an emotion tells us something of the person's ill ease and fear. Emotions in ourselves, and in others, can cause anxiety because we fear they may prove overwhelming, and so we may choose to be inauthentic about our emotions in a vain attempt to protect ourselves or others. A confident mediator is able to work with all emotions.

The mediator has to explore the meaning of the emotion so as not to misinterpret it. If the emotional aspects are ignored a great deal of important information can be lost. The more emotions are openly expressed and acknowledged the greater the opportunities for a creative mediated solution. A mediator will therefore invite openness and honest. In doing so, the mediator must commit to deal respectful with what is heard, even if in disagreement. This includes any personal criticism of the mediator, no matter how unfair. This does not mean that the mediator accepts all types of behaviour, but must remain alert to the level of tolerance of all involved in the dispute.

Understanding the power of emotions is extremely helpful in mediation. The mediator will be alert to a number of indicators as to what is important to each individual caught up in the conflict. One key indicator is the emotional expression of the party. The mediator will look out for emotions, whether they are being expressed overtly or subtly. By gaining insight into the parties' emotions, the centrality of a person's value system can be unearthed. People often feel at their most emotional when their beliefs or values are attacked in some way. The attack may come from others or themselves (when they find themselves behaving in ways which go against their beliefs). By understanding this, the mediator can identify emotional stressors and the values they are attached to. It may be appropriate to explore these with a party as emotions can become 'unreflected'.

We may always act the same way to a particular stimulus, but this may have become little more than an historic or habitual reaction, and if we ask ourselves in the moment how we are experiencing something, and what we are feeling, it may be very different from what we expect to feel.

The mediator must be tolerant of the emotional content, be it upsetting or provoking. It is not the role of a mediator to filter out emotional content they find disturbing, as it is likely this material will lie at the heart of the conflict. In understanding a person's emotional stance we gain entry into their psychological world, and this enables us to interact more effectively and empathically. It can be unusual for some people to have their emotions noted in this way and to experience being listened to. This can lead to a major shift in the individual's attitude towards dispute, and they may become more willing to move from a sedimented stance to a more fluid approach.

Although emotional expression is a gift to the mediator, the mediator is not seeking out or digging for emotions. They will not ignore any that are evident in the verbal or body language of everyone involved but will not suggest emotions or try to get a party to be emotional.

It is important that the mediator explores any emotion rather than believes they understand it through reference to self. What make one person angry may amuse someone else. A surface emotion such as anger may be disguising another such as fear. In any mediation, the mediator needs to check out and clarify any assumptions they are making. This is not done through direct questioning but through deep listening after they have bracketed any assumptions.

I shall move on to show when and how the mediator may work with these concepts in a practical way during the mediation process.

7 The psychological ebb and flow within the mediation process

Having introduced the importance of the psychological approach and how different existential elements are played out in a conflict situation, I wish to move on to explore how the mediator works with these throughout the mediation process.

The mediation day could be seen as being divided into two main components – tuning in and tuning out. The 'tuning in' process (through active listening) is the central element in building a trusting working alliance between the mediator and all parties. This is the core aim of the early part of the process. It is achieved by entering uncritically into the other's worldview, and so understanding something of their value sets, coping strategies, and emotional reactions.

The mediator has to be both a follower and a leader. In the early stages the disputant is the leader, and the mediator follows, slowly unwrapping the meaning of what is being presented. At the start of the mediation the mediator remains open to listen to everything the party wishes to tell them, even if it does not seem overtly relevant to the dispute. This enables the party to experience being fully heard without any initial judgement or censorship being imposed. The mediator is able to build a rich picture of each person's worldview, values, beliefs, hopes, and coping strategies, through following where the party leads. As the party realises it is safe to speak openly to the mediator, the necessary trust is developed, which allows the mediator to move on to the next stage.

Once the alliance is established and an understanding of the other's worldview developed, the parties in the dispute need to 'tune out' and become more focused on the 'world of the dispute' with its concrete and emotional implications. The mediator will look to identify potential areas of commonality amongst the parties, and explore solutions for potential agreement which are 'good enough' for both parties.

When mediating, I hold an internal image of a funnel (see Figure 7.1), with the early parts of the process being very open – the mediator

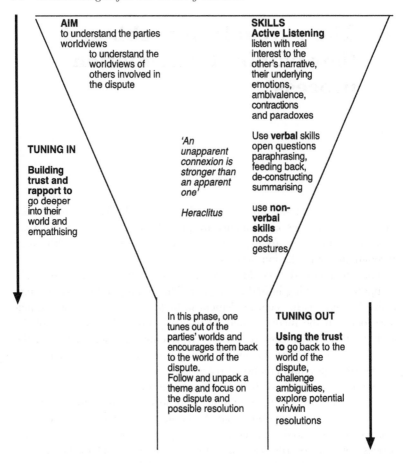

Figure 7.1 Funnel model: Hanaway (2012). To show 'tuning in' and 'tuning out' stages of mediation

following the party – whereas towards the end of the process the funnel narrows to become more challenging and more focuses on possible outcomes.

Unfortunately, the mediation process is neither chronological nor linear. The trusting working alliance may be built and lost a number of times throughout the process. When this happens, the mediator needs to acknowledge that trust has been damaged or lost and turn their attention to rebuilding it rather than trying to rush ahead.

Tuning in

Listening

In 'tuning in' the emphasis lies in consciously listening for descriptors of the inner world of each party, showing their emotions, values, beliefs, and coping and behaviour patterns. It is important to take everything which is said as being of equal importance and significance. Husserl (1913) uses the term 'the rule of horizontalisation' to describe this notion that everything is significant and there is no preordained order of importance. Husserl considered intuition to be the most reliable source of evidence, as it is permanently engaged with reality.

Much earlier Heraclitus (c.540bce–c.480) had found every 'unapparent' connection to be stronger than an 'apparent' one. When we do not immediately see the relevance of what is said, it is important not to dismiss it as irrelevant or disconnected. Freud and other psychoanalysts taught us to accept that all that is presented contains unconscious communications as well as conscious ones. The party may find it hard to tell the mediator things that make them feel vulnerable, stupid, or guilty, or where they feel the mediator may disagree with them. They may find it difficult to admit and to describe how they experience paradoxical responses to the dispute and/or the people involved. Such communication may be given subtly rather than in overt statements.

As the mediator listens and tunes in to a party they may begin to pick up themes. Each theme will have a level of relevance and so the mediator may decide to follow any theme, even if it seems very far removed from the actual dispute, and to go on to unpack it, controlling their own needs to find or offer a solution or to make 'inspirational' links. At this stage the party is the leader, and the mediator follows, slowly unwrapping the meaning of what is being presented through paraphrasing, reflecting back, and summarising without judgement. The mediator trusts in the process and believes that everything that is told to them in the early part of the process will prove to be relevant by giving indicators of the values, life strategies, and emotional stance of the speaker. This intense listening is a lot harder than we may think.

It is worth returning to Husserl at this point. Phenomenologists drawing on his works base their understanding about how we exist in the world on the premise that objects exist through the meaning that we give. This is known as 'intentionality', which occurs unconsciously. Husserl saw every act of intentionality as containing two parts; the 'noema', the object or 'the what' that we direct our attention towards and focus on, and the 'noesis', the 'how', through which we define an object. It is important in a dispute that we listen to both the noematic (content) and the noetic (the individual's unique emotional experience of that content) in all narratives we hear as a mediator. We can only begin to really understand when we listen for, and to both aspects. We need to remember that we will be hearing these things as they are interpreted by the teller and their perspective will be influenced by their familial, cultural, and individual experiences as informed by their value sets and the emotional context.

There are a number of simple skills which can help to elicit both the noema and the noesis. These include the use of encouraging body language, the use of silence, not interrupting, asking open rather than closed questions, reflecting back, paraphrasing, summarising, and the identification of themes which are tracked and deconstructed (rather than analysed). The mediator will feedback any contradictions they hear between noema and noesis, between the values and actions, between the body language and verbal content, or any other shifts in approach or outlook. They will explore the assumptions that are being expressed, and their emotional context.

To do this effectively, the mediator must set aside their own preconceptions and judgements (known in phenomenological terms as 'bracketing'), and listen in an open way. By doing so, they develop greater understanding of the individual's response to the dispute (e.g. emotions, value and belief systems, coping strategies, and factors influencing self-esteem) and their fundamental worldview. This facilitates a deeper and more authentic dialogue.

Identifying coping strategies

People are often afraid of experiencing powerful emotions, being confronted by different ways of thinking, or being challenged, and will develop coping strategies in response to life's challenges. Often these work well and the individual automatically employs them without being conscious of doing so. They become an automatic or default response.

Unfortunately, a coping strategy that works well in most circumstances can cause problems in others. In mediation the disputant can be enabled to explore a number of different ways of coping without losing self-esteem. To change coping behaviours may result in a person feeling vulnerable and exposed e.g. if they are used to leading and this role has become a problem in a certain context they may still find it hard to abandon that role to someone else. Learning that a role as 'follower' may be more effective can feel very challenging.

In mediation, the disputant can identify different ways of coping without losing self-esteem by identifying that they are in charge of their own behaviours and can abandon them if they have ceased to be suitable for purpose and may, in fact, in some contexts be working against them.

Tuning out

Once the mediator has clarified a party's worldview and priorities, they need to move on to enable the disputant to learn to understand and be sensitive to the perceptions of the other. The parties need support to identify what steps need to be taken to address the specific conflict and so move towards a resolution. This can only occur when trust has been established and both parties are respectfully heard. At this stage the mediator can invite the parties back into the 'world of the dispute' and begin to focus on possible solutions in order to facilitate a 'good enough' solution. This requires a move to the 'tuning out' phase, where the mediator shifts from tuning in to the individual worldviews and draws on the trust which has been created, to challenge assumptions, ambivalences, and ambiguities. At this stage the mediator may also choose to invite the parties to consider the implications, psychologically, emotionally, and financially of settling or not settling in the mediation.

By employing an existential approach, the mediator improves the chances of a successful and sustainable resolution. If a mediator ignores the emotional and psychological aspects they may succeed in obtaining a logical solution but it may be a solution which holds no meaning for the party.

Challenging

The mediator has to take care to get alongside each person, understanding their worldview, without colluding with their perspective on the dispute. Each party will seek to increase their self-esteem by presenting themselves, and their narrative, as favourably as possible to the mediator. A party's need to look after themselves emotionally, and to get the mediator on their side, may cause them to try to compensate by adopting either an assertive or even aggressive attitude, or alternatively be passive and helpless. The mediator must be confident to work with those different reactions and not be afraid to gently and constructively challenge.

Disputants may need reminding of their responsibilities and their potential for choice. Although they are unable to change the incident leading to the dispute, they can change their attitude towards it.

Understanding that they have choice may be uncomfortable, but also empowering, and does not allow the parties to adopt a position of passive helplessness or arrogant self-righteousness.

The mediator cannot challenge until people feel safe. A party will only feel safe when they believe they have been listened to respectfully and that the mediator has gained some level of understanding. Mediators can never fully understand another person but can give all their energy and attention in trying to do so. It is a false and potentially disrespectful claim to say to a party, 'I understand', and may well be understandably met with an angry backlash ... 'How could YOU possibly understand!' Challenge can come from the party as much as from the mediator.

Once the mediator has achieved a 'good enough' understanding then it serves no positive purpose to get stuck there. The disputant has to learn to understand a little, and be sensitive to the perceptions of the other, without getting lost in any newly found mutuality with the mediator, and/or other party, and ignoring the steps which need to be taken to address the specific conflict and move towards a resolution.

As humans are paradoxical creatures, it is likely a mediator will hear a number of ambivalent or contradictory statements of wants. It is very common for someone off work with stress to be demanding that they should have their job back, whilst at the same time they describe how they cannot enter the workspace without experiencing panic attacks. The mediator will not ignore these contradictions but will explicitly draw attention to them, challenging the party as to which is most important or stuck, recognising that one thing has to shift for there to be a resolution.

When caught up in a dispute we may lose our sense of time, and not notice that a proportion of our life is lost to the dispute. A mediator may choose to challenge parties to reflect on how much time they have given to the conflict so far and how much more time they are willing to give to the dispute to the detriment of other things in their life. It is not unusual for relationships to end because a partner considers that someone has become 'obsessed' in pursuing a dispute, and is no longer aware of anything or anyone else.

Another challenge the mediator may offer to help the individuals' progress is to explore what might happen if they choose not to agree to a resolution and had to go to court (e.g. loss of confidentiality, loss of their job, their family, their pride, their self-esteem, etc.). This is often quite a reality check which can change perception of the relative importance of the issue in dispute. This is known as the 'catastrophic what if' challenge.

It can be equally useful to pose the 'miraculous what if' challenge and ask the party to consider what will happen if they do get what they originally wanted from the mediation. Often other people will have told be what they should aim for from mediation; usually this is something financial or material. However, there is a growing recognition that winning can be twinned with loss. Getting what they thought they wanted may achieve material gain, but fail to bring the emotional state they were hoping for. They can be left wondering if all the time taken up in the dispute has been worth it.

Taking care of self-esteem

People in conflict often feel powerless; after all, they have been unable to resolve the conflict themselves and have needed to bring in, and probably pay, a mediator. This can result in lowered self-esteem. They may feel disempowered and have lost any sense that they have the power to choose how they respond to the dispute.

It is important to remember that this may be expressed through a quiet presentation or by arrogant, angry, and dominating behaviour. Both can be an attempt to guard against an attack on self-esteem.

The existential focus on relatedness will mean that the mediator is acutely aware of the need to respectfully honour the importance of their interaction with both parties and the need to take care of all parties' self-esteem. The relationship between the different parties and the mediator is built on trust and respect flowing from the authenticity and neutrality of the mediator. If the mediator can gain this level of trust they will be in a position to challenge gently without damaging self-esteem.

Concern for the parties' self-esteem starts at the beginning of the mediation process, with the mediator being sensitive to how the parties may interpret them giving more time or attention to one party than the other. Disputants are looking to gain the mediator's approval, and for the other side to be seen as the 'wrong-doer'. This sensitivity can extend to the length of time the mediator takes in a handshake, the seating arrangements, which party the mediator chooses to speak to first, or the different lengths of time given to each private session etc.

A mediator can damage a party's self-esteem through their tone or some of the areas they choose to explore. Sensitivity is required. To ask a party why they did not follow a certain course, which logically would have the obvious one to follow, can feel like an accusation. If we feel attacked we tend to move to one of three positions – fight, flight, or freeze. None of these positions are helpful to the mediator, whose main task is to form a trusting, working alliance with all parties to the dispute.

Whilst a psychologically informed mediator will seek to maintain the self-esteem of all those involved in the mediation, they need to haul in their own natural desire to increase their self-esteem by appearing to know the answers and to know the ideal solution. In most mediation approaches it is not the mediator's role to find solutions, to judge, or offer advice. It is important to remember that the disputants are always responsible for the solution; the mediator's role is one of facilitation, holding the responsibility for the process but not for the content. If the solution is so obvious to the mediator they must ask why the parties haven't already thought of it. The answer is because the dispute is not about logic, but about emotion. A good example of this is *Kingsgate Development Projects Limited v Jordan [2017] EWHC 343 (TCC)* in which much time and money was taken up in debate about the type of electric gate which may be fitted to serve adjacent properties. It would have been very easy for the parties to discuss which gate would serve them both best, but emotional factors stopped them from doing so.

As parties and mediator get tired and frustrated that a resolution still hasn't been found, it becomes harder to concern oneself with issues of self-esteem; it is easy to become frustrated because one or both sides are refusing to move. Indeed, the mediator also has to address their own self-esteem, having to deal with irritable parties and their own sense of failure. The parties may tell them that they are doing a bad job and yet the mediator must maintain their self-esteem, understanding the frustrations of all involved. A mediator needs patience and belief in the process, even when things feel very stuck. To maintain a good level of self-esteem we need opportunities for self-expression and respectful listening. A well-facilitated mediation provides this.

By employing an existential and psychological approach the mediator improves their chances of gaining a successful and sustainable resolution. If a mediator ignores the emotional and psychological aspects they may succeed in obtaining a logical solution, but it may be a solution which holds no meaning for the party and so be less likely to be adhered to. When we are in conflict we do not generally act in a logical manner, so a 'logical' solution is unlikely to hold if the underpinning more personal issues are not addressed. In my view it is a mistake to believe that there are any conflicts which are not emotional and psychological. If the solution is logical and obvious they would sort it out themselves without resort to a mediator or to litigation. Even when people attend mediations as a 'representative' they bring their own emotions, perspectives, and assumptions with them.

I hope that this book may in a small way encourage the increased the use of mediation, and of more attention being given to the psychology of conflict and its resolution. The 'studies' which follow show some of the many different kinds of disputes which can be successfully mediated, and hopefully demonstrate the importance of the psychological elements present in all disputes.

Part II

Studies in conflict and resolution

8   Introduction to the studies   65
9   Mother and daughters: a family mediation (a mediation
    taking place over two half days)   68
10 Fear and difference: a workplace mediation (a mediation
    taking place over one day)   89
11 Competition and challenge: a workplace relationship
    mediation (a mediation taking place over three days)   108
12 Disharmony: a musical mediation (a mediation taking
    place over one day)   131
13 Desires and drives: a marital mediation (a mediation
    taking place over one day)   148
14 Access: a family mediation (a mediation taking place
    over three half days)   161
15 Love and hate: a workplace relationship mediation
    (a mediation taking place over one day)   178
16 Hyperventilating: a school based work mediation
    (a mediation taking place over one day)   190
17 Warring cousins: a global family business mediation (a mediation
    taking place over four four-hour weekly meetings)   206
    Conclusion   220

Part II
Studies in conflict and resolution

8 Introduction to the studies

I have been involved in training mediators for 20 years. Students are often eager to know the historical background to mediation, the different styles of mediation, how the process fits both within and outside of the legal context, and how the mediation process is used. However, no matter how well versed they may become in these aspects, it is very clear that the most effective way for people to learn to mediate is through doing. For this reason, all the courses I am involved in use role-play to give participants the opportunity to 'feel' what it is like to mediate and to sit with, and be affected by the disputants' narratives.

If we commit to being fully present to each person then we enter into their world for the period we are with them; we experience how it is for them to be in their dispute. We feel empathy for their experience, whilst holding our neutrality. We may instinctively prefer one party in the dispute to the other. One narrative may be more convincing or in tune with our worldview and values than the other. We must learn to note these reactions and then bracket them. If we fail to notice them in the first place then they will inevitably seep out.

Having given our full uncritical attention to one disputant, entering into their emotional experience of the conflict, we are then required to do exactly the same with the other person. This is challenging as, having heard one disputant's story and explored its meaning with them, we then have to bracket this in order to be openly present to the other side. This requires the mediator to put aside any assumptions they may have unconsciously built about the individuals involved or about the 'rightness' or otherwise of their claims.

It is not possible to provide opportunities for role-play in a book. The nearest I can offer is to give a realistic insight into the way disputant's narratives are presented to the mediator. The studies which follow are drawn from cases I have mediated, which I have then written up as dramatic dialogues. This is the way they would be presented to a psychologically informed mediator. First you will 'hear' one voice telling their 'story', followed by the other person's experience. As you read them you may feel more fully connected with one side than the other. This is a natural reaction, which is more intense when physically with a person and experiencing their tears, frustration, anger, or aggression.

However uncomfortable being with some of these emotions may be, it is worth remembering that those attending mediation are unlikely to be feeling strong. The need to bring in a third party to mediate a dispute, thus acknowledging that they are unable to handle this themselves, can make the parties feel quite impotent. This often results in their self-esteem being low at the opening of the mediation. Different people react to feeling vulnerable in different ways. Some people attempt to hide it by trying to appear very confident, even arrogant and aggressive, whilst others can find it difficult to articulate their views. When faced with outwardly aggressive characters who may appear quite psychologically threatening it can help the mediator to consider that they are really showing their vulnerability just as much as a party who sits and weeps.

The mediation 'studies' which follow are very varied in the nature of their disputes and take place over different time periods. Some mediation providers claim that parties will only choose mediators who have experience in a specific type of dispute. I disagree with this stance and consider that it may be little more than an attempt to ring-fence certain disputes to mediators from particular backgrounds. As a neutral mediator, one is not offering a subject expertise, one is not required to make a judgement about what is right or wrong – I can mediate just as successfully in a shipping law case as I can with a street gang. The areas of expertise I do hold as a mediator are not limited to the nature of the dispute, but are focused on the ability to hold and use a psychological understanding of conflict, knowing the potential emotional impact of disputes, being aware of, and sensitive to the interpersonal dynamics, and having the ability to listen deeply and openly in a non-judgemental way. These skills are needed whatever the nature of the dispute. Indeed, it is often easier to mediate disputes in areas where one has little or no experience. In cases where you have subject specific experience and knowledge it can be harder to listen openly and non-judgementally to what the party is telling you. One's thoughts can be interrupted with questions as to why the party didn't follow guidelines or do things in the way you would have done them. When listening to these internal questions our thoughts are with our own brains, not with the party's unique experience. We are in danger of becoming judgemental. We are no longer tuned in to their experience.

Before moving on to the studies themselves, I just want to briefly address a question which often arises during training courses for mediators. Just how does one get mediation work? There is no one answer to this, but whatever the route it is not easy, and few mediators have enough mediation work for it to make up their full-time job.

Accredited mediators can apply to mediation panels or companies to be accepted as an associate and hope that they will be passed cases by that organisation. Most panels charge an annual fee for this service. It is usual for such organisations to require the applicant to agree to co-mediate or observe three mediations before being allowed to mediate. Some organisations will pay the applicant a small fee for attending, others will not, and there are some who will even charge for the experience. I have heard varying reports in terms of the number of mediations people have obtained through panels. Generally the people I have spoken with have felt dissatisfied, and believed that organisations have their favourites who get most of the opportunities that come in.

Many clients will seek out potential mediators through word of mouth recommendations or they may look to law firms, or to family and friends who have used mediation for recommendations. So, mediators may turn to their existing networks as sources of mediation work. If they already have a good reputation in a particular field then it makes good sense to market themselves through their existing networks.

Newly qualified mediators can contact local law firms, community projects, advice centres, etc., offering to run sessions on the importance of mediation and produce brochures to accompany the talk, thus building knowledge of their services in a particular geographical area. It can also be useful to try to link with existing (EAP) Employee Assistance Programmes. These programmes were set up to offer counselling and mental health support to organisations. Some have extended their services to include mediation.

Mediators also use social media by writing blogs or articles and using Twitter and other platforms. It is useful to set up websites to increase knowledge of mediation generally, and to market themselves as mediators. The profession is still relatively new and there needs to be a great deal more information readily available. It is not easy to make a living purely from mediating and most mediators offer mediation as part of a portfolio of other services.

After presenting each of the 'studies', I give a breakdown of how each case was mediated. The thought processes, analysis, and actions are my own and not offered as a template, but merely an observation of one mediator's practice. When working with a co-mediator one would debrief in this way after the mediation, reflecting together on what went well and what didn't work. I hope what follows gives you a taste for learning more about mediation.

9   Mother and daughters

A family mediation

Sarah

I really don't know how Mum could have done what she did. I hope to hell I will make a better mother to my children than she was for my sister and I.

We weren't short of money. I remember the family home well. It was in one of the better parts of London and I would sit in the window seat in our front bay window looking over our front garden, out at the tree-lined street, and feeling a wonderful sense of calmness. You could watch the seasons change from there, see the colour of the leaves change and watch as they fell from the branches, and yet all the time have a sense that little changed my side of the glass. Few people passed by, and most of those who did were neighbours. Several would give me a friendly wave as I watched them. I guess they must have thought I was a very serious young girl. I particularly liked seeing old Mr Smithson and his dog – a wonderfully scruffy thing with a huge tail which seemed to be constantly wagging, so that I always felt the dog was happy and pleased to see me.

Growing up I felt close to my Dad. He was a robust, cuddly guy and he always found time to play with us. He had an office job but he never spoke about it. I felt that me, my sister Marcia, and my Mum were the most important things in his life. His office was walking distance from our house which meant that he left home for work at the same time as my sister and I left for school, and arrived back shortly after we did.

When I got older I took pride in having the kettle on, ready to make him a cup of tea as soon as he walked in the door. It wasn't that often that I put him first. Like most Dads he acted as our personal taxi service, ferrying us to parties, cinema, classes, and meetings with friends. I always thought he was strong and healthy and would always be there for us. He was my rock. I thought I was the centre of his world.

I haven't got many strong memories of Mum from when I was very little, even though she was at home a lot in those days – only working part-time during school hours until I was ten. She was always generous if we needed anything but when we got to our teens she was very busy starting her own business and was often in her home office, working late into the night. I think she enjoyed her work. It seemed exciting to us growing up. It took her abroad quite a lot and she seemed to find it all very exciting and stimulating – certainly more interesting than my stories of what had happened at school, who my current best friends were, and who was refusing to speak to me. Those things I shared with my sister. Marcia and I loved helping Mum to pack for her trips. She always dressed superbly – everything matched and was of the latest season. The three of us would spend hours deciding what she would take with her. We would look forward to her return from these work trips as she would always bring us back some exotic present or other and show us photos of exciting places she had visited. I have kept many of those little gifts in a special box, but I can't bear to look at them. My favourite is a pair of butter-soft, cream gloves which she bought in Florence. They are gorgeous but too small – I don't think Mum really saw how we grew and changed. She was always ahead of the game with her work, planning for what she needed to do next.

Dad didn't seem unhappy when she was away. I think he was proud of her success and her absence meant we could do forbidden things like buying chips from the chip shop and eating them from their paper whilst watching TV!

On the whole, I guess I felt things were OK. We seemed like all other families with two working parents. At least we had the two! Lots of friends had lived through the very painful divorces of their parents and were passed from one to the other like parcels. One friend, Laura, had lost her mother to breast cancer and seeing the family go through that was almost unbearable. I would pray that nothing like that would happen to my family. My parents seemed robust and full of life. I would have preferred Mum to be more available but didn't think about it much and was thankful I had both parents.

My sister, Marcia, and I are very different characters. Marcia really enjoyed life in a very 'out there' kind of way, always the centre of things, usually laughing or loudly telling us of her latest adventure, perhaps a little bit spoilt. She certainly knew how to get Dad to do whatever she wanted and even seemed to have the knack to make Mum laugh and forget about work from time to time. I think I have always been the sensible, rational one – probably the curse of being the first-born. At school I studied hard and got good marks at GCSE. Obviously things were very hard when I was doing my A levels but despite that I was accepted at university, although with everything that happened I couldn't go immediately. I think I have got over the disappointment but I do feel that if Mum had been around to care for Dad I might have managed to go to Cambridge.

I couldn't believe what Mum did. First to have an affair! I know it happens and that she was working in the kind of job where you are away from your partner a lot but Dad was such a good guy. He was always there for us and never put himself first.

Marcia

I always felt in awe of Sarah. Like Mum she is sharp and clever. She knew, and still knows, what she wants and quietly seems to go for it and usually get it. I envy her calm. I have never felt that level of calmness. Growing up, my memories of Sarah are of her confidently being OK with being on her own. I remember her curled up on the window seat of our front room with a book, lost in the story she was reading, occasionally looking out of the window and perhaps waving to one of the neighbours, whilst I tore round the room whirling like a dervish and shrieking with laughter. She was always so quiet. She always seemed so self-contained and confident.

At school Sarah shone. The teachers loved her – 'a joy to teach' a regular statement on her reports. Everything seemed mapped out for her success – A levels, university, career, marriage to the right kind of guy, children ... she has still managed to achieve all those things despite everything that has happened, or at least she is well on the way, just the marriage and children still to come and everything in hand there too, starting with the coming wedding in July when she will marry Nigel. He fits the bill – handsome and successful. Actually, he is a lovely guy ... perhaps I am a bit jealous. Of course what happened did throw Sarah off schedule a bit, she didn't go straight to university from school and when she did go, it wasn't to Cambridge as she had originally planned.

And what of me? I notice I started right on in there about Sarah, not sure why. 'Needs to concentrate/talk less/pay attention' was the mantra from my reports. Wherever Sarah went there was calm and a sense of everything being in its place, There was no debris trailing her, whereas wherever I went I left the evidence – cushions I had accidentally knocked off sofas as I ran past, papers I had scattered, toys I left everywhere because I had thought of a new game to play but hadn't totally decided the previous one had finished, so why tidy up ... Growing up, the only way I had to take the attention from Sarah was to amuse people.

Unfortunately I wasn't always good at knowing when people had had enough. Dad would get tired but keep smiling, Mum would really enjoy a laugh, but not for long as she always had work to do or was preparing for, or returning from, a work trip. I felt that Mum and Sarah were very similar in those days – both clever and quietly making things happen. Both would give me attention but I always felt it was tinged with pity as though they knew I was different from them and not by choice. Dad and I were somehow more laid back, in that I don't feel either of us were very ambitious, I think that at some level we both felt that to be a failing and that we ought to be more like Mum and Sarah, but then why bother to get into a competition we knew we would never win.

I did have lots of friends in those days and when I got to my teens I came into my own. I loved going out to clubs with friends, shopping for the latest fashions. I started spending more and more time outside home. Sarah seemed to cling to the home – a safe and quiet place to study, especially when I wasn't there.

And now? I feel confused, sad and alone in all this. I feel abandoned by all of them. As usual Sarah has decided what is right for her and is going for it. I wish I had that much clarity. I want to survive but I'm not sure how. I haven't found a partner or a career. My biggest decision each day is whether, or where, to cut – it is my only relief. Can things that happened be wiped away, forgotten or forgiven? I don't know. It doesn't feel like it is that clean or clear and whatever happens I can't have Dad back and I no longer know who Mum is.

Kate

I suppose in the girls' eyes I am the total baddie here, a heartless bitch. I can understand that. I tried to protect them from the truth. I think I succeeded for a long time but in the end I just couldn't go on with it. I know how it looks to everyone from the outside but no one could see inside me. I still don't want them to know the full truth, I have hurt them enough already.

I met Gary, the girls' father, when I was 24. He was good looking, great fun, and very caring. I wasn't particularly interested in my work at that point. It paid for what I needed or wanted to buy but it didn't inspire me. It was just a job and I enjoyed the fun things of life – out every weekend; dancing, drinking, laughing. Work was just something to do whilst waiting for the next phase of life to begin. I was excited about the future but had no clear plans about how I wanted it to be.

I question the word 'love' now. What does it mean? I am not sure anyone knows. I know with some certainty that *I* don't. I do know that I 'fell in love' with Gary almost immediately. He was classically tall, dark and handsome ... well, probably not that tall but at least a couple of inches taller than me! He was quiet and a bit serious but was clearly interested in me and made me feel important. We had a lovely time getting to know one another and moved into a flat together after a year.

Gradually I began to see that although he made me feel secure in his love for me he had no ambition and I felt any decisions we had to make were left to me. I don't think we would have found the flat or ever had a holiday if I hadn't done the work to make things happen. I'm not certain we would even have gone out much at all. Despite that, I felt safe and comfortable with him and thought that was probably what was required of good husband material. When he did ask me to marry him I was pleased and excited and looked forward to us being together and having children some time in the future. As things turned out the 'future' came a little quicker than we thought. About three months after we moved into the flat I found I was pregnant. It will probably surprise you but I didn't really feel anything, not joy, not despair, just a kind of inevitability. We moved the wedding forward and I was five and a half months pregnant when we married.

I enjoyed being a stay-at-home Mum with Sarah. Gary had settled into a nine to five job, which he seemed OK with, and financially we could manage. I guess it was about this time, though, that I felt Gary change. We were still in our twenties but he seemed suddenly to be middle aged. There was no joy. He would go off to work, come back from work, have a meal and go to bed. It wasn't as though his work was tiring either. We seemed to have less and less to say to one another and so evenings would mean watching TV in silence once we had settled Sarah for the night.

It seems a bit of a miracle that I went on to conceive Marcia as I can hardly remember us having sex in those days! The pregnancy and birth were easy and she was a jolly baby and happy child. Once both girls had started school I felt really lonely. I missed them during the day and I also missed the 'old' Gary as by now we had very little to do with one another. I told him how lonely and unhappy I felt, at times I even felt I was suffering from depression but he just said that was 'par for the course' – what can you expect with two children to look after and that I just needed to get on with things and stop analysing everything and finding things wanting.

I felt I was losing any sense of who I was and took a small part-time job. This gave me some interest and stimulation and somehow made up for how I felt at home. Gradually I felt better about myself and gained confidence, so much so that I decided to start my own business and it just grew and grew. I expanded quickly which involved a lot of trips away. At first I always asked Gary whether he would like to come with me. He always said no, he 'didn't fancy' it, it was 'too much trouble', 'he didn't like the travelling' etc. I stopped asking and began to realise that, in any case, I no longer wanted him to come. His negativity and lethargy drained me. Looking back, though, to be honest I think paradoxically the time away allowed me to stay in the marriage as long as I did. It was a respite. When I was away I felt alive, I could laugh and enjoy life. I was treated with interest and respect, life wasn't 'par for the course' when I was in work, it was interesting, challenging – no day was the same and I enjoyed and valued that. At the same time the work was tough and I would like to have discussed things with Gary but he made it very clear he wasn't interested. He didn't discourage me in my work but he didn't encourage me either. It didn't seem to matter to him what I did or where I was and that made me feel invisible to him and of no importance in his life.

When I was away Gary was brilliant with the girls. They would do all sorts of magical things together. I was jealous, he couldn't be bothered to plan nice things to do with me – what a horrible thing to say – that I was jealous of my own daughters but I guess that's what it amounts to. At the same time he took less and less interest in his own job and seemed to lose all ambition. When the economy went into decline, without any discussion with me, he volunteered for redundancy ... at 37! I couldn't believe it. Everyone became dependent on me financially and although I loved my job, and still do, it became something I had to hold on to desperately, no longer a place where I was primarily seeking stimulation and fulfilment.

My relationship with Gary more or less ceased at that time. He seemed to enjoy being at home, took no interest in me – sexually or in any other way. I volunteered for more and more overseas work and some years later, I guess the inevitable happened – I fell in love with Tim, one of my work colleagues. The relationship grew slowly and wasn't primarily sexual at first. I just felt alive and interesting when I was with him. He was fun, we would share a laugh, enjoy being in new countries and trying new food whereas Gary was becoming less and less adventurous and stuck in his ways. The relationship grew and we decided we could not spend the rest of our lives looking forward to work and hating going home. Tim had been divorced for years so was a 'free agent', whilst I, in the eyes of most people, was a married woman being unfaithful to a loyal husband.

During this time Gary had become even more lethargic and began complaining of various pains. I didn't think it was anything particularly serious and went ahead planning to leave Gary and start a new life with Tim. I had to spend three weeks abroad and was determined to talk to Gary on my return, to leave and to move in with Tim. When I told him about Tim, he responded with 'I have some news for you too – I have terminal cancer'. I can't describe to you how I felt. I didn't hate Gary, at some level I still loved him, but I had felt unloved and let down by him and at this point had been looking forward to a new life with Tim.

I felt it would be dreadful for me to leave Gary at that point. Being honest, I feared what people would say. I told Tim about Gary's prognosis and he agreed I should stay with Gary and support the girls, who by this time were 18 and 15, and he and I would continue to see each other but put aside all ideas of moving in together for that period.

Sarah

I remember Mum's trip to the States really well. It was a new destination for her, an opportunity to further extend her business and she was really happy and looking forward to it. Most of her trips were short, usually two or three days but this was planned to last three weeks. You can imagine the amount of time Marcia, Mum and I took in deciding what she should pack. It would be the longest she had ever been away. I felt excited for her and wasn't worried about her being away.

I had asked Dad whether he fancied going and he said it was 'Mum's thing, not really of any interest to him'. I thought that was a shame but Dad never liked travelling or new things so I understood and I thought it would probably have been quite lonely for him as Mum would no doubt be busy, in meetings and socialising with work colleagues whom Dad didn't know. When I think about it I do remember Mum trying to get Dad to go along to social functions and business trips but he was never interested and was happier at home with me and Marcia chilling out in front of the TV. I think Mum gave up asking him. I guess I can understand that.

Anyway, once Mum was away, Dad really seemed to sink into a place where he didn't want to do anything at all. Previously when Mum was away we had gone off to theatre productions, the cinema, things like that. I asked him if he was OK and he told me that he hadn't felt well for a few months and had been to the hospital for some tests, but not to worry as he was sure it was nothing serious. I believed him and thought he was just run down.

Mum arrived back from her trip and everything went haywire. I wasn't there but I gather that the same morning Dad had been to the hospital and been told that he had inoperable cancer and was unlikely to live more than another two years. When Mum arrived back, the very first thing she did was tell Dad she was leaving him and going to live with Tim, a work colleague. Dad was shocked and furious and told her about his cancer. When I got home Mum was in the bedroom in floods of tears and Dad was sitting at the kitchen table looking more angry than I have ever seen. Before I got through the door he told me about the diagnosis and that Mum was leaving him. At first I thought she was leaving him because of the cancer and I just thought – the unbelievably selfish cow. When Dad told me she was leaving him for Tim, it didn't feel any better.

I went upstairs to talk to her, well, shout at her. I couldn't take in what Dad had told me about the cancer, I was so overwhelmed with anger towards Mum. She promised me that of course having heard about Dad's illness she would not leave and that she would stay and take care of him. At that stage I thought maybe things would be OK. I couldn't accept that Dad would die or that Mum would be as heartless as she showed herself to be.

Marcia

What do I remember about that day? The day Mum came back from her trip ... the day she announced she was leaving Dad ... the day Dad told us all he didn't have long to live! Well to be honest I don't remember a lot. I had been out with friends, larking about, having a drink, enjoying life. I was in a good mood when I got home, perhaps even a bit high, but as soon as I opened the door everything changed. Dad was sitting in the kitchen. His face was red and angry and he was just staring into space. From upstairs I could hear shouting and sobbing. The shouts were from Sarah, calling Mum all sorts of vile names and I guessed it was Mum sobbing. I had never heard Sarah shout and never seen or heard Mum cry. The whole atmosphere was terrifying.

I looked to Dad to see if he was going to tell me what was going on. He looked me straight in the eye and said, 'Well, you need to know, Mum is leaving me for someone else and I am dying of cancer...' That was all he said and then he turned and went out into the garden. I think I must have stood there for a few minutes not knowing what to do. Do I go to Dad, to Mum or to Sarah? I wanted someone to come to me and hug me and tell me all this wasn't real. Instead I turned round and walked back out of the front door. I found some of my gang of friends and got wasted. That was also the first time I cut my arm ...

Kate

I don't know how we all survived that night. I insisted Gary slept in our bed and I slept downstairs on the sofa. Sarah made her father something to eat and drink and then locked herself in her room and refused to speak to me. None of us had any idea where Marcia was. I had heard the front door slam when I was upstairs with Sarah, and Gary told Sarah that Marcia had come back, that he had told her what was happening and she had said nothing, just turned round and left.

The following day Sarah went looking for her and found her in a terrible state at a friend's house. She brought her home and Marcia wouldn't speak to any of us, just taking herself up to her room and staying there apart from trips to the bathroom or kitchen. After three days, she asked me if I was staying. It was the first thing she had said to any of us. I told her I was staying and slowly she began spending less time in her room and talking to us about mundane things. She never mentioned the cancer or the affair.

For the next three months I tried so hard to be a good wife to Gary and a great mother to the girls, but I failed. Gary was cold towards me and continually told me he knew I was only staying out of guilt but 'not to mind as he would be dead soon'. He repeatedly told both girls that I had someone else and that I had told him I wanted to leave on the same day that he had told me about his cancer. The picture he painted of me was as a heartless bitch – perhaps that is the truth and that is who I am, but I was trying to be different.

The girls were angry with me. Most of the time they refused to speak to me. When they did it was to shout at me for being cruel to their Dad. Each evening when the girls were out Gary would shout at and abuse me, calling me a whore and saying I was only there so the girls didn't see me for who I really was. On a few occasions he threw things at me but he never physically hurt me. I knew he was scared about the cancer and angry about Tim but I was trying. Eventually I felt it was impossible to stay. My being there seemed to make things worse and to be causing more pain when I had wanted to make things as good as possible for Gary and the girls in the time he had left.

I need to be honest though and confess that I was also missing Tim and the future we had planned together. I did not see how staying with Gary made anyone happy, at least if I went to Tim there was a chance of happiness for the two of us. I was surprised with the way Tim just hung on in there with me. He never contacted me but always responded immediately if I contacted him, trying to support me from a distance and telling me he would always be there for me. After three months I left to set up a flat with Tim.

At that time, although Gary was having regular visits to the hospital, there was no visible sign that he was ill. Neither of the girls has spoken to me since I left. I kept sending them letters, texts, and emails asking how they all were, inviting them for meals, asking what I could do to help and how Gary was doing. They never replied.

I was shocked when I heard from a friend that Marcia had been admitted to the local psychiatric hospital, as she had been cutting herself and not eating. I went to the hospital to see her but she refused to let me visit. Of course, this meant that Sarah was left alone looking after Gary. I went round to the house but Sarah shut the door in my face. Later I heard that Sarah had given up her place at Cambridge and decided to take a place at the nearest university and defer taking it up for a year.

I can't really imagine what it was like for Sarah. She effectively nursed Gary until he died. I heard from friends that Gary had moved to a hospice and I tried to visit but wasn't let in as Sarah had told them to refuse me entry if I asked to see Gary. I never said goodbye to him. I wrote to the girls and tried to express my concern for them and how sorry I was about Gary's death and me not being there. I got one sharp email back from Sarah saying she wished it was me who had died and saying I was not welcome at the funeral.

I understand why she hates me but I can't accept never seeing, or speaking with her again. I want to start a new relationship with both my daughters. I hear a little about them from other people. Sarah seems to be doing well and from all accounts has a lovely boyfriend but I worry about Marcia. She doesn't seem to have coped at all with me leaving and Gary's death, I really worry about her and want to help. I have spoken to Tim and he would be happy to have her live with us but she won't respond to any approaches I make.

Perhaps it was a mistake to have hidden from them how deeply unhappy I was in the marriage and how awful Gary's behaviour had been towards me a lot of the time, leaving me feeling profoundly alone. I don't want them to know that now ... it's too late. I don't want to damage their memories of their father, he was great with them, but I do want to be in their lives. I can't imagine going through life not seeing them.

Sarah

I had such hopes that things would be OK but they were never OK again. I think Mum tried. She took three months off work and was always at home. At first Dad didn't need any looking after and it was hard to imagine what it was like with just the two of them in the house whilst Marcia and I were out at school (or in Marcia's case, skipping school somewhere with her little gang). When we got back there was always a strained atmosphere between them although no rows, they were polite to each other as though they were strangers.

I couldn't believe that Dad was really ill. It all seemed like a terrible nightmare. There we all were all four of us carrying on as though Mum hadn't threatened to leave and Dad didn't have cancer. It seemed so unreal that although in my head I knew what was happening it was hard to really take it on board. Dad didn't seem ill, he never mentioned the cancer, and if he had hospital appointments they happened during the day when we were out and weren't referred to. I believe that Mum thought there would be a rapid decline and that she wouldn't have to wait long for Dad to go into a hospice or die. I think when she first heard the news she really felt she could be there for him, for all of us – that it wouldn't last long and she could stick it out for a short time.

As the time went on and Dad continued to seem OK, I think Mum began see the prospect of having to stay with him stretching out in front of her and she clearly couldn't stand the thought. One day I came home and she was gone. She left me a letter. When I first read it I wanted to shred it, together with all thoughts of having a mother but for some reason I still have it:

Darling Sarah,

I am so sorry. I know you are going to feel angry and disappointed with me but I can't stay in this house. It isn't doing any of us any good. When you and Marcia are at school your father and I just get into arguments. He hates me for falling in love with Tim and he can't forgive me. I can understand that.

I thought I could be there totally for your father and that for the time he has left we could find a way to get on together. I hoped he would let me look after him and enjoy the time he has left. I don't hate him but the truth is I no longer love him as a husband and partner but as a person who has been and will always be important to me. Together we have created you and Marcia and I hoped that the love we share for the two of you would have helped us through this time. Instead he is angry with me all the time and I can't believe that the anger will improve his recovery. I have decided that he would be better and happier without me and so I am moving out.

At the moment he seems well and doesn't need me to do anything for him. If things change there is help we can call on. I am not expecting you and Marcia to take care of your father. You are both young with your futures ahead of you. I promise you I will never abandon the two of you or your Dad. I just don't think living in the same house is helping.

I shall be staying with a friend at this address ... I will keep my mobile on 24/7 and the landline number is ... I am very near so can get to you within half an hour.

Let's meet up for lunch next week and see how I can support all of you from a distance.

Lots of love

Mum xxx

Can you believe it? She just wanted me to feel sorry for her and forgive her. It shows how selfish she is. How could she imagine that we could meet up for a civilised lunch as if my father wasn't dying and she wasn't leaving him for someone else. I wonder if she knows what she abandoned me to?

Marcia

I spent the months between Mum leaving and Dad dying either living with my friend's family or in hospital. I couldn't imagine life without either Mum or Dad and my calm, serene, sensible sister had turned into being either an angry monster, with her against the world, or a ministering angel to my Dad.

I was a coward. I couldn't stand seeing Dad in pain, being sick and failing to get to the loo in time. All his dignity was gone. I couldn't recognise him as my Dad. I know that makes me seem like a bitch but I really couldn't cope. At first I would try to visit him but I couldn't bear to stay longer than half an hour. He could hardly speak by then and so we would just look at one another. If I was feeling really brave I would hold his hand and make sure I wore sleeves that would cover my arms, so he wouldn't see the scars and me upset and worried.

I don't know what happened but I found myself in the local loony bin! I don't have any clear memories of being there. I know I refused to speak or eat. I just wanted to shut everything out that was happening to us. Each morning I was disappointed to wake up. I wanted to sleep forever. I know Sarah visited me a few times but that only made things worse. Knowing she was looking after Dad on her own just made me hate my own weakness more.

Kate

The months between leaving and hearing that Gary had died I kept trying to speak with the girls. I went back to work and was immediately very busy catching up on lots of things which hadn't been done in my absence. At the same time, Tim and I had found a flat and were busy trying to set up home together.

At first I had no idea Marcia was no longer living at home or that she was self-harming. I had tried to meet and speak with the girls but they refused to have anything to do with me. I was horrified to hear from a friend about what was happening with Marcia. When I heard she was in hospital I tried several times to visit her, turning up at the hospital but she refused to see me. No one would respond to me, no matter whether I phoned, emailed, wrote, or went round and hammered on doors. They just ignored me. I had left letters for both the girls when I left but I don't even know if they read them.

Most evenings I spent crying, not knowing what to do for the best. I was exhausted. Tim was sympathetic at first but it wasn't what he had planned for. He had hoped that when I finally left, or Gary died, we would have a wonderful carefree life together, enjoying working and travelling and creating a new home. My sadness, depression, guilt, confusion, whatever you want to call it was not what he had bargained for.

Sarah

Shortly after Mum left, Dad really started to decline. Instead of packing my bags to start a new life at university I felt I had to stay and look after Dad. I had months of wiping up his vomit and worse. When I wasn't with Dad I would get someone to sit with him. He was in great pain and I was very scared. He didn't want to spend time in hospital or go into a hospice. He said he wanted to die at home with his girls. Well, it was all too much for Marcia.

She moved out and went to stay at a friend's house. She began cutting herself and within weeks was admitted to a psychiatric hospital where they considered her a suicide risk. That just left me. At times, bizarre though it might seem, I was jealous of Marcia, she just vegged out and had people looking after her, I was trying to look after Dad on my own. At some level I was angry with her, saw her as selfish – just leaving me to it – to cope on my own but at the same time I could see how deeply hurt, confused, and scared she was and felt as the big sister I should somehow protect her.

I tried to visit Marcia in the hospital as much as I could. I don't think she wanted me there – my presence reminded her of Dad and everything that had happened. I felt rejected by her. It was as if, for Marcia, I had come to represent everything that had gone wrong. Mum was out of the picture and Dad was dying so who else was left for Marcia to feel angry with?

I want Mum to know all that. I want her to know what we all went through. I don't want her to have romantic ideas of me reading to Dad while he peacefully wasted away. It wasn't like that – it was horrific.

I know she did keep trying to phone and would write and email every day but that was just to get rid of her own guilt. It wasn't because she cared for me or Dad or Marcia.

In the end I couldn't cope and Dad didn't die at home as he had wished. Six days before his death he was admitted to the local hospice. I couldn't believe it when the nurses told me that Mum had tried to visit him. I made it very clear that Dad would not wish to see her and that they must not let her see him. Those last days were not the worst ones. Although I felt guilty that I hadn't managed to nurse Dad at home, the last days were not the worst ones. I still spent many hours with Dad, he wasn't fully conscious most of the time and there were lots of nurses around to look after him but for the first time in months I was able to breathe, take a walk, or go and have a coffee. Simple things, but they had come to be remote pleasures. I hadn't realised how much I had missed them.

Marcia was out of hospital and living with friends by this time and we were both with Dad when he died. I don't know how the hospice knew it was about to happen. When we got there he looked in the same unconscious but peaceful state he had been in the previous day. We held his hands and his breathing changed and then he was gone. That was it. After all those months it was over and I was left more alone than ever.

Marcia

Eventually, when I was in hospital I began to feel slightly better. I wanted to live but to me it seemed that in order to live I needed to get away, have nothing to do with my family. I felt that if I saw any of them I would tumble back into the darkness that I had just dragged myself out of.

I moved in with some friends who were very supportive and I started working Saturdays. Although I didn't want to see my family, it was too painful; I did need to know how Dad was. I knew he had gone into the hospice and I would ring them each day. They had my mobile number. On the day he died I got a call from one of the staff at the hospice who told me that they did not think he had long to live. They were talking hours, not days. I don't know how I did it but I put on my coat, headed out, got the bus, and found myself walking into the hospice. I was taken to Dad's room. I saw an old thin man on the bed. It was my Dad. I wanted to turn and run but something stopped me. I went and sat beside him, told him I loved him and said I was sorry for not being strong enough to be there for him. About fifteen minutes later Sarah arrived. We didn't speak but just hugged one another. We then each sat at Dad's side until he slipped away. It was very peaceful.

Kate

When I heard that Gary had died, all I could think of were the girls and what they had been through. I had wanted to support them but they wouldn't let me. I left a message for Sarah, saying that I couldn't bear the thought of them having to arrange the funeral themselves and that I wanted to help. It was the first message that she replied to saying she wished it was me not her father who had died and that I must stay away from the funeral and from her and Marcia ... that I no longer had a place in their lives.

I couldn't accept that. On a daily basis I tried to contact one of them. The day of the funeral was awful. I kept thinking of Sarah and Marcia and how brave they had been and were continuing to be. I was a coward. I had let everyone down. I didn't deserve a good future. That day I just locked myself in my study, I couldn't eat or even speak to Tim.

Eventually it got too much for Tim. He knew that I had stopped loving Gary before he became ill and he had supported my decision to try to stay with Gary during that time but once I left and we moved into a flat together Tim thought I could put my marriage to one side and begin to enjoy life again with him. One of the things that had attracted me to him was the way he enjoyed life, loved going out socialising, travelling, visiting galleries, going to the theatre. It was the life I wanted too but I couldn't stop thinking about the girls and whenever we did go out I felt guilty and couldn't enjoy myself. I wasn't surprised that seven months after we moved in together Tim told me he was sorry but it just wasn't working and instead of him helping me out of a depression he felt he too was sinking into one. He was right. I understood he had to leave; I wasn't the same person I had been. I threw myself back into my work and financially I am doing well. I am busy and travelling but I don't enjoy any of it. I miss the girls.

For three years I have tried to speak to Sarah but she has refused. Marcia too has refused to answer any letters or calls. With Marcia I gave up about a year ago. I know she has been ill and I don't want to be an added stress. I want to help but I know she doesn't want me. With Sarah, it's different. She has made it very clear how hurt and how angry she is with me, but somehow I held out a hope that over time she would forgive me and we could establish some kind of relationship. I have heard that she managed to resume her studies and that she has a very nice boyfriend who she now lives with. I can't imagine life just going on for her and me having no part of it. It is just too painful. I think of her having her own children and wonder what she will tell them about me. Will she say I am dead, or that I am evil and therefore to be avoided? I know it can never be the same between us as it was, but I still hope.

When you contacted me to say that Sarah wanted us to go to mediation so that we could have a safe place to speak to one another I couldn't believe it. I am still scared that she still just wants to tell me that I am out of her life forever. Even if that is the case, I would rather take that chance and have the opportunity to see and talk to her than never be in contact with her ever again.

Marcia

After Dad's death I just froze. I am ashamed to say I didn't make it to the funeral. I just couldn't, it was too much. I returned to stay with friends and I am still there. I hear from Sarah, although I never contact her. Mum tried for a year or two to get me to meet up with her but I just ignored her. I don't really want to remember 'family life', it is something which ended and I just want to move forward not think about it all, it is just too painful.

I really couldn't believe it when Sarah contacted me to say she wanted to meet up with Mum and that she had made contact with you about setting up a mediation. I don't see the point. Sarah says Mum needs to know what she did to us. It's too late. What happened, happened. I don't want anything to do with it. Thanks for talking with me but I don't want to see Mum. I don't want to see Sarah either, I just want to move on with my life as best I can.

Sarah

It must seem strange after all this time. Strange that I want to meet Mum and tell her face to face what she did.

Why now? Well, I hope to get married soon. I don't want Mum there but it has made me think about her. I wonder what I will tell my children about her. It is hard to explain to anyone why you chose not to speak to your mother for years and years. People sympathise with me about what she did and how I ended up having to nurse Dad but they seem to feel that because she is my mother, 'my flesh and blood',

imagine having her mother there, it did not seem right that she
could be present and enjoy the occasion, taking a central role as
mother of the bride, whilst her father was dead and unable to walk
her down the aisle. During these sessions she would move between
softer feelings towards her mother and a strong sense that she still
needed to punish her. When she and the mediator explored how she
would know when her mother had been punished enough she
couldn't answer. It was also explored whether this state of angry
limbo had also been any kind of punishment for Sarah too by not
allowing her to move on. It was clear that Sarah's fiancé would like
to meet her mother, his own parents being deceased, and he had
asked Sarah to consider what regrets she may or may not have if her
mother died without them really having the opportunity to know one
another as two adult women. Although Sarah began to remember
better times and to look towards a future in which her mother had
some presence, by the time she went back into joint sessions she
slipped back into her hard stance.

During the individual sessions on the first day, Kate expressed her
feelings of hopelessness and helplessness given Sarah's steely manner.
The mediator encouraged Kate to stay with the process, taking care not
to break any confidentiality by conveying the knowledge that Sarah did
want some kind of relationship with Kate in the future. The mediator
reminded Kate that after such a long time of refusing any contact with
Kate, it was Sarah who had requested the mediation, so something had
changed. This helped sustain Kate through the process.

As the mediation continued Kate became frustrated and impatient,
wanting to push things and to try to get an agreement for the two of them
to meet socially, or for her to meet Sarah's fiancé, even if only for one
time. She was caught between wanting Sarah to know how hard the
experience of being married to Gary had been for her and how angry and
aggressive he had been towards her when she had tried to nurse him, yet
at the same time she was conscious that she did not want Sarah to hear
her speak badly about her father. She could see that any negativity about
Gary was something Sarah would not be prepared to hear and so she saw
no point in trying to change Sarah's view of her father. With the mediator
she explored her understanding of what Sarah was saying and Sarah's continued need to punish her and refuse to accept her apologises. Although
she would have liked to give Sarah what she felt to be a more truthful and
balanced picture of her parents, she accepted that Sarah did not want to
hear this and that to push for that would further alienate her and Sarah.
She decided that she could live with being the one 'in the wrong' if that
would allow a new relationship with Sarah.

At the end of the first day, both agreed to return for another day of mediation. This surprised Kate as she felt Sarah had done what she set out to do – use the mediation to express her ongoing anger. To Kate it seemed hopeless, but she was prepared to do anything if there was even a slight chance of establishing some connection with her daughter.

The second day started with the mediator reminding Kate and Sarah that they would follow the same pattern as before and start with a short joint session where each of them could let the other know what they had taken from the previous day and where they were now in their thinking. In the event, things did not turn out that way. Sarah started by saying she had considered not returning for the second day and again talked of her anger, and her feelings of abandonment and hurt. Kate responded tearfully to this and expressed her love for Sarah and her desire to have just a small part in her life. From this a very lively dialogue ensued, during which the mediator remained silent, being alert to body language and checking in by eye contact with both Sarah and Kate to make sure that both were OK to continue.

Suddenly, something shifted. Sarah was talking about her forthcoming wedding and said 'Don't you think you can control it all and act out the full mother-of-the-bride bit, you certainly won't be sitting on the front row ...' This was the first acknowledgement that Sarah saw her mother as being present at the ceremony. Through the work she had done on the previous day Kate was able to contain herself and not press for clarification or to want more. She just let Sarah know that she had heard what she said and told her, 'I would be delighted just to be allowed to see you, all dressed up in your bridal gown ... you are so beautiful ... you will look so stunning ...'

From then on, the atmosphere changed. Sarah repeatedly told Kate she was not forgiven, not would ever be, but she suggested that they meet regularly every two weeks to see a film or a show and to slowly get to know one another again. Kate was overwhelmed as this was more than she had ever dared to hope for. Even at this stage Sarah was not ready to show any affection towards her mother but got out her diary and booked in the next couple of meetings and discussed where they should take place. She did not want them to leave the mediation together and by this stage Kate could respect and accept that.

A few weeks after the mediation Kate wrote to the mediator to express her thanks and to say she was not going to push but would follow Sarah's pace in developing a new relationship between the two of them. She had got more than she have could ever hoped for from the mediation, and trusted that if things progressed well with Sarah there may be a time in the future when Marcia might agree to meet her.

As with all mediations the key role for the mediator was to develop a trusting relationship with each party, helping them to feel safe in the process and to allow them to hear the beliefs/perceptions of the other.

10 Fear and difference

A workplace mediation

Leo

I just don't get it. What is the matter with all these women? I see them flirting with loads of guys but with me it's different. I'm a 'sexual predator' a 'potential rapist'. Have they any idea how it feels to be looked at that way ... wary ... as though they are just waiting for me to attack..

And what has it got to do with work? Why a grievance? I just don't get it ...

Sue

I really can't believe it. He has destroyed Sally's life. He as good as raped her. I don't think the senior managers have done enough. It shouldn't be left to the likes of me to take a grievance out in order for them to take things seriously. Anyway, they have asked that we try mediation so let's see if that can get through to him.

Leo

What happened happened out of work. It's no one's business except mine and Sal's. That Sue is just a nosy cow. I think she is getting off on causing trouble for me. Perhaps she is jealous that I didn't fancy her.

Sue

Sal and I have been best friends for years. She has been through a lot, has Sal. She had a terrible marriage, and then the struggle of trying to cope alone. Boy has she made good. She worked really hard to qualify as a mature student and I was amazed how she stuck that course out and got a job she really enjoys. She can't afford to give it up. She still has to work in the same building as him. Think what that must be like, day after day, worrying that she may see him. At least they are in completely separate parts of the complex, but I'm expected to work alongside him ... as though nothing has happened. It is all well and good being told that it has all been dealt with in the 'appropriate' way and that I am not allowed to know how – confidentiality, apparently!

Leo

I really liked Sally from day one. She was fun to work with and fit too. Very different from that stuck up man-hater, Sue. I am a healthy, full-blooded, single guy, if I like a woman, I let her know, treat her nice, and hope we can have some fun together. Sally seemed up for that. Several times after work we would go for a drink together, discuss work and have a few laughs. Occasionally we would ask Sue to join us but she was usually in a rush to get home so usually it was just me and Sally. It was good; we got along, had a laugh and a joke and would end the evening with a hug.

Well, we had been going for these drinks off and on for a few months. I really liked Sal so one evening instead of having a drink or two then heading home I suggested we went and had a meal. She seemed keen and we went to a local curry place. It was easy chatting with her and when the meal ended we were in the middle of discussing something or other and we wanted to continue the conversation so went on to a local pub for a few more drinks. After that I walked her home and we had a bit of a snog on her doorstep before I headed home.

The following week she asked if I fancied going for another meal and so we did. It was much the same as the previous week. We got on well, I walked her back and she invited me in. This time it was a bit more than a quick snog but we didn't have sex. I went back home quite early in the morning and when I saw Sal in work the next day she was really warm and saying how much she had enjoyed the previous night and we must do it again soon. She wasn't frightened of me or not wanting me around ... she was doing the pushing. I enjoyed being with her, I liked her, I thought things could develop. We arranged to meet for another meal the following Wednesday. Yes, I did want to have sex with her. We are adults; she had shown she was interested, I reckoned it was the natural next step.

Anyway, we had a great meal but instead of going back to her house we went to my flat. Things developed. I was pretty sure that she had come back with the intention that we would have sex. At first things were good and then she suddenly got cold feet. She had already got partly undressed, which I and most guys would see as a signal that we were on ... Anyway, she suddenly started saying she wasn't up for it and started to grab her clothes. I didn't get it. One minute everything was all systems go, the next she had slammed the brakes on. Why? I have no idea!

I was angry. I thought she was playing with me. I didn't understand what had caused the change. I know I shouldn't have but I grabbed hold of her clothes and told her that she couldn't have them; she couldn't leave. I was confused. I wanted to know what had happened. Why was I attractive to her one minute and not the next? Things had been going great ...

Sue

I know Sal rather admired and fancied him when they first met. I guess he is a good-looking guy, tall, strong, all those kinds of things and he certainly rates himself, walks with quite an arrogant swagger. Like Sal, he has had to work hard to get to the position he is in and I guess she identified with that.

I think many people were surprised when he was given the post as team leader. He had been good on the floor, working in the team but I don't think those of us who know him or work with him had seen anything to suggest he had managerial skills or qualities – he is too fiery and full of himself in my eyes. He has quite a temper. We all know he represented Great Britain in the Olympics, I guess he is right to be proud of that, even though it's some time ago, but that doesn't mean he is better than the rest of us, although he certainly acts as though that's what he believes.

I can only think he was promoted out of some idea of positive dis-crimination. It's true we don't have any other black managers but surely experience, skills, and some level of emotional maturity are more important than the colour of someone's skin. I guess the powers that be don't have to work under him; they just tick the boxes on their equal opportunities return and leave the rest of us to get on with it.

Leo

I really don't know what happened that night. I wanted her to explain. Had I got it completely wrong? Didn't she fancy me? Wasn't I good enough for her? Was she afraid what other people would say? I know I can get very het up about things and I probably did raise my voice. I wanted her to stay and at least explain what the sudden change was about. I really like her.

I wouldn't let her out of the room; I wanted to understand what had changed. I felt that if I gave her back her clothes she would never tell me what had happened and would just walk out so I hung on to them and stood in front of the door to stop her from leaving. I just wanted us to talk. She got pretty hysterical, I grabbed her and held on to her, I may have tried to kiss her, I honestly don't remember ...

Sue

I know Sal did like him. She was quite excited when they first started going for drinks after work. I think she had high hopes that something would develop. Although it's many years since her divorce she hasn't really dated anyone since. Not surprising really, it was a dreadful marriage. Her husband, Joe, was violent to her and she stuck it out for years. He was one of those Jekyll and Hyde characters – meek and mild in public but at home he totally dominated. He wouldn't let Sal work or train, she had to look after the house and him. You can hardly believe that it still is like that for some people. It was hardly as though they could afford for her not to work. Joe was in and out of work the whole time they were married. It was only after they divorced that Sal trained and started working. She was really proud of what she had achieved and rightly so.

I suppose that having the manager take an interest in her really boosted her ego and she did start dressing differently and looking after herself more. On the surface Leo is the opposite of her ex-husband. He seems handsome, uber-confident and a real success.

I think one of the reasons for his promotion is that he looks the part and is confident he is always right ... that and adding a black manager to the leadership team makes it look like the organisation is a good equal opportunities employer. It also gets the Black Support Group off Ted's back.

I sometimes wonder whether I might have progressed higher if I had been black, disabled, lesbian, or working class! I am none of those. I am an uppity, middle-class, confident woman, who won't be messed with. I guess Ted and others may find me difficult. They are more used to dealing with the likes of Sally, who is too scared of losing her job to question how she is treated.

Leo

I really don't understand. There are plenty of guys working here who are seeing colleagues outside work. Several are having affairs. I don't have a wife, Sal is divorced, what is wrong with us getting together?

All my life I have felt that people just look at me and see a big, black guy with muscles. They see me as a threat. Can you imagine what it is like for me? If I am walking behind a woman on her own I can feel her tension, I always cross to the other side of the street. I try to be sensitive to their fears but at the same time it really gets to me. Why should I be seen that way? They don't tense up when there are white guys sharing the pavement with them.

It's confusing, people seem afraid when they don't know me and see me in the street, but women are always coming on to me flirting and all that. They seem to like it when I am playful back.

When I was in the Olympic team they were all over me. I couldn't fight them off. For the first time in my life I felt confident. I could start conversations and not expect people to just stare at me and walk off. People listened to me. They wanted to talk to me. I was interviewed for magazines and TV programmes. Kids who had ignored me now wanted to be my friend. I began to enjoy life for the first time. I liked who I was.

It was hard when all that stopped. I had a few health issues and was told to stop boxing. I was very down. Being down for me also meant being very angry and I got into a bit of trouble. Eventually, though, I had to accept that boxing wasn't going to be my life. I had to deal with all those people, who had wanted to be seen with me when I had a taste of fame, just disappearing. Guess they found someone else's coat tails to hang on to.

I know it's different now. I'm older for a start. I have also been told by the doctor that I have to take things a bit easier, not so many visits to the gym, generally I've got to slow down. I am having checks on my heart. I don't want anyone here at work to know about it. I can still do my work fine. It made me feel real old when he said that. If you have worked hard to build muscles it becomes a way of life. If I stop the gym I turn to flab. It's as though everything that makes me who I am is being taken away from me.

I'm proud of how I got my life back together after boxing. I went off the rails for a couple of years and then I starting taking life seriously. Got qualified, got this job, got promotion.

That's why all this is so awful. I know I have been a bit of a player in my day. I could have behaved better but now I felt ready for a real relationship ... bit late at 40 to start growing up, I know ... and I really thought Sal might be the right person for me to settle down with. I like her. Neither of us have had it easy. I thought we understood one another.

I'm not letting that Sue destroy me, ruin my career, the life I have worked hard for. I feel she has 'stabbed me in the back'. It wasn't Sal who complained to the management, it was Sue, saying she didn't feel safe working in the same space as me. I was really shocked when Ted (the Senior Manager) told me what she said. Of course she is safe with me. I have never raised my hand or voice to her and never would. Until all this happened with Sal, Sue and I got on OK. I know we are very different and don't always see eye to eye but before we could joke about this, now she won't speak to me or even look at me. If I enter the room she leaves. People see that happening, I worry about what they think I might have done to her for her to act that way.

Sue

I guess, at first, Leo was good for Sal. Her confidence improved. She had a spring in her step. It was the first time she had allowed any man to get close to her since her divorce. I was really surprised when the two of them got together. I thought Leo would want someone glam, young, and out for a good time like him.

They did seem to get on. It was good seeing Sal with a smile on her face. She was really excited about their meals together and she was hoping something more would develop. She was looking for a steady relationship – she just picked the wrong guy with Leo. Everyone knows he is a player. He can't see a woman without flirting with her.

I don't really know what happened that evening. Sal won't talk about it. The first I knew was when she banged on my door after midnight that night. She was in tears and she had bruises on her upper arms. She kept saying she was afraid Leo was going to rape her. I finally got from her that she hadn't been raped but that he had really frightened her. I still wanted her to report it to the police. She had been assaulted ... she was bruised. She didn't want to report it and made me promise that I wouldn't go to the police either. I wasn't happy about that but didn't feel I could go against her wishes.

The next morning I went to see Ted. Sal hadn't said anything about not telling him. I told him what had happened and said I wasn't willing to work in the same place as Leo. Ted suspended Leo whilst an investigation took place.

Sal was angry I had spoken to Ted and wouldn't take part in the investigation and so Leo was back at work within a few days and looking as full of himself as ever. I am still so angry with him. Even though Ted has said it has been dealt with – there has been a disciplinary, it isn't dealt with as far as I am concerned. I can't work with the man. I don't really feel scared of him, I'm mainly angry about his arrogance. I can't stand to look at him, be in the same room as him and I certainly can't work with him.

Ted has said that I have to work with him or leave. He suggested this mediation. I think he just wants to be seen as trying to do something but he has made the bottom line clear enough – I'm out if I don't work with Leo. I know Leo doesn't want this mediation either. As far as he is concerned it's all over and done with. Although I don't hold out much hope of any change, I am interested to see what happens. Will he try to charm you as he tries with all women?

Leo

I don't think Sue would act this way if I was a white man. I see her with the other men at work; they are all white, she is quite happy to have a laugh and a joke with them, even to flirt a little. Sometimes I feel I want to stab her, poke some sense into her, make her see how it is for me.

Has she any idea what it feels like? If I see a white woman on the pavement in front of me I know she will feel uneasy. I see it in her shoulders and the way she clutches her bag more tightly. When that happens I cross to the other side of the road and quicken up so that I am in front of her, if she can see my back she has no need to fear me . . .

I have had to work hard all my life to try to get people to see me for who I am rather than a stereotype.

Sue

The worst thing about this whole business is what it has done to Sal. She feels so ashamed and worthless. She can't face going into work and just look at Leo . . . I mean just look at him . . . he walks around as though nothing has happened, he is totally unaffected by it all. If I could see some clue that he knew what he had done . . .

Reflections on the mediation

It was early in my career as a mediator that I was asked to mediate between Leo (an Afro-Caribbean man) and Sue (a Caucasian woman), who worked together in a highly charged creative environment. Both were the same age and held the same level of power within their organisation. I learnt a lot about them in our pre-mediation meetings and telephone conversations which took place in the two weeks leading up to the mediation day. I discovered that although they had reached the same point professionally, their backgrounds and aspirations were quite different.

Sue was the only child of middle-class parents. She had been born in the South of England and attended a single sex grammar school before going on to university, where she was academically successful and politically active. She had married quite late and she and her husband were hoping for a child; this was proving difficult and leading to some stresses in the relationship. Despite being in the same job for over ten years she wasn't looking for further promotion, although she was very committed to the work. Instead she was aiming to try to reduce her workplace stress in the hope that it would increase her likelihood of conception.

Leo was from the Midlands and was one of nine children. His parents had come to the UK to work in the car industry when their first child was two years old. For a while this eldest child remained behind in St Kitts, with his grandparents, whilst the parents found work and accommodation. The rest of the children, including Leo, were born in Birmingham. The eldest son did not come to the UK until he was 12 years old. Leo saw this brother as 'different' and 'foreign' and felt he never quite fitted in with the rest of the family. Leo attended the local comprehensive school but was never very academic and had been 'a bit difficult … getting into quite a few scraps …'

On leaving school at the earliest opportunity he became an apprentice engineer to one of his older brothers. He had a girlfriend at the time who, when they were both just 17, gave birth to his first child. The relationship was short-lived although he still has contact with his son who is now 20. He went on to marry when he was 25 and to have two more children before they divorced. He felt the relationship with his ex-wife was strained but that he had a reasonably good relationship with his children given that he had lived geographically distant from them for several years.

When he was still at school he had become very interested in boxing and showed enough skill to be chosen for the Olympic team when he was 19. This changed how he felt about himself. His confidence grew and he felt very proud of his achievements. In the event he did not do very well in the Olympics and on his return decided that he wanted more out of life and took an Open University course which qualified him to obtain his current post. He had been in post only one year when he gained promotion to his current managerial post. He was proud of his current position and felt that he 'had shown a few doubters that they were wrong about him'. Despite this confidence he had suffered a few 'run ins with some colleagues'. He felt many of those who had been there longer than him were jealous of his speedy promotion and he was 'on the alert to people who may try to screw him over and get him thrown out of that post'.

The working relationship between Sue and Leo had always been fairly strained, there were many things they did not see eye to eye on, but it had finally broken down following an allegation by another white female worker, Sal (a close friend of Sue's), of serious sexual harassment by Leo. Leo and Sue were aware that they had to continue to work together or one of them would need to leave.

I was brought in by the employer to offer a third-party intervention. The employer did not really care what the resolution contained as long as both parties were back in work and able to work together. There were no alternative posts that they could offer either Sue or Leo and so it was essential that they found a way of working together, which could be sustained. The organisation was not looking for any kind of judgement, as they felt they had already dealt with the allegation of sexual harassment through their disciplinary process.

When this case came up, I had just finished a piece of training focused on theories of conflict, so at the time I found it useful to check the reality against the theory by looking at this case using some theoretical frameworks. I am sharing these thoughts here as they may be of interest to those of you who like a more structured, academic, and systemic approach.

Many people have tried to analyse the steps which need to be taken to resolve a conflict. Vuchinich (1990) suggested that conflicts might be resolved by five different methods: compromise, third-party intervention, withdrawal, standoff, and submission. In this case, neither Leo nor Sue was willing to compromise. Both felt very strongly about the situation. Both were angry, and instead of looking to work together to find a way forward they had withdrawn from each other, refusing to speak to one another and thus creating a standoff and a desire to avoid submission. It is often the fear of being the one who 'submits' that keeps people from the mediation table. People in conflict find it hard to believe that a settlement can be reached which does not humiliate one side or one in which a judgement is formed that one person is right and the other wrong. In this case shame and potential humiliation were key themes and accompanied by anger on both sides. Both Leo and Sue had a strong belief in fairness as a value they held highly. When we can find commonality with another we can begin to empathise with them.

Empathy is one factor that can be called on to reduce and resolve disputes. In order to feel empathy we have first to 'meet'

ourselves in the other. It is not easy to feel empathic towards some-
one/thing we experience as alien. In this case, the 'otherness' of
each party was very evident; gender, class, race, cultural and moral
codes. Sgubini (2006) states that

> Mediation ... helps to bridge the gap between differences and this
> requires knowing and respecting the culture of people that you
> meet. When carrying on an international mediation or even
> a domestic mediation with diverse parties, a mediator must take the
> cultural differences into consideration.

As a mediator I have to be aware of the level of difference between participants, with the possibilities this creates for one party to identify and
project all that is dark, sinister, or negative into the other party.

I was aware of the degree of anger both felt towards the other, and
yet I was unprepared for the very overt way in which this was
expressed in the mediation. As I have shown earlier, it is usual for
mediations to start with both parties together in the same room with
the mediator. They are then each invited to say how they believe
they have come to this point in time where they find themselves in
mediation.

Sue started by saying she was angry about what had happened to Sal
and with Leo's 'arrogant behaviour since then'. She spoke clearly and
assertively but didn't shout and remained in her seat. Leo's anger was
even more apparent. He listened to Sue's comments and then, rising
from his chair, stated he was so angry with Sue that he felt like stabbing
her. He shouted about how white people always thought of black men
as 'sexual ogres, rapists, out of control'. This had been expressed in
a more controlled way in our pre-mediation conversations and I had
found it hard for me as a white woman to hear and I assumed it would
also be disturbing and difficult for Sue. Despite my anxiety I was pleased
that he had immediately touched on the sense of otherness he felt, and
the ways in which he believed others experienced him. It is interesting
that in his choice of metaphor, 'stabbing', he had chosen one which was
highly charged and if considered from a Freudian perspective, picked up
on the allegations of penetration implicit in the rape allegation. It felt
important for me to remember that I was not here as his therapist but
as a mediator and not to analyse the language but to meet and stand
strongly alongside his choice of language.

In this case race was clearly an issue for Leo who believed that
people, in particular women, chose to see him as an archetypal sexually
aggressive black man. Fanon (1986), himself a black African, describes

how white culture identifies the black man with the 'dark', 'animal' quality it fears in its own sexuality:

> European civilization is characterized by the presence, at the heart of what Jung calls the collective unconscious, of an archetype: an expression of the bad instincts, of the darkness inherent in every ego, of the uncivilized savage, the Negro that slumbers in every black man.
>
> Fanon (1986:187)

A mediator must take note of the level of difference between participants, with all the possibilities this may present for projection and projective identification, and the potential for identification of one party as bad, dark, unknown, and therefore threatening.

I believe the majority of conflicts, although perhaps starting with an objective disagreement, become enmeshed by virtue of identity issues and individual value sets, which need to be respectfully explored. This is true of both individual and small and large group conflicts. Rummel (1970) argued in relation to social disputes, the balance between order, power, and justice in society, and the need for security, protection, and autonomy are central. Jensen-Campbell, Graziano, and Hair (1996) proposed the 'realistic conflict theory', suggesting group conflict is based on prejudice related to inequitable distribution of resources i.e. 'instrumental conflicts'. As noted earlier, they suggested that conflicts might be resolved by five different methods: compromise, third-party intervention, withdrawal, standoff, and submission. In this case, neither party was originally willing to compromise and instead had chosen to withdraw from each other, refusing to speak to one another thus creating a standoff and a desire to avoid submission. In this case, mediation was sought. Aspects of these prejudices and conflict progression stages can also be seen in the dispute between Leo and Sue. We see 'non-instrumental' elements reinforcing identity and creating negative stereotypes.

As mediator, I needed to understand and take into account Leo's worldview and his emotional response to it, exploring the importance of how he saw himself and how this contrasted with how he experienced others seeing him. I also needed to explore his response to me as a white, female mediator. I had opened the discussion about my race and gender in the pre-mediation conversations and he had declared that it didn't matter to him but, given his opening statements, I explored this further in my first private session with him. He chose not to speak directly about his thoughts about me, merely saying that he 'trusted me to be an impartial mediator' but went on to say that many of his experiences with women had not been positive. 'You don't know where you are with them.'

My task with Sue was to explore her emotional and ethical response to the situation. It was important to understand what she wanted out of the mediation and what that outcome might mean going forward. For the mediation to succeed I needed both parties to take the other's worldview into account. This was difficult, as it may have seemed that they had to give credence to the other's position when it fundamentally differed from their own. In Sue's case I was also asking that she see Leo as another person with human vulnerabilities even though it was clear that she had dehumanised him and did not consider him to be worthy of respect or consideration.

There is not the space here to describe the mediation in full. However, it taught me an important lesson. After the first opening remarks, for which both were present and at which Leo made his outburst, I met separately with the parties. Sue told me that she was feeling much better! For her one of the things that she had found hardest to cope with was that the case had seemed to have no effect on Leo – 'he continued in his usual arrogant way, whilst her friend Sal was distraught'. Sue told me that 'I now see that he is really shaken by it and deeply upset … he has lost his cool … that means a lot'. She spoke of her anger at the way Leo had continued to behave as though 'nothing had happened, as though it meant nothing'. For her, his behaviour in the opening session had shown this was far from true and surprisingly for me, it seemed that this was what she was really hoping for in the mediation. The impact on her friend had been so great that she needed to see something similar in Leo.

When the mediation continued with private sessions I learnt of Leo's tension between 'the need to be macho and tough, not someone to mess with' and his desire to form an emotional relationship. He felt he was different to the tough youth he had needed to be, but was finding it hard to change without feeling he was making himself vulnerable. He spoke eloquently about the way he believed people saw him. He knew he was an imposing figure, indeed in the past this had worked for him – 'People don't mess with Leo'. He knew that although some people admired his toughness, others were just scared of him. We got to the point where he shared that most of the time he was emotionally frightened and only felt safe when he had demonstrated his own physical strength in some way. I asked him if he would be willing to share some of this with Sue. Initially he was very clear that he did not want to do this as it would give her 'ammunition' to use against him. We explored this fear and laid it alongside his wish to be more fully seen and understood by others.

In the next joint session Leo spoke about his own experience of being a 'big, black man in a world of white people'. He felt that he was always seen as sexual and this led to misunderstandings. This can be seen as an example of the type of cultural, social and racial stereotyping which can cause disputes. Kovel (1995), warns of the tendency for a psychic ghettoisation into different kinds of being: sex roles, general roles, social roles in general, to take place and Altman (2003, quoted in Totton 2006:34), describes how, 'black people represent the objectified human being ... suitable containers for our sense of oppression'. Zizek (1989:127) goes further, focusing on some of what may be feared in this objectification, 'We always impute to the "other" an excessive enjoyment ... what bothers us about the "other" is the peculiar way he organizes his enjoyment'.

Leo described how he saw white colleagues 'playfully flirting' in a way which he felt would be interpreted as sexual harassment if he behaved in the same way. He spoke softly about his sensitivity as to how he was perceived e.g. crossing the road to avoid walking behind white women in case they were scared he would attack them. In speaking in this way he unconsciously spoke to Sue's value system.

I encouraged Leo to bravely speak to Sue about his experiences and perceptions. When Leo was able to be vulnerable and share these things with Sue she respectfully listened. She hated inequality, and she saw that Leo occupied a less secure place in the world than she did. She was able to express empathy for his position. This in turn led to Leo saying he was sorry about the way he behaved towards Sal, that he really liked her and had acted out of frustration because he felt once again he wasn't being seen as human, just as a sexual predator. He asked Sue to pass on his apologies, saying he would like to do that himself face to face but he doubted Sal would be willing to be in the same room as him. Sue thanked Leo and said she would speak to Sal and let her know what Leo had said.

The parties left the mediation together and spent some time talking calmly in the car park. Although they will never be friends they are able to work together and behave professionally with one another. With Leo's permission, Sue shared with Sal what Leo had told her in the mediation, and all three met for coffee where Leo apologised to Sal.

This case stayed in my mind for a long time and I checked back with the organisation some three years later to find that Sue, Leo, and Sal were all still there and working together.

For those of you who like to understand more of the theory, I thought it might be interesting to look at Leo and Sue's tale and see to what extent it maps onto one prominent theory of conflict which I was studying at the time of this mediation. Freidrich Glasl (1999) proposed that conflict escalates through an identifiable number of phases:

Hardening
Debate and polemics
Actions not words
Images and coalitions
Loss of face
Strategies of threats
Limited destructive blows
Fragmentation of the enemy
Together into the abyss

I shall look at these in the context of this case.

Hardening

In the initial stages both Sue and Leo felt they had tried to make their views known to each other but had failed to be listened to. As Glasl postulates, 'standpoints attract adherents, and groups start to form around certain positions' (1999:148). In this case this was particularly disturbing as it split male/female and black/white. More effective early interventions from management could have helped at this stage but the manager was young and inexperienced and very worried about being seen as sexist or racist. Thus the habitual behaviour patterns of which Glasl writes began, firstly with verbal sparring, moving to a position where neither party believed in the humanity of the other, or the possibility of resolution, and thus the conflict moved to stage two.

Debate and polemics

By now, both were locked into inflexible positions, moving on from the initial incident and beginning to focus on what each perceived to be the intrinsic personality of the other. Each chose to label the other with an 'ism'. For Sue, Leo was sexist; for Leo, Sue was racist, and they each portrayed the other's followers as absurd. At this stage, if they had not shared common goals within their work it would be difficult to see how this could resolve.

Actions not words

From here, Leo and Sue refused to speak to or acknowledge each other; fitting Glasl's description, they began to 'see themselves as being held captives by external circumstances they cannot control. They therefore deny responsibility for the course of events. An increasing part of their own actions are regarded as necessary responses to the behaviour of the other' (1999:132). In seeing themselves in this way, Leo and Sue moved away from the existential requirement to take responsibility for their own perceptions, decisions and actions, and the consequences which may follow.

Images and coalitions

The previous phase was followed by increased reduction of the other to a fixed archetype. By now these negative images had become so strong and sedimented that they made it impossible for the parties to see each other in their common humanity. They only saw the other party as a fixed alien force, intent on defeating them, and so denying the potential for change.

They both tried to involve supporters in identifying these stereotypes in the other. Leo turned to the Black Workers Support Group, which in this organisation was entirely male. Sue was already acting as 'rescuer' for Sal, and so was already in coalition with her. Together, Sue and Sal also looked to other female workers for support, although they did this informally and not through any organised group. In the choice of their coalitions they were all reinforcing gender and race differences. This made it harder to relate to the other person as another human being with common fears and vulnerabilities. Each group sought to define 'their member' as the victim – Leo of racism, and Sue and Sal of sexism and sexual assault. By default the other then became the perpetrator.

Loss of face

The conflict quickly moved into Glasl's stage 5. The stereotyping, which had been reinforced by the coalitions, left Leo in particular feeling he was being seen not as his true self but as if through the mask of the other. This is a state in conflict which divides people into angels and devils, with one side representative of the good forces in the world and the other representing all which is destructive, subhuman and bestial. This mirrors Fanon's 'uncivilised savage' motif. Leo's fear of 'loss of face' thorough showing hurt or vulnerability paradoxically led him to act in a way which was perceived as 'arrogant' and reinforced the image Sue had built of him. The beginning of the resolution of the conflict occurred when Leo showed his vulnerability even if this was expressed through verbal aggression. Fortunately Sue recognised it as such. We often see aggression used as a defensive response to fear, and in 'macho' cultures the only 'acceptable' response if they wish to retain respect from their social group. In my work with gangs this has often been a key motivator.

Strategies of threats/limited destructive blows/ fragmentation of the enemy

One could say that it was the threat of damaging action (i.e. the grievance procedure), which provided the motivation to move things on to the next stages. The threat created a pressure to act rapidly and radically, as it carried with it the desire to 'eliminate/destroy' the other through seeking to engage the management in taking disciplinary action. Leo and Sue rapidly moved to a position where their primary desire was survival. They sought to have their view validated by the mediator while the other's views were denied.

The mediation process seemed to prevent them moving into Glasl's 'together into the abyss' stage. It has been suggested that there are seven main reasons for negotiations failing, and although my example resolved successfully, I wish to take the opportunity to explore the case in relation to these suggestions. The first is the premise, held by both sides, that the other party does not deserve to win or gain anything. In this case, both parties had to continue to work together. Following the line of my mediation plan, we made this common need explicit at the start of the mediation.

Secondly, it is often suggested that emotions can disrupt negotiation. In this case, emotions were highly charged. Neither party started with respect for the other. Feelings of hatred were overtly expressed and Sal spoke of her fear of Leo and endeavoured to paint a strong picture of his 'otherness' during the private sessions. Leo's shame about the original allegation led him into a defensive rage. For me as mediator, the client's emotions provide a valuable tool with which to work, although I was concerned in this case about the impact Leo's opening statement may have had on Sue.

Many psychological minded mediators see the expression of emotion as a gift they can work with:

> every emotion is connected with the givens, and each emotion is a manifestation of an aspect of people's worldview. Indeed, emotions are the most useful tools for the mediator and for the parties to gain insight into aspects of their own worldview ... they can highlight some of the ambivalences each party holds ...
>
> (Strasser & Randolph, 2004:146)

Scheff & Retzinger (1991) drew our attraction to the emotion 'shame', which we can identify in Leo. He identified a core sequence in emotional conciliation which requires that one party expresses shame or remorse and that allows the other to move to the first step towards forgiveness or acceptance of the other. Although not disagreeing with this in relation to restorative justice practices, I believe it is important to consider what shame means within the culture of the individual. Culturally it was difficult for Leo to openly express remorse, but his shame was apparent in his emotional responses. I would also question whether 'forgiving' is necessary for a resolution. One may come to an understanding and an acceptance, allowing one to let go, without forgiving the other person for actions one continues to believe to be unacceptable.

Glasl also emphasised the importance of 'justice'. Leo had become 'the other' in Sue's eyes and in his own. He did not feel that Sue saw him as fully human, but merely as a stereotype and so not to be trusted or deserving of equal treatment. Leo was a boxer and believed that one defended oneself through attack (not necessarily physical) and his racial, cultural, and class background meant that he saw an admission to vulnerability as a failing in his masculinity. A mediator must always be impartial, but as a white woman I had to explicitly demonstrate impartiality and fairness throughout the process, ensuring that both parties had equal opportunities to express their views and these were held to be equally important. Neither Sue nor Leo felt safe when they agreed to the mediation and I was careful to choose a neutral venue to which both parties agreed and to make the non-judgemental aspect of my role clear.

It was essential that I maintained both parties' self-esteem. Leo's self-esteem and self-concept seemed the more vulnerable of the two, and I had to bear in mind the need to take care in relation to this even when I challenged him with possible outcomes if he stuck rigidly to his current stance.

It is accepted that negotiations may often lead in unexpected directions. This was certainly the case here. What Sue required for a successful resolution was different from what I had anticipated. For her, it was good enough that she saw Leo affected by the allegation. She saw him move from an apparently confident and aggressive stance, to one demonstrating that the event had impacted on him and so made him vulnerable. In Leo becoming vulnerable, Sue became strong. This emphasised the importance of mediators being truly open and bracketing their own assumptions.

On the surface, both parties had equal power. However, both felt power imbalances in relation to their gender and race and these played an important part in the dispute and needed gentle exploration. In the one-to-one sessions it was apparent that both considered that despite doing work they liked, others might consider them to have failed because they had not 'progressed' their careers. Both held a need to be superior to the other, and in the eyes of the mediator.

The mediation allowed both to express their concerns, including some difficult feelings and perceptions which each held towards the other, and to identify points of commonality. Breaking through deception and secrecy allowed the real issues to be discussed. Sue's fear of Leo subsided once she had seen his vulnerability and her own feelings of strength grew. She was then able to treat him as a fellow human being, thus removing one of his major grievances.

Both parties had hoarded negative judgements about each other, and reduced the other to a stereotype. It is common for there to be multiple resentments, wounds that hurt, and moments when the parties seem repugnant and barely human to each other. In this mediation these feelings were safely explored. Once the strength of these emotions was acknowledged this led to the possibility of change which in turn made working together possible.

Hicks (1996) and Tantam (2002) both propose models which involve meeting the parties separately before the mediation in order to consider whether the conflict is about issues or identity, This was particularly relevant in this case. It was not possible to meet either party face to face before this mediation, although I engaged in pre-mediation phone calls with both. In my call with Leo I checked how he felt about the mediator being a white woman. He brushed this off as being of no importance to him. However, my question did demonstrate an acknowledgement that I did not share his gender or race but that I was aware that it may influence the level of trust he felt he could place in me. I don't think a pre-mediation face-to-face meeting would have improved the outcome of the mediation, as it may have prevented Leo's emotional outburst in the opening statement, an emotional outburst which paradoxically marked a breakthrough for Sue.

As the mediation started with an expressed attack, in that Leo felt 'stabbed in the back' and wanted to 'stab' Sue, I chose to pick up on the flavour of these words and to speak of 'wound' and 'feeling wounded' when talking to both parties. Although I challenged both to explore the worldview of the other and inviting them to interpret actions through that view, I was careful to use their language and not to be confrontational in the way the parties had been in the opening.

In these emotive mediations, which are often found in workplace conflicts, it is important to understand the assumptions, values, beliefs and behaviours of both parties. My own experiences as a white woman inevitably inform my worldview, and so I must be conscious of what this may bring into any mediation. Despite the differences between Leo and myself, we were able to build a trusting alliance. The mediation was helped by the parties shared believed in the importance of the work they did and their acknowledgement that ultimately they needed to continue to work together whatever happened. The current situation was damaging the work and having a negative impact on the clients they both cared about. In reminding them of this shared belief and need throughout the sessions I was able to maintain their commonality and therefore their connectedness.

Through encountering and gaining some understanding of the other's worldview and being brave enough to show their vulnerabilities, Sue and Leo were able to see each other as fellow humans with strong commonalities as well as differences. For a mediation to succeed it does not require acceptance of the other's views, just a greater understanding of how they come to hold those views. Earlier I expressed the importance of emotions; here we see that the success of this mediation was almost entirely due to Sue finally seeing an emotional reaction from Leo.

11 Competition and challenge

A workplace relationship mediation

Jane

I'm not interested in mediating. I'm Sarah's manager, and I can sort this out. I don't know why the HR department have brought you in. If she wants to take out a grievance against me, then let her. I haven't done anything wrong. She is difficult and lazy, that's basically all there is to it and I am not prepared for it to continue like that. She needs to get her act together and get on with her work, or leave.

I think she has asked for this mediation just to embarrass me in front of you. It is another attack on my seniority. She hates the fact that I am her manager.

Sarah

It's been unbearable. The woman is out of control. She has a lot to teach Hitler. She expects us to greet her with a salute each morning! I don't feel this mediation will change anything, it's just who she is, but I don't want all the hassle of going through with the grievance so I'm going to give it a try.

Jane

It seems like I have no choice. The HR department have said I have to take part in this mediation. They are afraid that if Sarah took them to an employment tribunal it would look bad if they hadn't tried mediation first. I think Sarah has them scared and wrapped round her little finger.

I don't see the problem. Sarah is lucky to be in a job. We both are. Lots of people were made redundant in the restructuring and she should be grateful she wasn't one of them.

I have worked here for over ten years. For the last five I was PA to Mr Sym, who is Head of Department. Well he was, he took the opportunity that the restructuring presented to take early retirement. Before he left he told me how much he respected me and that he felt I could do his job after all the years I had spent looking after and supporting him. It was true that during that time I had pretty much learned how to do his job. I wrote his letters for him, minuted his meetings, organised his diary. I was essential to his success.

When I heard about the restructure I was a bit worried as they were changing the administrative system to use a shared services model which meant that personal PA posts were not going to exist. Now all the senior officers have to share a pool of senior admin staff rather than have their own PA with whom they could build a strong working relationship. I always prided myself that I knew Mr Sym's needs almost before he knew them himself! That kind of professionalism isn't possible in the new system.

I shared my fears about how I would fare in the restructuring with Mr Sym, who put my mind at rest and told me I was highly respected and valued by the organisation and they couldn't afford to let me go. He created a new managerial post which he encouraged me to apply for. I was so pleased when I saw he was on the interviewing panel and delighted when I heard I had got the job. It's a tremendous opportunity for me and although I haven't previously managed staff I have had plenty of experience in helping Mr Sym manage his teams. I am a good manager. I know what is needed and I don't take any excuses. My motto is step up or ship out!

Sarah

It has been a very scary time. I was happy in my previous post. For four years I managed the IT team. All guys, but I liked that. They were straight, said what they thought, and just got on with things. They did their jobs well and I respected that. We would discuss new ways for delivering our services and they would always have good creative ideas. I was their manager but I was always happy to learn from them and not too proud to ask if there was an area of expertise in which one of them had more experience than me. We got along really well and I was sad when it became clear that the restructuring meant the organisation was going to outsource the IT support function.

It's a shame as we were all great at our jobs. Everyone started and finished work on time and we succeeded in structuring the day so that there was never anything left outstanding. This was helpful to me as

I have a disabled husband who over the past two years has been very ill. I work hard during the day at work and in the evening I work hard at home too, caring for Mike. We value that time together. It is important to me to spend time with him. The prognosis isn't great and I don't want us to waste what time we have.

I don't want to sound like a martyr. I do things for myself too. As the IT manager I signed on to Management and Leadership evening classes. I guess that might have helped me come out with a better job in the restructuring but I have never really wanted more responsibility. Although my job certainly isn't my life, just a small part of it, I have always wanted to do my job to the best of my ability. I loved managing the team and I think the course helped me with that. I know I don't know much about management but I sure know more than Jane. I can't believe how she does things. She seems to think she is a Sergeant Major and that when she says jump, you jump!

It is not just me who has a problem with her. There are several people who have put in grievance procedures against her but they are all on hold pending the outcome of this mediation. Although there are all those others who find her difficult I do think she has something personal against me – I don't know what it is but she certainly has it in for me, I can't do anything right.

Jane

Although I enjoyed working for Mr Sym I always wanted a more responsible managerial post. No one really respects you when you work in 'admin', they think you just file and photocopy things. Certainly my husband doesn't think much of what I have done so far.

My husband is very high up in his company and we often have his work colleagues over. He has told me how important it is that they should view us positively, it all enhances his promotion chances. I never have much to contribute to dinner party discussion. They are all high flyers.

I think I am a pretty good cook and hostess. The house looks wonderful. There are always fresh flowers on the table, and I take real care over the food – only the best ingredients and unusual recipes – I scour magazines looking for interesting ideas and file them away. When I serve up the food there are often positive comments but then it is as though I just disappear. The 'grown ups' start talking about their work, plans for expansion, business trips abroad, new strategies for business development etc. It has always made me feel out of my depth and very boring so I just go quiet. No one seems to notice, no one tries to draw me into the conversation. I just top up the wine glasses and replace one course with the next.

I know that sounds bitter. It isn't really that bad and anyway things are changing ... have changed. This job has changed my status. I am no longer the wife who earns a bit of pin money with a cosy job in an office, I am a manager, I have status, and I have something to say. I can join in the conversations. I can talk about the restructuring and how I am improving the quality of the work here by taking no stick and ensuring everyone works to their full capacity. As Tim (my husband) would say 'there are no slackers on my watch'. He is very strict with his staff, he won't let anyone take advantage or not pull their weight. I think Tim is amazed to know how well I can do this job.

I haven't told him about this mediation or the trouble with Sarah and the others ... You know there are five of them conspiring against me, they all have grievances pending which are on hold whilst the mediation goes ahead. If Tim found out about all this I would be back to being the 'little wife' again. I don't want him to find out about this. I don't think he has ever really believed I could do a managerial job and it is important to me that he isn't proved right.

Anyway, enough about Tim. I have no idea how I have ended up talking about my home life. One of the things that makes all this worse is that Sarah is one of the few people I felt I could talk about personal things with. Of course when I moved into management and she was in my team, I had to stop that, it wouldn't have been appropriate to the manager/employee relationship which we have now.

She knows that at times things haven't gone too well with Tim and I ... but then no marriage runs smoothly all the time and it is hard when your husband is away a lot on business trips abroad with colleagues ... some of whom are very smart and attractive women. I am not saying he has affairs but a couple of years ago I did wonder if something was going on and I did talk to Sarah about it. She was very understanding and helpful but now I am embarrassed that I ever said anything to her about my doubts. When I ask her to do something and she doesn't do it, she gives me a look which says she knows the truth about me and has no respect for me.

Sarah

Jane has always seemed a bit on the hard side, closed off and a bit aloof. A few years ago we were both on the company tennis team and I did see a slightly different side to her. A few of us would sometimes go for drink after a match and she would talk to me a bit about her home life. She is hugely proud of her husband. He has done really well. They aren't short of money and they have a beautiful house ... not that I have ever been inside. I think she felt as though she had to work hard to be a credit to him. I gathered that all their social life revolved round his friends from work. Apart from the tennis, as far as I know, she didn't see anyone from work socially and she never mentioned friends of her own, just friends of Tim's. I know he works abroad a lot and that it has been hard for her. She was never 'Mrs Sociable' but she wasn't like she is now.

The promotion has made her worse. There is a definite 'us and them' now. She is on the management side and the rest of us ... well, we are of no consequence. We are just cogs in the wheel which she is driven to ensure keeps going round and round. She stopped coming to the tennis club, saying it wasn't appropriate for her to socialise with people she managed! She thinks she is above the rest of us now.

Despite all that, I think she is struggling with the new job. She has never managed anything. I don't think she has ever had any training. I offered to lend her some of the books from my course but she nearly bit my head off! She was really insulted but I genuinely wanted to help her. I have lots of ideas about how things could be done more effectively but she isn't willing to listen to anyone. I think she is scared that if she asked for or accepts help, people will question whether she is up to the job.

In many ways I feel for her but she has no excuse to treat people in the awful way she does. If she were nicer she may find the job a bit easier.

Jane

The trouble with Sarah is that although she is lazy and shows little interest in her job, she thinks she knows all there is to know about it ... she even offered to lend me some books she has for a two pennyworth evening course on management she is doing – the cheek! She has ideas for everything. Anything I ask her to do she just comes back with ideas of how it could be done more efficiently or even questions whether we need to do it all. She doesn't seem to get it. We aren't here to ask questions and waste time; we are here to do what we are told and to get on with it, without question.

I never did like all that studying which she seems to enjoy so much. I found school tough. I have learnt what I need to know from Mr Sym. His way of doing things served him well for many years. I learnt on the job – the best way to learn. Tim wouldn't encourage me taking time in the evening to study or attend classes. We have a busy social life, lots of dinner parties to prepare. The socialising helps with his business and I'm a very good hostess.

I was so pleased to get this new job, it's a wonderful opportunity for me but I am worried. There is talk of a merger and I think I will be very vulnerable if that happens. I was OK with the last restructuring because Mr Sym was looking out for me but he has retired and I feel sure that the people in similar managerial positions within the company we are planning to merge with will be better-qualified and more experienced than I am. It makes me feel quite vulnerable. Sarah is probably quite sensible to be gathering further qualifications. If I think about it she does seem to have picked up some ideas from that course but it is not her position to decide strategy, that's my job!

Perhaps that's what her studies are all about ... perhaps she has got wind of the merger and is positioning herself for any managerial opportunities, probably ensuring she would be seen more favourably than me ... very clever! That explains a lot of things, she is hoping to undermine me, lower my confidence, make others aware that she has got ideas, training, etc.

She also has more managerial experience than me. She managed the IT team before the restructuring. I had sort of forgotten that – I guess she can't feel too happy about me getting this current post ahead of her. I haven't really given that much thought. Mr Sym more or less promised it to me and I really never considered anyone else – whether they would be interested, better-qualified, etc. I saw it as a reward for the good work I had done for Mr Sym. I do deserve this post and I am good at it but they are all making things very difficult for me.

You would think when I was given this position the company would have arranged some training or induction for me but there was nothing. I guess they recognised my talents and didn't think it would be necessary but I think it would have helped a bit, at least people like Sarah wouldn't be able to say I had no training or experience. Do you think it's too late to ask for some training now? If it takes place in work-time then Tim can't object. I am still scared at the thought. In truth I admire Sarah, the way she has just constantly, over the years, gone about adding to her skills, taking any training opportunities available and even studying in her own time. I know things aren't easy for her at home. Her husband has been very ill for years.

Sarah

I don't know how Jane got her job. I don't think they advertised or interviewed for it. I never saw anything on the noticeboard or in the internal post. Suddenly the new structure charts were sent round and

there was Jane, moved from a PA post to a managerial one. I was
shocked. What did she know about managing people? I know she was
a brilliantly efficient PA, and I could learn a lot from her about managing systems but her previous job never required her to manage
people. I would have applied for the new post if I had known about it,
I have been doing this management course and I am really interested in
all the management theories …

Mind you, reading about it isn't the same as doing it. Jane's job is much
more complex than managing the IT team, they were a great bunch of
guys. They had been there for years and didn't really need any management. We loved bouncing new ideas off each other, trying new things and
not being over-worried whether they worked first time or not. The restructuring seems to have brought a load more admin; creativity and lateral
thinking don't seem to have much of a place here anymore. It is rules, policies, form filling now. I guess that's partly what Jane is responding to. It
makes her into a 'jobsworth'. She doesn't want to take any risks, get anything wrong, she is afraid to forget even one form in case that is noticed
and it shows up her weaknesses. She must feel very vulnerable.

I wonder if they gave her any training for the new post – my course
stresses how important that is and how important it is to have a proper
induction period and not just to be thrown in to do things you have
never done before. Come to think of it I haven't had any induction for
this new post either. It's totally different from my last one, it is dead
easy, but that's not the point. There has been no induction, no support,
and no regular supervision meetings – nothing other than Jane wanting
to check that I have done everything she has told me to and in the way
she wanted it doing (even if that was the less efficient way).

Well perhaps I wouldn't want that additional bureaucracy and responsibility at the moment with my husband being so ill. Yet it is very frustrating
to see her struggling with no ideas and not willing to listen to ideas from
other people. The more I think about it the more I feel sort of sorry for her
but it doesn't excuse her behaviour. If only she would let us act as a team
we could support one another. I know she needs us to accept her as the
boss. I haven't got a problem with that but she doesn't need to keep shov-
ing it down our throats. If I ask why we are doing something, which seems
nonsensical and time wasting to me, she just responds with 'You are doing
it because I'm the boss and I am telling you to. End of!'

Reflections on the mediation

For this mediation I was called into a large organisation to mediate
between two work colleagues, Jane and Sarah, who had become very

stuck in a dispute, following a large restructuring programme within the company. Various interventions from senior colleagues in the organisation and from the HR department had failed to elicit any movement on either side. Initially we agreed to try a one-day mediation. There was no opportunity to extend the agreed end time for the day as prior commitments meant I had to fly back immediately after the close of the mediation. During the discussions the real sources of the dispute began to be clarified and we were able to agree a resolution to some aspects of the conflict and signpost a way forward.

On the first day of the mediation I followed my usual model of working together with the parties in dispute. I spoke to both parties by phone in the weeks leading up to the mediation. Jane was very sceptical about the usefulness of mediation and felt that her management role was being challenged by the organisation's decision to bring in external mediators to deal with an issue she felt she should be able to resolve. She did not express much willingness to engage in the process but felt she had no option but to attend. Sarah was more emotional during these calls and keen for the opportunity she saw the mediation as presenting.

The background to the dispute focused on the fallout from the recent restructuring. Both women were required to work closely together in the new arrangement. Jane had recently taken up the post as Sarah's line manager, following a major restructuring in which both had faced possible redundancy or redeployment.

Before the restructure, they had been on the same level in the organisation. Sarah had worked independently managing an IT section. Reluctantly she had accepted a move to an administrative post, which she believed to have lower status than her previous post but she had been redeployed on a protected salary. Jane had moved from a PA role to manage five staff, of which Sarah was one. This was quite a leap for her in both status and salary.

This mediation focused on the breakdown in the working relationship between Jane and Sarah. Jane considered Sarah to be a 'slacker', doing the minimum amount of work possible, being reluctant to tell Jane what she was doing because 'she probably wasn't doing anything' and questioning Jane's authority. In turn, Sarah considered Jane a 'jobsworth' with no management experience. Jane's post had never been advertised and Jane had, in Sarah's words, 'merely been given the post', there had been no advertising and no interviews. In the mediation, Jane confirmed this, saying 'a new post was created for me'.

Jane saw the promotion as a unique opportunity to move into management but was given no training to prepare her for the new role. She was determined that she be accepted as a manager and awarded the respect she felt was due to the managerial status. Jane valued hard work and organisational commitment and saw success in life as being achieved primarily in the workplace. She spoke of her previous position and the way she had always behaved respectfully towards her manager, always doing what was asked without question. She saw this new post as a reward for being dutiful, respectful, and available to her previous boss, who had made the case for the new position she now held. Her values contained a 'just rewards' belief, with high value placed on (unquestioning) loyalty. Her self-esteem rested largely on her ability to second-guess her boss' needs and to respond to them before being asked. She felt a great deal of pride in this skill and could not understand why Jane was not intent on pleasing her. In work she found meaning in her sense of serving the other, in this case the organisation, rather than in the nature or purpose of the work. During the mediation we were able to explore whether loyalty was always a good thing and found many historical examples when it had proved to be the opposite.

Sarah found Jane's managerial style overbearing. She was irritated that whenever she asked Jane why she was being asked to do something, Jane replied, 'Because I tell you to, and I am your boss'. Sarah felt she had experience which could be useful to Jane but that Jane refused to consult anyone or respect team members.

Throughout the mediation I was able to establish a good working relationship with both sides. At the end of a fairly tough day of mediation Jane and Sarah reached agreement on a number of issues. However, many concerns had been raised which could not be fully explored within the time constraint. Some of these were personal and the parties were reluctant to discuss them with their employers, others flowed from the lack of experience and training which should have been offered to each of them when they took up their new posts. It was agreed that a further day would be set aside to bring them together for a second mediation session.

This presented a further new challenge. The organisation was keen that the second day should happen soon. Unfortunately this wasn't possible and the second mediation day happened a week later. I followed the same format as previously, starting with individual sessions. During the intervening week Jane had approached HR and told them that she felt she needed some support and training in order to improve her performance as a manager. Jane gave the HR department permission to tell me this and it was agreed that if appropriate I could incorporate some coaching elements into the individual sessions.

Jane had been insistent that the main issue was Sarah's 'insubordin-
ation', 'secrecy', and 'lack of engagement with the work' and that
Sarah needed 'to do as she was told and not question it'. During the
mediation, I was able to introduce Jane to a model of explorative listening. She experienced the power of being listened to and the power
of feeling the authentic desire of the listener to understand. She was
then able to employ these skills in her subsequent meetings with
Sarah.

We were able to explore what lay at the heart of the frustration both
parties felt with the other and how this seemed to stem from a clash in
value systems. Through our work during the day we were able to identify some areas of commonality in their value systems. Although they
shared some values, the ways in which these values were manifested
were very different.

Both shared a strong belief that one should be rewarded for good
behaviour. However, they differed in what they believed to be 'good
behaviour'. For Jane 'good behaviour' meant doing what one was told
without question, whilst for Sarah it meant developing and using skills to
do a good job. Sarah had taken a number of courses to improve the
skills required in her previous post and was still undertaking a course
one evening a week. For both women good behaviour was also about
loyalty and being engaged with their work. Jane believed that engagement with work was demonstrated through long hours and doing what
was asked to ensure that deadlines were achieved. Sarah's desire to stick
to her contracted hours was seen as demonstrating a lack of engagement
in the work. Sarah's ideas of commitment were very different and she
saw her willingness to undertake training outside of the work place and
to offer ideas for development as clear evidence of engagement. She
experienced Jane's reluctance to discuss what for her were the more
meaningful aspects of work – whether processes were worth doing, or
could be done differently were perceived by Sarah as demonstrating
Jane's lack of engagement in the work. Jane's primary loyalty was to the
organisation and she perceived any questioning of what they did to be
disloyal. Sarah valued loyalty to her husband higher than to the organisation and believed the organisation hadn't shown her any loyalty in its
handling of the restructuring.

The importance of justice was also a common value for Jane and
Sarah. Jane's promotion was perceived by Sarah as unjust, both in the
appointment process (or lack of) which went against Sarah's commitment to equal opportunity and because Sarah could not see what Jane
was being rewarded for. She felt her own commitment to professional
development was not respected or rewarded and her value systems not

understood – she was expected by Jane to be happy that she was still in a job, whereas she was finding it a struggle to find meaning in the new work and the accompanying loss of independence. The redeployment had struck a harsh blow to her self-esteem and self-identity. For Jane her promotion was entirely just and a result of the unquestioning devotion and hard work she had shown in her previous post. For her it was clear that commitment to serving the organisation and non-questioning obedience should be rewarded.

Both women prided themselves on working hard. For Jane this was demonstrated by the long hours she put in, often working several hours beyond the official requirement of her contract. Sarah always arrived on time, worked her full contracted hours and believed that she did everything that was asked of her. The working day didn't finish for her at 5pm, as at home she continued 'to work', helping her husband or attending classes. For Sarah, hard work was not confined to what she did for her employers or to the working day and environment.

For both Sarah and Jane being respected was important. Jane believed that status should automatically bring respect and that respect would be evidenced by obedience. Whereas for Sarah, respect came from the way in which one treated others. Both craved respect from the other.

During the individual sessions I was able to learn more about Jane. She had a high achieving husband who was often away on business, so she would return to an empty house after work. She was encouraging of her husband's ambition but wanted to match his success. She spoke movingly of dinner parties where she had felt she had little to offer to the high-powered conversation which lowered her self-esteem and hoped that this would change now that she too was 'a manager with staff working to her'.

Jane's self-esteem was heavily invested in the new managerial role. She resented the fact that Sarah did not seem to recognise her status, and saw work as less important to home life.

It unfolded in the individual sessions with Sarah that she had a partner with a serious long term illness and so stuck very closely to her contracted working hours so that she could spend as much time as possible with him. One of Sarah's complaints was that Jane never enquired about her partner's health even though she was aware of the situation.

Through our dialogue Jane realised that she too might wish to go home on time if there was someone waiting for her. In many ways she too resented how much time and energy work was taking and acknowledged that part of her would like to be more self-disciplined (a word she never thought she would use about Sarah) and set aside at least one evening a week for some non-work related activity, just as Sarah did in attending her evening course.

She spoke with concern about Sarah's husband's health but expressed her view that Sarah was a very private person who would not wish her difficulties to be spoken about at work. In thinking further about this she began to understand that her perceived lack of interest in Sarah's home situation was experienced as cold, uncaring, and disrespectful, and so was having an impact on their working relationship. She resolved to 'be brave' and to occasionally 'check in' with Sarah about how her husband was doing. In understanding that Sarah's priorities lay in the home, Jane also saw that Sarah was not a competitor to her on the career ladder.

This allowed Jane to be brave enough to share with me her fears for the future. A further merger and restructure were due, with her employers taking over another organisation. Jane knew that the person occupying her role in the other organisation was an experienced and well-trained manager who was held in high regard and she feared that the merger would result in her redundancy or demotion. Sarah's complaints about her management style had been threatening on many levels but she feared that she would be seen as an ineffective manager and so had become increasingly more demanding and authoritarian in the hope that she could 'force Sarah into line'. Although it was clear that this was having the opposite effect to the one hoped for, with Sarah digging her heels in deeper, Jane had no experience, management training, or knowledge to draw on and felt stuck, disheartened, and scared.

Sarah too expressed common feelings of fear, frustration, and stuckness. She had no knowledge of Jane's insecurity and saw her merely as a bully. She could not understand why Jane responded so defensively to any questions she posed about why they were doing things in a certain way. In the coaching piece with Jane, she began to see that Sarah's questions were no threat and that she could choose how to respond to them. She began to see strength in admitting that there were things she did not know and understand and that by owning this she could effectively use the skills and knowledge of others whilst building on her own knowledge.

Most of my work with Sarah focused on exploring her communication style and helping her so see that she too could be experienced as aggressive. She was also able to forcefully express her anger at the way she felt she had been treated by the organisation and realise that much of this anger was being projected onto Jane.

Both recognised that they had been thrown into new roles without any training and both felt unsure about their abilities in these roles. They began to recognise that they were both 'victims' of the restructure and that they had much in common.

I was able to offer Jane a day of leadership coaching, sharing key approaches which she could call on to help her achieve her objectives. She identified that through the lack of knowledge of other approaches and her own feelings of inadequacy she had automatically taken on a very transactional, directive style which emphasised punishment for non-compliance. To adopt a more questioning transformational approach, allowing others to question her actions would have made her feel very vulnerable to exposing her lack of experience and knowledge. I introduced her to Connective and Existential Leadership theories and the concept of Negative Capability within which leaders no longer have to hold onto the illusion that they can solve all problems. The coaching day turned out to be a rich learning experience for both parties and myself.

I was very aware of how Jane changed during this phase. She moved from a very cynical distanced stance, which she had stayed with during the first day's mediation, to allowing me to see her vulnerabilities and fears and showing a willingness to train and understand management and leadership strategies.

Sarah, Jane, and I met together the following day to resume the mediation. As the day progressed, the parties openly talked to each other about their shared frustrations with the organisation. They were able to identify and tell one another what they admired in the other. Jane was able to talk sensitively to Sarah about her husband's illness and for Sarah to receive this as genuine concern rather than pointing out a weakness.

The mediation concluded with an agreed plan for the ways in which the parties would resume working together. They had learnt more about who they each were as individuals and what was important for each of them in life. Working models for achieving the best outcome for work goals were identified and as both had ceased to see the other as a threat they were able to establish a positive way of communicating. They set regular meetings in place and decided to hold these in the coffee area in a bid to alter the negative dynamics that had been established in previous meetings.

For Jane and Sarah much of the dispute was not about the concrete day-to-day relationships within the workplace, but about issues of self-identity, tensions regarding priorities, and fears for the future. My approach to mediation is based on the philosophical framework of my training as an existential psychotherapist and so it is essentially a psychological one.

I aim to understand the parties in a mediation by exploring their worldviews – what makes them tick, what makes them who they are, and why the conflict has caused pain and become stuck.

The role of existential thought

As explained in part one, I bring existential philosophy to my work as a mediator. This means focusing on a number of things we all share and which are termed 'existential givens'. These include:

- We are emotional.

  Emotions are intentional – they are about something. If I can identify the 'something' I am identifying a person's value.

- We need to be heard.

  This is a gift to any mediator. If people need to be heard, all I must do is truly listen.

- We will die and have to deal with time and temporality.

  We each experience time in a different way. In mediation we have limited time to resolve the dispute. The mediation is a 'moment' in time. The dispute has already taken time out from our limited time on this planet. What is the temporal worth of seeing this dispute resolved for the disputants, allowing them to move from 'stuckness' to re-engage with life?

- We experience anxiety.

  Anxiety is a normal emotion, which we all experience. The focus of the anxiety will differ with individuals and can help identify existential concerns, values, and beliefs.

- Our behaviours are influenced by our values and belief systems.

  We develop behaviours as ways of coping. Sometimes these behaviours serve us well throughout life but it is also true that sometimes these behaviours become sedimented and we continue to employ them although they no longer work for us.

I seek to 'tune in' to the values and beliefs of each party in the disputes. To some extent all our behaviours are coping mechanisms, filtered through our value systems. One way into discovering a person's values is to provide space and safety for the individual to express their emotions. All emotions are intentional, that is they are about something, and that something will be linked to inherent values and beliefs. It is not my job as a mediator to try to change these values but by understanding what is really important to the individual I am better placed to facilitate a settlement which has meaning for that person, rather than one which looks good to me or the 'outside world'. Often a lawyer or mediator can congratulate themselves on having achieved an excellent settlement (usually judged by monetary value) whilst the disputant goes away financially richer but unsatisfied.

An existentially informed mediator attempts to understand the dispute not just in terms of the facts (noema) but also in terms of how those facts have been experienced, perceived, and made sense of by each individual (noesis). After all, we cannot in any dispute, change what happened, we can only change our perception of that event and move on. How we perceive things will be very different according to our individual worldview. One way to help us gain some insight into another's worldview is through considering how they are in the world. We can identify four core dimensions in which we operate – physical, social, spiritual, and psychological. Some dimensions will be fully and richly inhabited at one time whilst others may appear quite barren.

The arrows in Figure 11.1 seek to remind us that the degree to which each dimension is prominent for the client will vary over time.

Physical dimension

On the physical dimension (Umwelt) individuals relate to their environment and to the givens of the natural world around them. This includes their attitude to the body they have, to the surroundings they find themselves in, to the landscape, climate, and the weather, to objects and material possessions, to the bodies of other people, their own bodily needs, to health and illness, and to their own mortality. The struggle on this dimension is in general terms between the search for domination over the elements and natural law (as in technology, or in sports), and the need to accept the limitations of natural boundaries (as in ecology or old age). People generally aim for security on this dimension (through health and wealth), but much of life brings a gradual disillusionment and the realisation that such security can only be temporary. Recognising limitations can bring a great release of tension.

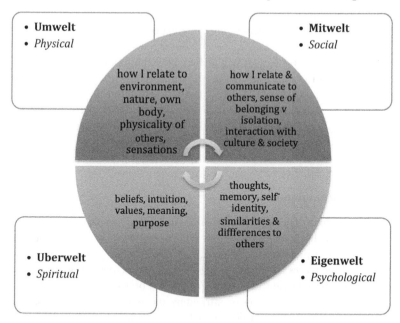

- **Umwelt**
- *Physical*

how I relate to environment, nature, own body, physicality of others, sensations

- **Mitwelt**
- *Social*

how I relate & communicate to others, sense of belonging v isolation, interaction with culture & society

beliefs, intuition, values, meaning, purpose

thoughts, memory, self identity, similarities & diffferences to others

- **Uberwelt**
- *Spiritual*

- **Eigenwelt**
- *Psychological*

Figure 11.1 Hanaway (2012): existential dimensions

Social dimension

On the social dimension (Mitwelt) individuals relate to others as they interact with the public world around them. This dimension includes their response to the culture they live in, as well as to the class and race they belong to (and also those they do not belong to). Attitudes here range from love to hate, and from cooperation to competition. The dynamic contradictions can be understood in terms of acceptance versus rejection, or belonging versus isolation. Some people prefer to withdraw from the world of others as much as possible. Others blindly chase public acceptance by going along with the rules and fashions of the moment or they try to rise above these by becoming trendsetters themselves. By acquiring fame or other forms of power, individuals can attain dominance over others temporarily. Sooner or later, however, everyone is confronted with both failure and aloneness.

Psychological dimension

On the psychological dimension (Eigenwelt) individuals relate to themselves, and in this way create a personal world. This dimension includes views about their own character, their past experience, and their future possibilities. Contradictions here are often experienced in terms of personal strengths and weaknesses. People search for a sense of identity, a feeling of being substantial and having a self. But inevitably many events will confront them with evidence to the contrary and plunge them into a state of confusion or disintegration. Activity and passivity is an important polarity here. Self-affirmation and resolution go with the former, and surrender and yielding with the latter. Facing the final dissolution of self that comes with personal loss and the facing of death might bring anxiety and confusion to many who have not yet given up their sense of self-importance.

Spiritual dimension

On the spiritual dimension (Überwelt) (van Deurzen-Smith, 1984) individuals relate to the unknown and thus create a sense of an ideal world, an ideology, and a philosophical outlook. It is here that they find meaning by putting all the pieces of the puzzle together for themselves. For some people this is done by adhering to a religion or other prescriptive worldview, for others it is about discovering or attributing meaning in a more secular or personal way. The contradictions that have to be faced on this dimension are often related to the tension between purpose and absurdity, hope, and despair. People create their values in search of something that matters enough to live or die for, something that may even have ultimate and universal validity. Usually the aim is the conquest of a soul, or something that will substantially surpass mortality (as for instance in having contributed something valuable to humankind). Facing the void and the possibility of nothingness are the indispensable counterparts of this quest for the eternal.

In this mediation, we see that all areas were in play.

Umwelt

Jane

Given her long working hours, Jane had stopped being involved in exercise and her sexual life had also suffered. She had previously enjoyed swimming and been a regular visitor to the gym but her working hours no longer allowed for this. Her professional life focused on work tasks and trying to succeed as a manager and in her home life she was focused on working hard to keep a perfect house for her husband to entertain his business colleagues. She had no clear sense of her own space either in the workplace or at home – nothing was chosen to address any aesthetic or spatial needs of her own. From her description, her home looked like something from a magazine – very smart and minimal, although Jane really longed for comfort and a scruffy dog which would be allowed to lie on an old sofa – something her husband would never tolerate! Even her clothing was now chosen to match what she considered appropriate for a manager (navy skirt suits and white shirts) rather than clothing which reflected her personal identity. Her physical world had been eroded.

Sarah

For Sarah her husband's illness had curtailed their love of outdoor walks with the dogs but the dogs still needed walking and this provided Sarah with times of peace where she enjoyed being alone and exploring the countryside. Her home environment was also important to her and she had worked hard to make it comfortable and welcoming. You could easily pick out which workspace belonged to Sarah. It looked quite chaotic and was decorated with photos of her husband, the dogs and herself. She also had many postcards on display from friends around the world. Despite the seeming chaos Sarah knew where everything was. She had a clear sense of her own identity and seemed comfortable with it.

Mitwelt

Jane

Jane's work left little time for anything else. She would often not leave work before 7pm and later if her high achieving husband was away on business as there was only an empty house to return to. She was encouraging of her husband's ambition and wanted to match his success. For many years, at home, she had devoted herself to helping him achieve. Whilst in work, she was doing the same for Mr Sym, her boss. Although outwardly a strong and assertive woman, she had no friends of her own; they were all colleagues of her husband, and socialising was always seen as networking and ways of improving her husband's chances of promotion.

Sarah

Despite her husband's illness Sarah continued to find time to see old friends and to make new ones through the courses she took. To maintain these social networks and to enjoy time with her husband Sarah would leave work at 5pm, her contracted work time. In work she had always enjoyed social chitchat with the men in the IT team. In the new structure Jane discouraged this kind of talking, seeing it as getting in the way of the work. Sarah experienced this as a closing down of her social world.

Eigenwelt

Jane

She had little sense of herself but wanted to project herself as disciplined, hard working, and successful. She wished to be respected and obeyed. She saw herself as very different from most of the people she worked with and also from the successful women she knew through her husband. When hosting dinner parties she could 'talk the talk' and put on the 'uniform' of the successful hostess but she never felt comfortable in her own skin, being over conscious of how she may be appearing to others. She felt she had little to offer to what she perceived as the high-powered conversations enjoyed by her husband and his colleagues and hoped that her own move into management would change this. In many ways she envied Sarah her sense of self and the way in which Sarah was willing to take risks for what she believed in.

Sarah

She is clearer about her own identity and what she wants and values, although she still carries some ambivalence about whether or not she should have applied for Jane's post. Sarah knows who she is and what is important to her. Although she had previously enjoyed work and it had interested her enough to take further training, her primary identifier at this point in time was as partner to her sick husband. She is clear that professional ambition and development are important steps for her in defining who she will be without her husband when that time comes.

Uberwelt

There were a number of values which both women shared but their ways of behaving in alliance with these values differed greatly. For both women, loyalty, respect, and fairness were all very important. Although expressed very differently, both desired respect and believed in 'fair play' and being rewarded for good work.

Jane

Jane saw loyalty as being focused on an unquestioning obedience to the organisation and she saw her promotion as a just reward for that obedience. For her, respect was linked to achievement – if a person had achieved in their profession and had status and money then she respected them. She believed that her new managerial status should automatically be met with respect from members of her team.

Sarah

Sarah prioritised loyalty to her husband but also believed that her willingness to seek Continuing Professional Development opportunities showed her commitment to the organisation and a willingness to do her job as well as she could whilst continually seeking to improve her skills. Sarah believed that if things were fair Jane would not have got a job for which she had no experience. Her sense of fairness made it impossible for her to accept the way the post had been 'given' to Jane rather than openly advertised. Sarah respected people who were open to discussion and who were continually trying to question both themselves and others in an endeavour to improve their own knowledge and skills.

There were also areas of difference in how the women encountered some of the key existential dilemmas of life e.g. freedom, uncertainty, and anxiety.

Freedom

Jane

Jane had never consciously thought about her own freedom. To a large degree she accepted what life brought her without taking any ownership of her own decision-making. She felt she had drifted into marriage with a man her family approved of. She had never asked herself what she sought in a partner and whether Tim was that partner.

Indeed, Jane had gone through school without gaining any real picture of herself – what she was good at, what she enjoyed, what she may want in the future. When it came to work she had just seen a job as an administrative assistant in the organisation she still worked in and had applied because it was near the house she and Tim had bought. She was dedicated to her work and had gained promotion to the PA role and then, with help from Mr Sym, to her current position.

She was now very scared to start asking those questions of herself as it would force her to take responsibility for her own future and not make assumptions about her limitations. These areas of her life came up in the mediation but it was outside the scope of the mediation and the role of the mediator to attend to any of these outside of the boundaries of the current dispute. However, just hearing herself voicing some of these things in the mediation led to Jane making changes such as seeking training.

Sarah

Sarah valued freedom, particularly the freedom to think and question things. She was also very aware that there are limitations to our freedom, some of which we choose and some we are dealt; this would be termed existentially as 'thrownness'. Her husband's illness and the time remaining to him was outside the control of Sarah, yet she was acutely aware that she was free to deal with this tragic limitation in a number of ways. She chose to exercise this freedom by spending as much time as she could with him whilst still engaging in a life of her own, knowingly preparing for a future without him.

Uncertainty

Jane

In the same way as freedom was disturbing for Jane, she found uncertainty equally hard to bear. She had remained in the same post, as PA for Mr Sym, for many years and it was only the restructuring that brought about change. She was now very concerned about the forthcoming merger and also about any possible reaction her husband may have to changes she may make that could impact on him e.g. undertaking further training which may make her less available as a dinner party hostess.

Sarah

Sarah could not ignore the reality that we must all live with uncertainty. Her husband's illness forced her to face this. Not even the medics could tell her what would happen or when and she had no idea how she would respond. She did not fight this uncertainty but was trying hard to live in the moment. Equally she was aware that she had perhaps not been 'present' to what had been going on at work and hadn't considered whether she would like to put herself forward for promotion.

Anxiety

Jane

Jane hid her anxiety through her aggressive 'I am right' stance. Like many people who present this way, Jane was far from being convinced that she was right but was terrified of people knowing that. She was anxious about many things, but was particularly anxious about how she was perceived by other people – her husband's business colleagues, her husband, her fellow workers, and potential employers. This was made worse as Jane had not developed a strong sense of self, always looking to others to provide feedback as to who she is. She was also very anxious about the future – what would she do, was she good enough, etc.

Sarah

Sarah was more accepting of uncertainty and thus less anxious. Even in this situation with Jane she was more angry and hurt than anxious. Having to face her husband's illness and accept that it was terminal had put her strongly in touch with her own temporality and although aspects of this were anxiety provoking it had been a rallying call to do more with her life and not to put up with the situation that had arisen with Jane. None of the other team members who had brought grievances against Jane could overcome their fear of her to attend the mediation.

Through our dialogue in the mediation, both Jane and Sarah could hear and reflect on their own words and come to recognise their many shared values and concerns. This allowed them to empathise with each other and to move from a position of alienation to one where there were identified commonalities. Both craved respect from the other and were able to share what they admired in each other and even areas of jealousy.

Through better understanding the values of the other they were now in a position to serve those values. For Sarah, being authentic was extremely important and at times this amounted to her being brutally honest and showing her frustration. In allowing Sarah more openness in their interactions, instead of experiencing it as a threat to her authority, Jane was increasing the respect Sarah had for her, rather than diminishing it by seeming weak, as she had originally feared. In turn this removed the aspects of Jane's behaviour which Sarah had not respected, allowing her to show respect for Jane's new skills.

They acknowledged their differences too, and in doing so they became less threatening. Sarah's focus on home and husband meant that Jane had no need to see her as a competitor or as a threat to her career ambitions. Sarah came to understand that Jane's 'bossiness' stemmed from her concerns to do a good job as the 'boss'. The aim to do a good job was one they both shared although their interpretation of what 'doing a good job' entailed remained different.

In addition they came to see that they were both poorly served by the organisation in respect to support and training, particularly induction in relation to the restructure. Together they decided to join forces to have this addressed by the organisation.

12 Disharmony

A musical mediation

Alan

I feel totally disrespected. Who does he think he is? I was there at the start. I got everyone together and now he acts as if I have no importance at all, nothing to offer, just someone who must bow to his greater knowledge and experience.

Steve

I am really brilliant at what I do, and have a track record of lots of successes to prove it. Artistes seek me out. I don't have to go looking for work. You can ask anyone, anyone who is anyone in the business knows me and knows my reputation. They know that I am successful and that I can make them successful. I know what it takes to make something a hit.

Alan is a pain in the arse. He hasn't a clue and I am fed up of his moods and negativity. If he wants success he should listen to me and be grateful. He can learn a lot. I can help him. He just needs to get on with it, do what I suggest and he will be part of something good and successful. He knows that deep down, so what is his problem?

Alan

I don't know if you are into music but a few years ago I was in X [a famous band]. We were really successful. Lots of tours – Japan, US, and everywhere of importance on the music scene. We did lots of festivals all over the world ... got lots of number ones ... were on TV and radio and in all the music journals. Generally it felt we had made it. I felt I had made it. It is never seen as glamorous to be the bassist like me ... but it could be worse ... I could be a drummer! The important thing for me in that band was that I also co-wrote all the songs. I knew they needed me. I was important to them. It was never in question that I was key to the success we had.

We had known one another when we were at school. Simon and I were friends from primary school. We both lived in the same village and he would come over to mine. My family had an old outbuilding and we would go and practice our guitars and sing out there where we weren't disturbing anyone. He was like a brother. I have four older sisters and my Dad died when I was ten so it was great to have some male company. I could talk to Simon about anything – how I missed my Dad; stuff like that. My Mum really struggled when Dad died and I tried to be the man of the family. With Simon I could just be me.

At secondary school we met Sam and Jamie. They weren't particularly friends of ours at first. Jamie was full of confidence, a good mover with a great voice and he was also good looking – all the makings of a charismatic singer, so we invited him to join our band. Sam was a brilliant but shy drummer and Simon and I were interested in getting our songs out there and heard. It seemed like the magic combination. Throughout our school years we rehearsed and played local small gigs, we were quite well-known locally. It was good fun but when we got to A levels we all had different plans. Both Simon and I wanted to study art, and were accepted to take a foundation course at the same art college. Jamie was going off to do a Performing Arts degree at the other end of the country and Sam just wanted to start earning money.

Just before we all left to go our separate ways we recorded an EP and to our great surprise and excitement we were picked up by Z [a famous record label]. It just went from there. After one term at art college, Simon and I packed it in, Jamie, who had started travelling for his gap year, never took up his degree place, and Sam left his job so that we could give all our time to the band.

Before we knew it, everyone knew who we were and it was sex and drugs and rock and roll all the way! Because we all knew and liked each other we agreed to split any song royalties evenly between us. On reflection I probably regret that, after all, it was Simon and I who did most of the song writing. As time went on Jamie wrote a few songs too, although Sam was never interested and was happy just playing his drums ... and he was brilliant at that.

We quickly got a manager and we had our record deal so at first we had a great time. Gradually Jamie became quite a pin up and all the attention was focused on him. It went to his head, he would send people out to score for him, pick out girls he liked and get the roadies to have them ready in his room for him after the show. Whenever there were photo shoots or interviews to do, Jamie was first in line. He even did some modelling gigs and was given cool clothes by some upcoming designers. He got to be quite a handful. He was so up himself.

Simon liked the lifestyle too and made the most of it. For Sam it was an ordeal. He was so shy. He would try to hide himself at the back and on tour would just bury his head in books. I was a bit more ambivalent about it all. I was up for everything at first and got a bit too much into coke. Then I met Alana and couldn't be bothered with all the groupies and all the women Jamie needed to have around. She was quite spiritual in a hippy kind of way. I wanted to make things work with Alana but that was a mistake. I think she was with me because of the band I was in, not for me, who I am. We had a great fun time but she wasn't the settling down type. For a couple of years she would just come with us wherever we went, just up sticks and follow us wherever but gradually the novelty of it all wore off for her and we split up.

After that I started seeing Saskia. She was very different. She was quite a bit younger than me. She didn't have any interest in all the media stuff and she didn't want to go out much. She was happy to support me and stay at home when I was away on tour. She was insecure but in some ways that made me feel more important and secure. I never had to worry about what she was up to when I was away on tour. We have had our ups and downs but we are still together. Sometimes I look at some of the confident girls the others spent time with – models, artists … I sometimes feel I would like a bit more excitement and stimulation but at the same time I like knowing Saskia will always be there.

Women can be really troublesome in bands. Jamie met Annabel, a model who also fancied herself as a singer. Her father had been a really well-known singer until his drug use took its toll. Annabel was used to life on the road from her childhood and she came with Jamie everywhere we went. When we were on stage she was in the wings, when we were on tour she was on the tour bus. Jamie had no time for the rest of us, didn't turn up for rehearsals or contribute to the song writing. He was mesmerised by her and I think the kudos of her father's name also attracted him. He spent more time 'being seen' and courting photo opportunities which he hoped would 'help Annabel's profile'. He started to write songs 'requiring a female voice' and pressed that Annabel should join us to sing a duet with him on stage … a touch of the Kate Moss and Pete Doherty syndrome! They began to write songs together too and it was clear that these were intended for the two of them to sing together either by Annabel joining the band, or Jamie leaving it and setting something up fronted by the two of them.

Eventually we all got fed up with him. Unfortunately he was the frontman and without him the band couldn't exist. We were doing really well and there were lots of gigs lined up but it was clear we couldn't go on. Sam, Simon, and I would meet to discuss the situation and we were about to confront him and demand that he gave more time to the band when he announced he was leaving to go solo and that he already had a publishing deal and contract sorted and a tour organised. We were pissed off. We felt completely abandoned. It was clear that Annabel had had a lot to do with his decision. She was always telling him he was wasting his time with us. I haven't really spoken to him since.

When he left the band fell apart. Sam went back to his old job, Simon went off to France and holed up for a time writing songs and developing his own style as a solo artiste. I tried to continue writing songs but mainly got along finding work as a session musician. It felt like a big fall. It was awful seeing Jamie's career take off. His pictures were everywhere and his songs haunted me – whenever I put the radio on there was Jamie, even if I went into a shop they always seemed to be playing his music. He did lots of work which Steve produced and most of them were huge successes. I met Steve about that time too. I was covering for a bass player, in a well-known band. I stood in for him and have awful memories of Steve shouting and being aggressive with everyone when that band was in the studio. I knew I was only a temporary member of that band and although I felt put down by Steve it didn't really bother me at the time because it wasn't my music I was playing and I wasn't invested in that band.

I heard that Steve wanted to move from the back room to the front of the stage but I was surprised when he contacted me to see if I was interested in getting a new band together. We didn't really know each other and I wasn't sure I liked what I had seen. It seems Jamie had suggested he contact me. At that time Simon had managed to sell some of his songs to other people and had some success in his solo career but it hadn't exactly taken off and he jumped at the chance to join us when I asked him. Sam wasn't interested. He had got married and had a small child, he had been promoted in his job and wasn't up for taking any risks. He never really liked the limelight anyway.

Simon became the joint lead singer with me in the new band. I'm also the bassist, I got Stu in as the drummer and Steve ... well Steve just believes he can do everything. He is lead guitarist and now he is insisting on producing everything and singing the lead on several of the songs. He is a bloody good producer. He has had a lot of hits with some famous names but the sound he likes to produce isn't really what

Simon and I like. The production takes over, we like something more stripped back but will Steve listen? No, he knows best. We are in the middle of recording our first album and I can't stand the guy. He's an arrogant bully with no respect for anyone else. He thinks only *his* ideas are any good ... he knows what is best. He has no interest in discussing our ideas.

If things don't change I can't see us finishing this album and that will be another failed band. I need some success. I need to get my name back out there.

It has really come to a head, Steve and I had an almighty row and I stormed out of the studio. This mediation seems like the only chance for us to get things back together. We all have a lot to lose if we don't finish this album – a lot of time and money down the drain – but I am not sure I could face trying to get another new band together and I haven't a clue what I would do if I wasn't out there performing.

Steve

I first met Alan when he was in X. I knew Jamie the lead singer really well. I've known him for years. He's a great guy. I never really got to know the rest of them. I might have a drink with Alan and the others but that was about it. At the time I was really busy producing for most of the successful bands of the time. Anyway, when Jamie went solo I produced all his recordings for him. He was really appreciative of my ideas. Whatever I suggested he went along with. We had loads of successes. I can see why he left X. Simon isn't too bad but Alan is a real pain. He is over sensitive ... he can't take criticism. He thinks that creative suggestions are criticisms. He doesn't seem to get that you pay a producer to add something special. He knows how successful I am. I've still got bands badgering me to produce them. He's stupid if he tries to block my ideas. I know what works commercially. When I suggested to him that we start up a new band he knew that I intended to produce everything we did, not just be the lead guitarist.

I am keen to get out on the stage, to be seen a bit. Production gives me a buzz but I want some of the limelight. I have plenty of recognition from musicians but a fancy a bit of fan worship before it is too late!

Alan

I was hoping this band would be a place where I could have a bit more space to try new things. I have written lots of new material since X disbanded. Many of the songs are quite different. I think they are good and could do well with those who appreciate something a bit deeper.

I have enjoyed commercial success with X. I don't need to play it safe ... turn out commercial rubbish; I want some critical acclaim from those who appreciate vision and a bit of risk taking. Steve just wants commercial success. I guess it's his last chance. He is getting on a bit. He is about five years older than the rest of us and we aren't spring chickens.

Every track we work on he tries to change it into some kind of dance track or film score. He wants to lose what we have created in overblown production. He won't listen to the rest of us. He needs to decide whether he wants to be a band member or our producer. It is becoming clear he can't be both. Personally I would be glad if he were neither. He stresses me out.

The others want to stick with him. They keep going on about how successful he has been and how we ought to listen and take on board his ideas. He is causing tension between all of us.

Steve

I have always wanted to front a band. My family is basically a bunch of old hippies, but successful ones. My Dad is quite well-known; he started a well-known festival and has run all kinds of events. Mum was a singer herself when they met but stopped to have kids. There is my elder brother and my sister. If I told you their names you would know both of them. They are both musicians but play very different stuff to mine.

In many ways it was great growing up in that family. We had a lot of freedom. There were lots of things around to interest us. The place we lived in was amazing. Outside it was quite wild with lots of places to make dens or swing from the trees. We even had a little lake in the garden and canoes we could go out in. In the house it was all very 'ethnic'. I'm sure you can imagine. Lots of cushions covered with bits of old saris, woven wall hangings, lots of warm red walls and an over-powering perfume from joss sticks. There were lots of musical instruments around – piano, violins, guitars, a saxophone, even a harp. We were all encouraged to just pick them up and play with them. It was quite a busy household with lots of adults coming and going. There always seemed to be a lot of pregnant women around as my Mum ran Natural Childbirth Trust sessions in the house. When I was small I loved it but when I went to school it all felt very embarrassing.

I remember the first time I brought a friend home from school. I thought he would love the place but as soon as he came in he started sniff-ing and asked what the strange smell was. He also wanted to know where our TV was and I felt real shame when I said we didn't have one. He didn't seem to know what to make of it all. The next day when I went into school he ignored me and I kept getting funny looks from some of the other kids. I think he had told them that we were weird. After that I tried hard to fit in more and didn't bring people home. I have always had that sense of difference.

As I grew up that difference became a more positive feature. I started to like it. I could see that our family were bright and interesting even if my parents didn't do the kinds of jobs other parents did. By the time I got to my teenage years I had become 'cool'. I wore the latest gear and looked the part. By then my brother was very well-known in his field and had moved from a musical prodigy to a world-renowned success. I wasn't too sure where my talent lay but I was determined to be as well- known as him. As a child I was rather overlooked because of him. People would tell me what a brilliant brother I had but they had nothing much to say about me.

I worked hard and became good at guitar. Like every teenage boy I was in local bands, none of which lasted long. I gradually realised that I was good at production and moved across into that area of work. I've done really well at it. I have worked with some of the biggest names and produced loads of hit albums. It's a good life; I travel the world and have my own studios in the UK and France. I enjoy the work but I have been missing the immediacy of gigging, being out there, seeing the audience and how they are reacting. Being a producer means always being in the background. People in the music industry recognise my talent, know me and want to work with me but the punters ... the fans ... they couldn't care less who has produced a record, they just fall in love with the guys in the band, those out there on stage, in the spotlight.

I have been doing a lot of producing for Jamie recently. I have spent time with him and Annabel in his house in France and that got me wondering what the rest of X were up to. I got in touch with Alan. I knew he had been writing stuff and I wondered if he was planning to get a new band together. We met for a drink and things went from there. He contacted Simon and found Stu and we formed the new band. I feel this is my last chance to make it in a band ... to be seen, instead of being behind other's successes. Alan knew that I wanted to take a more central place.

My voice isn't bad. I want to be lead guitar and to have some opportunities to take the lead singing on some tracks. I'm tired of being in the background. I know Simon and Alan are lead singers, although I think I am as good as them. Alan's songs are good. He doesn't seem to want to lead on all the singing, so I don't see why any of this is such a problem for him. He must know that I'm the expert when it comes to producing but everything I suggest he argues with. Its madness, I have a proven track record of successes, he should be pleased I want to work with him. He doesn't understand what it takes to make something a commercial success. He just seems to feel that people should listen to his work and doesn't care if it is only appreciated by a few.

Alan

I found it hard when X split. I think I was depressed for quite some time. I didn't want to go out as people would ask what I was up to and expect to hear exciting news of record deals and world tours when in fact I was just sitting at home. You can imagine how different life was – before we had world tours, it was all go – there were drugs and girls and adoration. As I have said the drugs and the girls were a bit of a problem for me once I met Saskia. It was hard keeping a relationship going but we did it. Although truthfully I do miss that sense of feeling special – that people knew who I was, were interested in me, wanted to talk to me, thought I was great. Now I am afraid of being recognised and having nothing to tell people about, and I am also scared of not being recognised – of being a nobody. That has been really hard.

Anyway ... eventually I got my act together and started writing songs again. I think my 'depression' actually helped my writing. It is deeper and more meaningful now. I guess you could say it's more 'grown up'. There is pain in there, not just a good beat.

Whenever we have laid down a track on this album and I am satisfied with it, along comes Steve and wants to mess with it, tart it up, make it more commercial. We are not teenagers, we are not a 'boy band', we have had life experience, we have something to say ... he is only interested in creating a commercial success. If *Top of the Pops* still existed he would be desperate to be on that, at the front of the stage instead of tucked away in a dark recording studio, where he has been for the past ten years!

It isn't that I'm not interested in commercial success. I need this to be a success but I know how fragile that kind of success is. I have had it and lost it before and I very nearly lost myself in the process. Part of me is very ambivalent about the whole thing ...

This time the most important thing for me is that I want the music to be about my experiences and feelings and not just a formula to make as much dosh as possible. I want to be respected as a musician and songwriter.

Steve

I think Alan is bitter because after X split, Jamie was so much more successful, whereas he wasn't in demand anymore. I haven't had any of those real fallow times, myself. I guess it must feel very hard. He must have quite a lot riding on this album. He won't want to be forgotten. I can understand that but he doesn't seem to get that if he just listened to me and did what I suggested he would have a hit on his hands and he would be back in the spotlight.

Alan

I do wish Steve would get it. This isn't his band. We are not asking to be moulded by him.

I do believe he has a lot to offer. He is a brilliant producer – when he listens to what the band wants. He is a good guitarist and his voice is fine. He needs to look in the mirror – we are old for the music world and he is even older than the rest of us. I know it must be difficult for him to see all the bands he has helped become successful out there in the limelight, getting the praise. Those in the industry acknowledge his contribution but the public who buy the music haven't a clue who he is and aren't interested … at least I have had my fifteen minutes of fame … but I wouldn't mind some more minutes!

I am not willing to sell my soul this time. In X we started out writing music that we believed in but as we became more popular and got 'proper' management we were not encouraged to progress. We were selling records and making tons of money – mainly for other people – those who were making money out of us were keen that we remained 'commercial', not to risk anything new or different. We were churning out a successful product and 'hiding' the more meaningful stuff, as the management didn't feel it would sell. I want it to be different this time. I want to be proud of what I produce, whether it goes down well commercially or not. I guess I would rather be known and respected by a few than have crowds of people buying stuff I am not proud of. I guess that is where Steve and I differ, his skills are in knowing the market and providing stuff which will sell well, my skills are in writing music which has some depth and meaning to it.

He wants the big crowds, he wants to be seen and known by as many people as possible. I don't know if you know but he has a world famous brother, I guess that must be hard – quite something to compete with and no matter how hard he tries he isn't going to win that battle. It feels like he and I are engaged in battle, perhaps he feels he has more chance of winning this one but I am determined he won't. I won't be bullied. If we can't find a way forward together then he is on his own – I will walk and the others will too. It will be thousands down the drain, we have paid lots for the studio and we do have some good tracks down. If he would leave them alone they will be fine but he keeps wanting to tinker with them, tart them up.

Reflections on the mediation

It is very common in mediations for people to give very long and often non-linear and non-chronological accounts of what brought them to their current conflict. It is important for the mediator to remain open to what is being said. It is all relevant to building an understanding of each person's worldview and allows the mediator to develop a picture of what their priorities are and what they may need from any settlement.

I have worked a lot with creative people. This has often included working with bands. Bands, no matter the music genre, share important commonalities. They require people to work together towards a common goal and to make decisions which impact on all members. The structure for this decision-making can be conscious or unconscious, formal or informal.

Most bands experience internal conflict. Potential sources of this strife are common across the array of band styles. Disagreements often occur due to the differing aspirations of the members, the different amount of time members contribute to the group, musical direction, egos – upstaging one another, substance use, relationship with management/ record companies, the type of decision-making structure which is in place (or indeed, absent), competition among the participants, monetary issues – share of royalties/bills/money, workload, punctuality, career conflicts, who to hire/fire, relationships with families, girlfriends, boyfriends, partners, etc., what will be worn on stage/for photo shoots etc. (Kramer & Yahn, 2010; Thomas, 2011). The list is endless. Often at the core of all these conflicts lie issues of self-esteem and a perceived lack of fairness, empathy, and/or acknowledgement. Some of these conflicts create more acrimony than others, but a band that wishes to survive must find ways to mediate these differences.

Although stemming from personal issues between the two, and relating to their prior experiences as members of bands and of families, Alan and Steve's tale is reminiscent of many I have mediated. Some of the toughest issues in bands have nothing to do with writing, recording, or performing music. They have to do with the other people in the band and how you work with them. Band conflict can arise in any group for different reasons, and there are many different ways to resolve it (or avoid it in the first place). Common methods of reconciliation and conflict prevention include encouragement of open communication, the ability to selectively ignore unsolvable disagreements, and active group mediation. Thomas (2011) speaks of more drastic solutions, involving the adoption of more hierarchical leadership-based political structures. I shall say more about this later in relation to Alan and Steve's battle for leadership.

Whenever I work with bands, or indeed theatre or dance groups, I am always stuck by how much the group reflects a family dynamic. Group members often have to spend long periods of time together, often 24/7. When touring they are away from other support systems and live within a small, intensive group of band members, roadies and hangers on. It is difficult to step outside of the 'norms and conventions' of the group – to do drugs or not, to enjoy casual sex, or try to maintain a relationship, etc. The fear of being the odd one out, or even worse, of being cast out seems ever present. In the band, the individual's long established patterns and ways of being in a group, particularly a family group, tend to come to the fore. Groce and Dowell (1988) wrote of musical performances as social interaction, best understood in a group context and they see this sociality, and collaboration of multiple perspectives as being a fundamental in contributing to the richness of the musical material created (Conlon & Jehn, 2010; Ferguson, 2002; Groce & Dowell, 1988; Murnighan & Conlon, 1991). To be successful, to write music or even to perform at any level, a band must spend a good deal of time together practicing, writing, devising performance routines, and learning new material. These activities provide abundant opportunities for the development of interpersonal problems.

We bring our past experiences and the assumptions we have drawn from them into any group we join. We don't become someone new when we join a new enterprise. The closer in nature the enterprise is to previous experiences at an overt or covert level, the more likely it is that we will be influenced by past experiences, expectations, prejudices, and bias. Both Alan and Steve brought a lot of strong emotions, hopes, and fears into the new band.

Alan had found the break-up of his previous band and the subsequent loss of identity very difficult to cope with. He had experienced fame, but also the fall from fame which had taken him into a place where he couldn't define himself for others, or even to himself. This led to him leading quite a reclusive life for a while. He was looking to the new band as a place where he could re-establish himself and to rebuild his self-esteem and this time he hoped it would be in a more authentic way.

With X he had felt out of place towards the end, not wanting the rock and roll lifestyle, and yet he felt some shame that he had gone along with some of the more commercial products they had produced. During his time in X he had often felt criticised and not understood. Unfortunately the musical world is one which is full of criticism. This can come from the public and management but also from fellow band members. Creating new material is a difficult and stressful process which inevitably involves criticism and sees work being altered, and possibly, in the eyes of the creator, compromised to some degree, in order to fit the material within the capabilities, taste, and style of the rest of the band members. It may also be compromised to increase its marketability. In his study of bands, Thomas (2011:27) noted that 'this can create a situation in which a disgruntled band member may anticipate criticism and react pre-emptively without knowing whether they would have actually been criticized at all'.

It seems very probable that Alan entered into the new band in this emotional state. It also transpired that Alan had worked with Steve before when Steve had been the record producer for a successful group in which Alan was covering for a member of the band who was ill. During that recording session he had felt continually criticised and put down by Steve. He believed that if there was anything to criticise it was for the leader of the band (the singer songwriter) to do, not the producer. Yet here he was, now the leader and singer songwriter of his new band, again feeling criticised by Steve whom he perceived as being desperate to control him and his creativity.

Alan's past experience meant that he had encountered conflict with band members before and it had resulted in the band breaking up and Alan entering a very painful period in his life. In the mediation Alan spoke a lot about those experiences. He had found touring stressful when the band members, roadies, and management crew were in constant contact with one another as they flew from country to country and drove from town to town. They had little time to themselves and it was easier for everyone if they were seen as one entity rather than a group of individuals. It was easy to cater if everyone liked the same food, took the same drugs, and shared the same sexual requirements. Even simple things like what to go and see when they had any free time in a new country could lead to arguments. Both touring and recording require group members to be in extremely close spatial contact with each other, often for extremely long periods without a break. Some bands I have worked with have worked 24/7 over a long period without breaks because they wanted to ensure that they got their full benefit out of the money they were spending to hire recording studio time. It is not surprising that the current dispute came to a head when they were in the middle of a month's recording, away from family and friends, and living and working together 24/7 in a remote recording studio.

Both Steve and Alan had needed to strive hard to develop their own identity in their childhoods. For Steve, he battled to be accepted in school, where he was seen as different, and also needed to find a way in which he could equal his brother. For Alan, the loss of his father meant he grew up in an all female household, where at an early age he had to be the man of the house. Both were the youngest child in the family and both had struggled to establish where they sat in the family hierarchy in what were fairly unconventional families.

Identifying the hierarchy in a band is often fraught with difficulty. Even the most egalitarian band needs to have elements of clear leadership and delegation of duties. Some bands manage to achieve a high degree of equality with everyone sharing song writing duties, being paid equally, and holding equal say in decision-making. Alan had experienced an attempt at that with X, although ultimately Jamie became the clear leader, leading to resentment from Alan and other band members. Although politically Alan's values included wanting the new band to be egalitarian, his experience and self-esteem made it important for him to step into the leadership position, he did not want a repeat of what happened with Jamie. This was welcomed by everyone except Steve. Steve had his own reasons why needed to see himself as leader. He had always been on the periphery of success; he was never on stage receiving the adulation of fans. He had spent his professional life in the fairly lonely position of producer. In his previous times in the recording studios he had taken the lead, telling various bands he produced how to make their music more commercial. Thus a battle for leadership, focused on the style of musical production, ensued between Steve and Alan. Both believed the other saw himself as better than the rest of the band members.

Unfortunately, it is not uncommon for a band member to believe their talent surpasses those of their band mates. This can result in them expecting special treatment and believing they are excused from certain more mundane parts of the job. This certainly seemed to apply to both Alan and Steve. Alan believed his song writing and past experience of being on the road in a successful band gave him precedence. At the same time Steve believed his production skills and his experience of enabling many well-known bands to gain commercial success made him more important and valuable to the band than Alan. Alan had also had the experience of Jamie, in his previous band, beginning to see himself as being more important than the rest of the band when he started receiving more media attention and fan adoration than the rest. Added to this Jamie formed a relationship with Annabel, who had parents who were well-known and successful rock musicians. Jamie seemed to feel that this gave him an elevated status, not just in the band but in the wider musical sphere in which the band operated.

In addition to these professional experiences both Steve and Alan had needed to battle in their families to be seen for who they were as individuals rather than 'little brothers'. In Alan's case, at a very early age he had needed to take on a quasi-leadership role in relation to fulfilling some 'male duties' in a female household. Steve had been given pretty much free rein in his liberal family but had experienced his brother as leader with whom he would have to compete. His fear of failing to win that sibling battle meant he chose to tread a different but related path to his brother so the opportunity for comparison would be minimal.

A frequent cause of band conflict can be the different level of time commitment members contribute to the group; however, this was not an issue here as both Steve and Alan were committed to making the band work and were willing to put their all into achieving that. It was easier for Steve who was in a financially more secure position and did not have a partner or children. The need to maintain other employment in other bands or jobs as well as family obligations can make it difficult to meet the band's expectations. Alan's partner was very encouraging of him putting a lot of time into the new band and their first album, as she had supported him through his depression and saw this new project reenergising him. She was concerned that the conflict with Steve would take him back into a depressive state.

During the mediation, which at times became highly heated and emotional, both Alan and Steve eventually were able to listen openly to each other. Both had seen the other as arrogant but once they heard each other speak they began to see that they both felt vulnerable and that they were both investing a lot, emotionally, in the success of this new band.

Neither had spoken to the other about their childhoods, and listening to how it had been for both of them made them feel more warmly towards each other. In many ways they had been lonely young boys. They were able to recognise that both found being in groups (and not just the musical variety) quite difficult. Steve always felt in competition, as he had with his brother, and his coping strategy was to seek a sole leadership role, which made him an important and integral part of the group yet at the same time separated him. Alan sought brotherly companionship from his group members and recognised that to some degree he felt a sense of bereavement and abandonment when X disbanded.

He was desperate not to repeat this experience and so had sought out more control in this new band and tried to shield himself from forming too close relationships with the other band members, preferring to prioritise his relationship with Saskia.

As the songwriter Alan had to work closely with Steve and so the success of their relationship became essential to the success of the band. Unfortunately both had felt that in previous musical endeavours with other bands, their skills had not been fully recognised and both saw the new band as a place for this to be addressed. Both felt this was the last opportunity they were likely to have. Success for Alan required his compositions to be produced in a way which was true to his intentions rather than changed to make them potentially more commercial. For Steve this was his first opportunity to be out there, on the stage, in the spotlight, and he desperately sought commercial success and public recognition. In the discussions during the mediation Alan saw that to have his self-esteem restored, some degree of public recognition was required. Whilst wanting to stay true to his musical ideas, he did not want his work to go unnoticed. Steve expressed his admiration of Alan's songwriting and spoke of his own unsuccessful attempts and his sadness that his skills lay in the less visible field of production.

Although they are never going to find their musical partnership easy Alan and Steve were able to use the mediation to agree a number of things which allowed them to complete the album they were working on and to plan a tour. Through the mediation it became clear that Steve needed personal public recognition and that this could be enabled by giving him more guitar solos where he could literally take centre stage. It was also decided that two of Alan's songs had the potential to be real commercial successes, and that this kind of success could benefit everyone. Alan agreed that Steve's ideas for these songs were good and didn't compromise what he was trying to express in them.

The rest of Alan's compositions were recognised as being more likely to appeal to a more discerning and thoughtful audience. Although Alan had agreed to use some of Steve's ideas on two tracks it was agreed, by all band members, that another producer would be used for the rest of the album. Steve could see that this also met some of his needs; in order to be seen as a performer it was best not to try to combine this with producing. He continued to produce for other bands but agreed that there was a conflict of interest in doing so for Alan's band.

When planning the tour they intended to combine performances at some small intimate venues, where Alan's songs could be better heard and appreciated, with bigger venues where the music needed to be more commercial and where people were encouraged to get up and dance and where Steve's expertise could be brought in to play. Once this vision was agreed things changed quite a bit and Alan and Steve even worked together on a number of more commercial up-tempo numbers to be played at the bigger venues.

The regularity of tensions in bands has made it the subject of a number of studies (Arts & Ashdown, 2015; Thomas, 2011). It has sensibly been suggested that a lot of conflict in bands could be avoided if certain questions were discussed when the band is formed. These would include checking they share the same aspirations and goals; in existential terms this would cover whether they shared values as well as vision. It may feel appropriate to consider whether band members share the same cultural, religious, and political views, and if not whether any differences may cause problems? Each member should be clear about their expectations of the others and what is expected in return.

It is almost unheard of for a successful band not to have conflict, so it is realistic and not negative to consider at the start how conflicts or differences of opinion will be respectfully handled. To prevent conflict an atmosphere has to be created in which it is safe to talk with total and complete openness, to discuss potentially uncomfortable subjects, express strong emotions, and not feel judged. Each member may be able to identify sensitive issues and behaviours and share these with their band mates, so care can be taken when these areas need addressing. In addition to these more interpersonal concerns, being clear about financial and practical issues is essential from the outset.

Unfortunately, in my own experience bands are not always very logical when they come together. They are often driven by romantic ideas of shared creativity. Sometimes little thought has been given to whether they all want the same thing. One person may be looking primarily for an outlet for their creative writing and wish to keep as close as possible to their creative values, whilst maintaining purity of message (Alan in this case), whereas another group member may be seeking fame at all cost (Steve, in Alan's view). At an unconscious level they may be aware of these differences but fear of losing an important band member at this early stage, when enthusiasm is high, can prevent them asking the necessary questions or even acknowledging these inner doubts. It is also hard to confront difference in people you have known for a long time and have perceived as being 'like you'. Outside of *The X Factor* and other reality TV shows where bands are manufactured, band members have often known one another for years and may even have been school friends. As a result they will feel they know each other and it can come as a shock to realise they have differences. No matter how great the differences may be there will always be some commonalities which the mediator may help to identify. Once the sense of alienation and otherness is met with some sense of sameness, it is easier to facilitate a useful dialogue which can lead to a resolution.

Both Steve and Alan shared the need for this band to succeed. Once they began to see this through listening to the other's experiences and perceptions they began to be less hostile and to see both shared hopes and individual hopes and needs. They discovered that not all the individual needs had to be compromised and they were able to find ways of helping each other get what they needed without giving up what was important to each of them as individuals.

13 Desires and drives

A marital mediation

Ian

Well, it seems my wife wants to leave me. I don't get it. We have every-thing any couple would want. I have worked hard to ensure we have everything.

We have a beautiful house, which Rebecca chose and she has every-thing in the house that she could ever want. She can decorate it how-ever she likes, I am happy to go along with whatever she decides. She is great at making things look nice, she has a real flair for interior design. I don't really care as long as we have somewhere to sit! We really do have a house and garden to be really proud of. Rebecca is a really good homemaker.

I do my bit too. I'm doing really well in my job. I work really hard. I leave home at 6.30am and get back around 8.30pm – she can't say I haven't done my duty and worked all hours to ensure she and the chil-dren have everything they need. I know we had both hoped that I would have progressed further up the pecking order and to be honest I don't know why I haven't. I put more hours in than anyone else; I work harder. Perhaps I should spend more time socially with my colleagues – the promo-tions seem to go to the bosses' drinking pals. Anyway, even though I haven't been promoted I am on good money so we don't go short of any-thing we need.

Every autumn we go skiing (even though I'm not keen myself) and in the summer we go to our house in France or spend some time in Italy. I know Rebecca doesn't like it that I can't spend the whole summer away with her and the children and that she has to spend time in France on her own but I do have to put the hours in to ensure we can afford those holidays. Despite me not being there much she has made a beautiful job of renovating that house too. It looks really lovely. She speaks French fluently, unlike me, and knows most of the people in the village. She loves the local market, all that kind of thing. She is quite a member of the community there. I doubt anyone in the village would say they know me. When I am there I like to take it easy, to sit in the garden and read, although we do, of course, go out for a few meals and take the children to the beach. I can't say the village itself interests me, or the people who live there, I prefer England.

We have two great children. The boys, James and Henry, are doing well at school, they are at a splendid school and board there during the week but come home at weekends. They are both good at sport and so a lot of the weekend Rebecca ferries them to various sports activities. I don't know where they get their athletic abilities from, certainly not from me; I am totally useless, not very coordinated. I hated all the sports stuff at school. It was tough really; the school I went to didn't appreciate boys who weren't interested in sport, so I was a bit of an outsider. I am still not interested in any sport, even as a spectator. I am glad the boys are good at it; it will make life easier for them in many ways. Fortunately academically I was quite successful. I did pretty well in my exams and went off to do a degree in psychology – people have always quite mystified me and I had hopes that learning more about psychology might help me understand people better. It didn't work, I still find it hard to understand other people and now it seems I can't even understand my own wife. She has really been the only person I have ever met who seemed to understand and accept me. We get along fine, or I thought we did. I am sure this is just a phase. She will come round. She can't really intend to give everything up.

What is the problem? We aren't short of money. We have a lovely house and a good lifestyle. Both Rebecca and I are successful – or reasonably successful – at work. I never stop her doing anything she wants, she goes off to lots of conferences and workshops and I look after the boys when she needs me to.

None of it makes sense. We have been together 14 years and now she wants to leave me. I can only think she has another man.

Rebecca

He really doesn't get it. Sometimes I think we haven't been living in the same marriage!

I blame myself. When we married I knew things weren't quite right, but I guess, like many women I thought I could make them right. No one is perfect and I thought I could improve on the Ian I was getting and develop him. He was shy and inexperienced when we met, he doted on me and I liked that at the time. He had fallen out with his family and was very lonely. I was lonely too, I had come here on a work placement from my university in Australia and I didn't find it easy to settle or make friends. I had just split up from my first real boyfriend and not feeling particularly good about myself. Meeting Ian was great for me. He made me feel I belonged here in the UK and that someone wanted and needed me. He made me feel important.

He is not a bad man and he works really hard, but he is absent. I don't mean he is away a lot, although his working hours are horrendous ... and I have checked with his boss ... it's Ian's decision to work 7am-8.30pm, not a requirement of his work ... what I mean is he is emotionally absent. I don't think he has really experienced anything deeply. That is partly why I can't take seriously his threat to kill himself if I leave him. He doesn't take any notice of me most of the time, so what difference would it make to him if I wasn't around?

When I think about it, he could easily replace me with a PA. I can understand he doesn't want me to leave, I can understand that he is scared because he can't see how he can manage on his own but I don't think it is me he will miss, just my role.

Ian

I know Rebecca is disappointed in me but I don't really understand why. She says I am unemotional but I really love her. Surely love is emotional. Doesn't she see that I love her, I can't imagine life without her; it is as simple as that. I am proud that she is my wife.

I know I haven't really done my share. She gets frustrated that I don't want to socialise, why would I want to? I like it just being the two of us, it is enough for me but clearly it isn't enough for her. I probably should have made more of an effort with the boys' schooling. I pay their fees but I have left her to go to parents' evenings and meetings, I hate that sort of thing – lots of parents trying to outdo one another with how well their child is doing or how much they contribute to the PTA. It is just not my thing.

Everything about me seems to irritate her at the moment. She goes on and on about me never having learnt to drive, that I don't want to go to the theatre or cinema. I am tired when I get home, it's too late to go out, I just want to sit down with Rebecca and have a good meal and some quality wine, maybe watch a bit of TV to wind down. Isn't that what most people do? I don't see what is wrong. I am happy with life; we have everything we need.

I am sure we can sort things out. If she just tells me what she wants me to do I'll do it. I can't imagine who I would be without her.

Rebecca

I think it was a mistake for me to marry Ian. I was so lonely and I was on my own in the UK. As I said he is basically a good man. I was young and didn't really know what I wanted or could expect from a partner. I had had one very bad relationship and it was partly to get away from that that I came to the UK. I feel bad. Ian hasn't changed, I have. I knew what I was taking on with Ian. He was never the life and soul of the party but that didn't matter earlier on in our relationship. In fact, I quite liked it. It was better than being with my previous boyfriend who dominated me and thought a huge amount of himself. In those days it was me that didn't want to socialise because when we did I just found myself in a corner watching my boyfriend flirting outrageously with everyone. Ian is safe; I don't have to worry about him going off with someone else – he hardly notices that people exist.

Something has changed in me and I have become more and more interested in people and what makes them tick and my own self-development ... Surprising when I have a husband who behaves as though he wished other people didn't exist. I have taken up yoga, been on retreats, attended courses, anything where I have felt there may be some opportunity to be with some people with some emotional intelligence. I have asked Ian to come too but he is always 'too busy'. He has never wanted to get involved in community life or even in stuff to do with the boys' schooling. Gradually I have stopped expecting him to come, or even asking him along and more and more I have done things on my own. Now, I am not even sure that I want him to come – he would just be a square peg in a round hole. I would just have to look after him. I would feel embarrassed by him.

We just don't share any interests anymore. In fact I am not sure what interests we have ever shared – except that we were both lonely. I don't look to him for much anymore. It doesn't help that he has never shown any interest in learning to drive so if the boys need taking anywhere that is down to me too. It also means he doesn't meet any of the other parents who are acting as taxi drivers for their children. There is quite a lot of socialising and chatting goes on while we are waiting for the boys to get their kits together. I have become quite friendly with many of the other parents. Basically, I have learnt to make a life for myself separate from him and I can't imagine him in that life. He just doesn't fit. When both the boys started school I went back to work. Ian didn't want me to; he couldn't understand why I needed to be with other people. I would have dried up and died without work. I take any opportunity I can to go to conferences or on work trips abroad. I enjoy being with my work colleagues, they are interested in what is going on in the world, we also have a laugh. I'm not going to give my job up, like Ian wishes I would.

The boys board during the week and that's fine but if I am away at weekends I have to pay someone to come in and help Ian look after them – his own sons! He hasn't a clue how to talk to them, how to play with them, even what to feed them. He doesn't cook anyway, that's something else which is my responsibility and if I am too tired then we eat out. When I really think about it, he doesn't take responsibility for anything much. I make sure the bills are paid, that holidays are booked, family birthdays remembered, clothes bought (even Ian's clothes). I am more like his mother than his wife.

Ian

I think Rebecca must be having an affair. I think that is what this is really all about. Nothing else would explain it.

All these conferences and retreats she goes on, I think they are covers for meeting up with her man friend. She is always very excited when these events are coming up. She buys new clothes, gets her hair done and all that kind of thing. If it was just about work, why would she do all that?

She never wants to go anywhere with me these days. I know I don't want to go out but if that is what she wants we could do that. I'm not sure what she would like to do – the theatre, cinema, a meal, whatever, I would go with her. We could ask Loretta to look after the boys. When Rebecca is away at weekends and the boys are home from school Loretta comes in to help me with the boys, so they know her already. I can't drive so when Rebecca is away Loretta takes them to any places they need to get to, she cooks, keeps the place tidy, shops, all those sort of things, so I don't think there would be any problem asking her to come in of an evening if we wanted to go out.

Rebecca

I know it is hard for Ian. As far as he is concerned everything is fine. He is miserable but he seems to think that is just how life is. I haven't given up yet. There is still time for me to make a new life with some enjoyment in it. The trouble is that Ian brings me down; just to think about him makes me miserable. I can't bear the thought of the rest of my life being like this.

I do feel sorry for Ian. He is like a big child. A big child who makes lots of money, and can hold down a responsible job, but still a child. He hasn't a clue how to do the most basic things. I think his helplessness is one of the reasons I haven't left before now. It makes me feel guilty and I worry how he will manage but that is no way to think about your husband. A husband should be an equal partner, not someone you feel responsible for, like a particularly hopeless child. It is no good staying with someone out of pity. My resentment will only grow if I stay.

Ian

I'm sure we can sort this. If Rebecca owns up that she is having an affair I am sure we can come through that and I can forgive her. I think it was a mistake her going back to work when the boys started school. She doesn't need to work; I can pay for all we need.

Perhaps she is scared and worried that if she tells me about this other guy I will divorce her and because she would be in the wrong she wouldn't get much money out of me or custody of the boys. That's probably what it is. She is mistaken if she thinks she will get the boys whatever happens. We should all just be together, a family. I won't let her leave and take the boys away from me.

Yes, I am absolutely sure there is another man. I even think I know who it is. I know it's a terrible admission but I have been going through her texts and email. Since she was at a conference in the States last year she has been receiving lots of texts from a man called Samuel. I have looked him up on Google. He is a doctor and seems to be into all that alternative medicine. He has a yoga retreat (which Rebecca has been to several times) and he offers holistic healing ... I can guess what that entails! Their emails are very intimate ... 'How are you coping darling? ... I think of you all the time ... I can't imagine how awful it must be for you ... etc.' Surely that's evidence of an affair.

I haven't told her I have looked at her emails, and I'm not even sure that it might not be illegal, so don't say anything to her, but I have asked if she is having an affair. She always denies it but I know she is lying.

It would solve everything if she has been having an affair. I can forgive her and she will be grateful. I could always remind her if things got difficult again.

Rebecca

Because he thinks our life is OK he has convinced himself that I must be having an affair. Nothing else makes sense for him. He keeps going on and on about it. Whenever I am on the phone he hovers about and asks who

I am talking to. Part of me feels he would be happy if I were having an affair. That would somehow make things make sense for him. It would be his fault; he could blame me, or my imaginary lover. He can't believe that I want to leave because this just isn't enough . . . I feel I am suffocating, dying . . . I'm too young to give up on life. I want to get out there and live.

Ian

I know she hasn't been happy and I'm not a bundle of fun, but I am sure we can work things out. If she gives up work and stops going on all these retreats and conferences, than I can forgive her being unfaithful. What she needs to know though is that I am not letting her go and she is not taking the children from me. They are mine.

Rebecca

I am not having an affair but there are men I am a lot more intimate with, more connected to, than Ian. I make the most of the time I am away to get to know people, men and women. I need to feel that I exist, that people are interested in me, that I am not some walking zombie or robot who just gets up, sees to the children, goes to work and then goes to bed. I can't live like that.

When I was in the States I met a man who really showed me what I was missing. He seemed to understand me and to share my interests. He runs a retreat and yoga centre there. The first time we spoke to one another we talked and talked for hours and hours, it was amazing. He is horrified that I am 'wasting' my life staying with Ian. He finds it hard to believe my life here. He can see it is slowly killing me. Every day he emails or texts just to see how I am doing. He encourages me to be myself and to make something of my life but he doesn't ask anything of me. He knows more about me than Ian ever will. We laugh and cry together, we share our thoughts and hopes. We aren't having an affair in the way people think of as an affair but he fills my thoughts and gives me hope. He shows that being with me, or away from me, makes him feel things, he owns his feelings, he shows them, he talks about them honestly and encourages me to do the same. Ian, well, Ian, one wonders whether he has feelings at all.

Ian

I know Rebecca thinks I am without feelings but it isn't true. I love her and it hurts to see her become so distant, to write me off. I can tell she doesn't even want to be in the same room with me these days.

I can change; I can show my feelings more, if that is what she wants. I know she says I don't have feelings, that I am a cold fish but I can't explain how hard this all is. We have everything we could have ever wished for. We can be happy again. I just ask that she gives me a chance to show that I am emotional ...

In fact, I am emotional – I have changed already. I would never have imagined that I would fall apart in the way I have. Until this last month I have never had any time off work and now I have been away for three weeks and I have had to see the occupational health doctor, who was the person who suggested I contact you. I never saw myself as anyone who would have any truck with psychologists and all that sort of thing but here I am ... lost ... tearful ... scared. Rebecca has never seen me like this before, I am in tears most of the time, I can't eat, sleep, or work but she just looks at me and says she wants out. She is the one showing no emotions, she is being hard and not caring.

Rebecca

It's too late now. I can see he is upset. Every evening when I get back from work, he is just sitting there shaking and I can see he has been crying. I think he is just scared and feeling sorry for himself. Whatever these new emotions are about they are too little, too late. I have made my decision, I want out of this marriage before I curl up and die. I have grown to hate Ian and myself for all the years I have wasted by staying with him. I need to get my life back, I need to breathe and find fun in living again.

What I want from the mediation is Ian's agreement to a separation. I would like a divorce but if it is easier for him to take things one step at a time I will go with that. It's not thinking time, or changing my mind time ... I know this is it ... but if it gives him time to get used to the idea, I am fine with that. I don't have another man in the wings or a new life to run off to – I just need to find myself again and move on. I would really like to do that with Ian's blessing, without threats of suicide and histrionics. I want him to behave like a man and not a child and be adult and mature about this. I know it would be a first for him, but it is what I want.

He needs to help me find somewhere for the boys and I to live and he needs to share with me the task of telling the boys what is happening why. I don't want to move far from him, I want him to be a presence in the boys' lives. He is their father, I respect that and I don't want them to grow up without a father or feeling angry with the one they do have.

Reflections on the mediation

When Ian initially rang to discuss the possibility of mediation he sounded very cold and business-like. I was surprised, when I met him in person, to meet a very vulnerable and emotional man who cried many times during the mediation. Rebecca, who had been quite emotional on the phone and spoke a lot about the need to 'own one's emotions' presented a much colder picture in the flesh. It reminded me yet again to try not to make any initial assumptions as to what the people may be like, who is most upset, who holds the most power, etc.

It became apparent that in order to leave the marriage Rebecca had taken a very conscious decision to disengage from Ian. If she allowed herself to feel anything for him, she feared she would be stuck in an unhappy marriage forever. In the mediation she repeatedly made it clear that she had made her mind up and was leaving despite any changes Ian may promise, or indeed, evidence.

Both Rebecca and Ian had fundamentally different hopes for the mediation. For Ian, the mediation signalled the hope for a new beginning in which he could relate more openly, honestly, and emotionally, not just with Rebecca, but with everyone he came into contact with. For Rebecca the mediation was not about a new beginning for her and Ian, but an ending to the marriage and a new beginning for her as a single woman. She wanted the ending to be as clear and painless as possible. Ironically it was Ian who discovered a new identity during the process of the mediation.

Initially Ian would not accept that there was anything fundamentally wrong with him or the marriage. He felt that Rebecca's head had been turned by some 'new age guy, much more attractive and emotional' than him. For Ian, it was easier for him to accept that Rebecca had been unfaithful than to except the truth that she found the marriage stifling and she believed she had to leave for her own wellbeing. It was impossible for Ian to envisage that for Rebecca the single state was preferable than being married to him.

During the mediation it became very clear that loneliness had played a major factor in bringing them together as a couple. Rebecca had come to the UK for a fresh start following the breakup of her first real relationship. In talking about this relationship she was quite tearful, in a way which wasn't evident when she spoke of her relationship with Ian. Her partner had been a charismatic and untrustworthy socialite who enjoyed life, parties, and women and in many ways put Rebecca down so that she retreated into her shell. In the end this had proved too much for Rebecca and although she felt the loss of excitement which the relationship had brought, in Ian she found the polar opposite – a man who was unsure of himself, not comfortable socially, wanting to make a commitment and, in his own way, devoted to Rebecca.

In talking about the early days of their relationship, Rebecca was clear that she was looking for safety and for a relationship in which she knew she was important and loved. Over the years she questioned whether this was true in the long term, and she was left pondering whether she had just convinced herself that it was what she wanted, or whether it was just because that was what Ian could offer her. She now wondered if all that happened was that she rescued Ian from being alone and that he would have 'loved' any woman who had done that for him. When she heard herself say this, she also recognised that it had been true for her too. She had never 'fallen in love' with Ian but had thought he was loyal and kind and she believed she could change him and 'make him more like the man I was looking for' through encouraging him to be more sociable and interested in the world.

She had never been happy with Ian's wish to just stay at home and watch TV nor in the way in which he just designated everything about the choosing and decorating of the home to her. Again, on reflection, she remembered that she had originally liked these things about him. Unlike her ex-boyfriend, he didn't flirt with other women, in fact he showed no interest in them. She didn't have to worry about him 'going off with someone else'. For these reasons she had initially quite encouraged his solitary nature when they had first got together and even when their children were very small. As the years passed, Rebecca felt the need of more company than that of a silent Ian and her two boys. She tried to get Ian to accompany her to social events but even when he did so she found it painful as he 'made no effort to talk to other people' and just 'hung about' by her side, 'inhibiting' her so that it often resulted in her becoming bored and the two of them deciding to go home early. Eventually she just decided to attend these kinds of functions on her own and discovered she enjoyed them and could be the 'life and soul of the party'.

To transport herself to all these new interests Rebecca learnt to drive and bought herself a 'fun' car. She loved the freedom that being able to drive and owning her own car gave her. At first she had no desire for Ian to learn to drive and acknowledged that this gave her a certain degree of power and freedom in the relationship. However, as the boys grew older and needed to be ferried around more she began to resent the fact that this task always fell to her.

She also acknowledged that she had at first been pleased that she could choose the décor for their homes in the UK and France on her own. She didn't have to argue with Ian about the colour of the furniture and walls, she could do as she pleased and know that Ian would always compliment her on her choices although she believed that he would have done so even if he had thought they were hideous. Her feelings about this changed as she began to feel very isolated and wanted Ian to take more of an active interest and to choose things for their homes together. Although she believed that she had expressed this clearly to Ian, nothing improved and she began to wonder why she was putting so much energy into homes her husband didn't seem to care about and nobody visited because Ian discouraged visitors.

Rebecca's newly found social side became very important to her, particularly with the boys away at boarding school and Ian spending long hours at work. The more time she spent with people the more intrigued she became with how people functioned and the importance that many of her new friends gave to self-development. This led her on a new path of reading, attending courses, retreats, and conferences, and taking a very serious interest in yoga. These were activities which took her further away from Ian, to a point where she could no longer see any similarities between the two of them, and became fearful of what remaining in the marriage would do to her psychologically and emotionally.

She began to forge close friendships with people who shared her new interests. She became particularly close to Simon, who ran a retreat centre that she would visit two or three times a year. She spoke very passionately about the interests they shared, the close fit in their values, and their hopes for the future. She spoke of the way in which she felt whole and totally different when she was with him. She expressed her love for him and for what he had taught her but maintained that they were not sexually involved with each other. During the mediation it was difficult to know what hopes Rebecca might be holding for this relationship developing further.

Ian's solitary existence meant that although he felt he 'got on all right' with his colleagues at work he had no friends (nor desire for any). He was estranged from his parents and so his family – Rebecca and the boys 'were all he had got'. He had never spoken openly or shown his emotions to anyone before Rebecca told him she was leaving. He had now discovered a very different part of himself which was very emotional and vulnerable. He spoke of how amazed he had been when he had found himself in tears when speaking to the occupational health doctor and his shock at hearing himself tell his boss that he needed time off from work because his wife was leaving him and he 'was falling apart'. He didn't recognise the side of himself yet discovering it was proving liberating for him and he rather liked this 'new self'.

During the mediation he talked about having taken psychology as his first degree but finding it impossible to get a job when he graduated. During college holidays he had worked at an accountancy practice run by a friend of his father. He found the work very easy and he discovered that he was much quicker than his more experienced colleagues. When they invited him to join them after he graduated he had jumped at the chance, even though he had planned to find a job more closely related to his psychology degree. He now held a high status accountancy post in the banking sector. He had never questioned whether he enjoyed it or whether it bored him. He found the hours long but the work easy and he earned good money with which he could give his family 'a good life'; therefore it made sense to him to stay there.

As he listened to his wife describe him as unemotional, and heard her speak of the excitement which she was finding in her new self-development activities, Ian started to wonder what life would have been like if he hadn't moved into accountancy. He spoke quite animatedly about some of the things he had learnt on his degree course and told me that he was 'enjoying' the mediation as it was giving him the 'first chance I've had in a long time to think about who I am and what I want in life'.

The discussion in the private sessions moved away from his desperation to hang on to his marriage and took on a more self-reflective character. He began to consider returning to his psychology studies by enrolling in evening classes and seemed very animated and excited at the thought. He felt he had surprised himself by actually enjoying the dialogue with the mediator during the private sessions and regretted that he had distanced himself from other people and shied away from social encounters. He was determined that he would change and still held out a hope that Rebecca would see this and give the marriage another chance. He still believed that she had been unfaithful but this did not seem to be an issue for him, in fact he saw it as something which 'evened things out and gave him the moral high ground' if there were future difficulties. Although there was some consideration of whether 'holding something in reserve' as a potential weapon was a positive thing, Ian felt strongly that he needed something to give him 'the upper hand if need be'.

From the start Rebecca focused her dissatisfaction on Ian's lack of 'intimacy and emotional intelligence'. During the mediation Rebecca saw a very emotional Ian and said that if he had shown this side of himself even three years ago they may not have got to the point of her seeking a separation but she was adamant that it was now too late and that she had to leave.

Something had shifted in Ian. He was now much stronger. He reiterated that he did not want the marriage to end but that he understood that Rebecca would have difficulty believing in 'the new emotional Ian' and his ability to sustain his new openness. For this reason he would support her moving out of the family home with their sons but would not agree to her immediately starting divorce proceedings. He hoped that during their separation they could go out together, without the boys, at least once a week, and that this may allow Rebecca to see that he had really changed and that the change could be sustained. Rebecca agreed with this suggestion but made it very clear that she still saw the separation as the first step towards obtaining a divorce.

Despite this agreement, Ian couldn't leave matters there and ended by telling Rebecca he knew about the affair but would forgive her! Fortunately, despite despairing looks from Rebecca, this did not sabotage the agreement and both left feeling they had gained from the mediation.

14 Access

A family mediation

Francesca

It was a difficult decision to make – to have children with no partner but I knew it was something I had to do. Since I was a small girl I have known that I wanted children but having lived through my parents' marriage and seen the damage my father did to me and my brother and sisters, I was very unsure about allowing any man to play a big part in my life.

I think I have learnt what not to do when bringing up children, from how my own parents were with me.

James

She used me to get what she wanted and now she sees no further use for me she just wants to cast me aside and never set eyes on me again. I don't care if we never see one another again but I damn well won't allow her to deny me access to my own child. She is controlling. She will damage Billy. Billy needs me to protect him from that mad woman – all her aspirations for him, her rule and regulations. She is used to getting what she wants and she thinks I am weak ... well she got it wrong this time. This is one fight she isn't going to win.

Billy

It makes me sick. If they could chop me into two, I think they would. Well Dad would as long as he gets exactly one half. He is always going on about how it should be 50/50 with them each getting me for equal hours, minutes and seconds in the week. It's a bit different with Mum; I think she would prefer 100/0, with Dad not having anything!

Isn't there a story in the Bible where two mothers argued over who is the mother of a baby? We learnt about it in RE. I think King Solomon had to rule between two women both claiming to be the mother of a child. He tricked the women into revealing their true feelings … I think both women lived in the same house and both had baby boys. One of the women accidentally smothered her own son while sleeping, or something like that, and then she claimed that the surviving child was hers, which obviously the other woman denied. If I remember right, King Solomon called for a sword saying there was only one fair solution and that the remaining baby must be split in two, each woman receiving half of the child. The true mother couldn't bear for her child to be split in two so she told Solomon to give the baby to the other woman whereas the other woman preferred that if it couldn't be hers, that it was divided and neither woman got a living child. It was obvious that the true mother who really loved her child would rather give up her baby to another than hurt or kill him. Look at my parents … I think they would do anything to avoid losing out to the other. They would even cut me in half if they could!

Francesca

I have always seen my future as involving children. I have always known I wanted to be a mother. What I thought I knew was that I never wanted to be married or in a long-term relationship with one man. I still can't see myself ever marrying but probably would like that long-term relationship now but certainly not with James.

James and I knew each other through mutual friends and would often find ourselves at the same political rallies or social functions. We seemed to get on well and began to have a sexual relationship although I was always clear that we were not boyfriend and girlfriend. When I got to 30 I became really broody and talked to James about wanting to have a child.

I made it very clear that I wanted to bring that child up alone, to be solely responsible. James told me he had no intention of having children as he felt they would tie him down but that he would be prepared to father my child on the understanding that I would not expect him to take any responsibility or to relate to the child as a father. This suited what I wanted and seemed a good way forward. I took him at his word, we never wrote anything down about how we saw it working but everything changed when Billy was born.

James

I have known Francesca for years. We have hung around in the same crowd. We share the same political beliefs, or so I thought. We have both put time and energy into the Cooperative movement and local

Labour politics, that's how we got to know one another. It is strange that we share those ideals as we come from very different backgrounds.

Francesca's family have money and are very educated and middle class but as dysfunctional as they come. Her two sisters don't talk to her parents. Jan, the eldest, has had serious drug problem for years and is in and out of rehab. It seems to work for a while but as soon as she is put under any kind of stress she relapses. Her brother Simon, the middle child, accused her father of sexually abusing him when he was small. Apparently he had no memory of this until he went into therapy, in his 20s, to explore some issues about his sexuality. When he raised this with his family his parents and Jan didn't believe him. Francesca sat on the fence and has never said whether she believes him or not. Fran has never liked her father, she finds him difficult and controlling and thinks he behaves very badly towards her mother but I really don't think she believes he sexually abused his own son. He seems pretty clearly hetero to me, he has a history of affairs with a number of women and I don't think anyone has seen anything that would indicate any interest in men or boys. Despite all this and the fact that her family are mad she is desperate to present a picture of a united family and so she is the one that has kept in touch with all of them, tries to arrange family parties and get togethers. She sees herself as the sane one ... and compared to the others she is but that upbringing seriously screwed her up.

It is strange really that she is so keen to try to keep that family together whilst never wanting a 'proper' family of her own. Not that I saw that as a negative. I didn't believe in the nuclear family. I never wanted to marry or have children and when Fran asked me to father a child for her it seemed like a good idea. It is always nice for a man to know he has the ability to father a child. A macho thing, I suppose. Although we agreed that I would father her child and then not be involved I don't think I really gave it any serious thought. In fact, I doubted Fran would get pregnant, I don't know why I thought that, but I did. I am not sure whether either of us would have given it more than one try but amazingly that is all it took. Probably not such a surprise because Fran is so controlling and so planned the whole thing meticulously, checking her temperature every day, working out the best times to have sex – when she was most likely to conceive ... all that stuff. Like most of what Fran takes on, she succeeded; she got what she wanted.

I never thought I would want any involvement in raising the child but I was with Fran when Billy was born and I can't describe what I felt once I saw him. To have a son, it felt amazing. I knew I wanted to be a father, not just a sperm donor!

Billy

They both tell me they can't bear to be without me but that's not true. I can't bear it, them arguing all the time. I think they forget what they are arguing about – me! It is more an argument based on their need to win out against the other. I wonder how they ever came to have me.

My Mum tells me that she had always wanted a child but never met someone she loved enough to get married to and to stay with. She had been going out with my Dad for months, then they split up but remained friends and she asked him to get her pregnant! I think it's a disgusting idea, it was all about what she wanted, she never thought what it would be like for that child – me. I can't believe that Dad went along with it. What did he think would happen? According to him, he was shocked with how he felt when he saw me for the first time, according to him it was love at first sight and he said at that point he realised he couldn't go ahead and just be my Mum's friend – he wanted to be a Dad to me. I know this isn't how Mum had seen it. She has very clear ideas on childrearing, I think that is one of the reasons she didn't want anyone else involved. I know she was shocked when Dad didn't just disappear after I was born.

I understand Dad even asked her to marry him but she was adamant that she did not want to be married and that she wanted to bring me up on her own. Dad refused to go away and although they have never lived together he has remained involved.

They are very different. Mum is a strong person and I think she bullies Dad a bit. Some of my friends say Mum is a snob and I know what they mean. Mum is clever and helps me loads with my homework and that kind of thing. She is very anxious that I do well at school, keep up my music practice and private German lessons, she is very strict about all that – she doesn't like me watching TV or hanging out with friends but she does spend lots of time doing things with me, like reading, playing board games and she takes me out a lot, we go to museums, galleries and we also camp out a lot. Mum loves the countryside and knows loads about wildlife, insects and that sort of stuff. Dad is much more laid back, lot quieter and less sure of himself.

I have my own room at both houses and in my room at Dad's I have my own TV and games consoles so when I am there I spent a lot of time in my room playing on those kind of things. Dad will pop in from time to time and check I'm OK but mainly he just does his own thing – watches different programmes on the TV downstairs. He hates the countryside and the places I go to with him have usually been towns, with the visits planned around football matches. It is quite exciting; we go for the whole weekend and meet up with some friends of Dad's and their boys. We stay at one of their houses and Dad goes on about old times. I enjoy those weekends and I am very friendly with the other boys, we keep in touch through Facebook and text one another a lot.

I'm 11 now, nearly 12, and all I can remember is them arguing about me. They are meant to be grown up but I feel as though it is me that has to act as the grown up whilst they behave like children.

Francesca

James has no idea how to bring up a child and throughout the time we talked about me getting pregnant he showed no interest at all in being part of any child's life. He was happy that I didn't intend putting any father's name on the birth certificate. In fact he was pleased as he felt that would safeguard him from taking any financial responsibility for the child. He is very tight with money but I have never wanted him to take any responsibility. I wanted a child of my own. I know a lot of people don't understand that and disapprove, thinking I was being very selfish, but I wasn't being selfish or silly, I had thought it through. I have my own house and I am financially stable, I have a job and I have family money to fall back on if I absolutely need to. I thought about it a lot before I went ahead with it.

I think he liked the idea of fathering a child, proving his manhood. To be fair he was also my friend in those days and he knew it was very important to me to become a mother. I think he saw helping me to have a child as something a good male friend would do for a female friend. We had been in a sexual relationship with each other before and I guess it could have just happened at that time but I was careful, I didn't want a man involved in bringing up my child and I was very upfront and clear about that throughout. I thought we had a very clear mutual agreement that his involvement was limited to helping me to conceive. As a friend I knew he would be around as Billy was growing up but I didn't see his relationship with the child as being any different from all my other friends.

I was a little surprised when James said he wanted to be there at the birth but I was OK with it. I gave birth at home and I was shocked that the midwife handed Billy to James and he was really reluctant to let go of him. He insisted on having several photos of him taken holding Billy in those first moments. I was surprised but didn't really see it as significant, I didn't recognise that things were going to be different. Giving birth and being present at a birth is mind-blowing but I thought his enthusiasm would soon die down. Anyway, it seems that at that point, the birth, James changed – he became besotted with Billy. This was never what I had envisaged or wanted. It wasn't how we had agreed it would be. I am really angry with him for changing his mind; he is being awful and demanding. He just wants his own way and his way is the wrong way for Billy. We don't agree on anything about Billy's future or what is important in the way he is brought up.

James

I am quite frightened by Fran. She is very articulate and can run rings round me in any argument. I'm not dim but I don't have the gift of the gab. Fran makes me feel small and stupid, even uncouth. I don't have her sophistication. I wasn't brought up surrounded by books and classical music. My family are pretty straightforward. Dad worked in the factory all his life and was a strong trade unionist, Mum stayed home with me until I was old enough to go to school and then she got a part-time job, one which meant she could see me off to school in the morning and be home when I got back in the evening. They are no great intellectuals but I always felt loved. Every Saturday I would go to the match with Dad and every August we had a week at Butlins. It was fine. I didn't suffer because I wasn't surrounded by books or made to do homework and go to after school clubs. I learnt to play the trumpet because I wanted to. I went to university because I wanted to, not because my parents made me. I want Billy to grow up with a mind of his own, not to be brainwashed by his mother. Life is about enjoyment as well as work and achievement.

Billy

I worry about Dad. He seems so unhappy. He doesn't seem to do anything except go to work and come home again. I'm not sure he even enjoys his work 'cos when he gets home he usually moans about all sorts of things that have gone on in the office. I don't think he likes it there but he has been there since before I was born. He talks about the time when he will be retired and seems to be looking forward to it but I can't imagine what he will do all day.

I worry about him, I think he is lonely and I think he needs me more than Mum does. She has quite a few friends and she is always busy. She takes courses in all sorts of things and loves painting and making things. Each evening I'm there she spends time helping me with my homework and making sure I do my music practice. She spends a lot of time with

me and we talk a lot. She knows I am worried about Dad – that I think
he is unhappy and lonely. He is better when I am there and when we
go off to football matches, then he does actually seem happy ... unless
his team loses! I think if I spend more time with Dad he may be a bit
happier but if I did I would upset Mum.

Francesca

I am not just being difficult because James went back on his word.
I really don't think he is a good father. Yes, he wants to see more of his
son but he doesn't really pay any real attention to him. When Billy stays
at his father's, it's inevitable that he will lose things – socks, underwear,
that kind of thing. Does James ever just replace them, go out and buy
some more? No, he expects me to just buy anything Billy needs and to
replace things that get lost. James knows that my family have money but
I don't have personal money, just what I earn, the same as James.
I don't want to ask my parents for financial help. He wants his son but
he doesn't want to do the things involved in raising a child.

It's not just the money. I bet if you asked James what grade Billy was
up to with his flute, he wouldn't have a clue. He shows no interest in
Billy's education. I worry when Billy goes round there that he won't do
his homework. James does turn up at parents' evenings but I think that
is more about staking his claim, he never asks any questions and if there
are any problems he ignores them.

James

She is so used to having everything her own way. Francesca says jump
and you jump, no question. Well this time I am not going to jump,
I am sticking in here for what is my right and because I believe it would
damage Billy to spend all his time with her.

I think she dislikes all men. She looks down on us and resents us.
How can she know how to bring up a boy? Does he really want to
spend his time playing the flute and learning a lot of foreign languages
he is never going to use? I worry that he will get bullied at school. She
doesn't encourage him to go and play sport with the other lads. No, it's
'homework and school are more important than anything else'. Doesn't
she see that she is making him an outsider? If he had been a girl, she
would be less damaging but he is a lad.

When he is with me we can do lad things, play football together ...
I have even bought him an X-Box which we play games on, but that
has to be kept a secret from his mother. She would hit the roof if she

knew about that. She doesn't even have a TV in her house. Just think what that is like for him – how can he have chats with mates when they are all talking about what they are watching on TV? Well I have just got Sky with a box we can record programmes on, so at least he can catch up a bit when he is at mine.

Billy

Sometimes I wish Dad would get a girlfriend. I would worry less about him if I didn't think he was on his own, just sitting there watching TV. I can't see that happening though; he isn't really a fun person to be with. I don't know if that is because he is upset about me and Mum and him, or perhaps he is just like that? I wonder if he is depressed.

It's funny me saying I would like Dad to have a girlfriend as last year my Mum did get a boyfriend, Mark. I hated it and I think they split up because of me. Whenever he came round I made sure that he knew he was in the way and that I didn't want him there. I was jealous, I am used to having Mum's attention and even though she still did everything with me that she did before it just didn't feel the same. Mum did ask me to be nice to him and asked me why I didn't like him. I remember just saying he was horrible but that's not the truth, he was really quite nice. He tried to be my friend, bought me things, took me on trips, talked to me and all that. Perhaps if I had been nicer they might still have been together and Mum wouldn't mind me spending more time with Dad.

It's not that I prefer being at Dad's, although it's much more relaxing there. He never asks have I done my homework, have I practiced the flute, that kind of stuff. We can have quite a chilled time. Sometimes, even on a school night, we might get a Dominos and just watch telly, play computer games or play football in the park. Mum would go mad if she knew that. Sometimes though I worry when I go to school from Dad's because I have usually left something behind or forgotten to do something.

That never happens with Mum, she knows exactly what my timetable is for each day and checks I have everything I need before I go off in the morning. That's kind of comforting, I don't have to worry about it but I do think she is a bit of a control freak – it's almost as though she is watching me the whole time and if I don't get top marks at school she is in there double quick wanting to speak to the teacher, asking what went wrong and telling them to give me extra work to do at home. You should have heard her when I said I wanted to give up the flute – she just went mad, told me I would regret it in the future and blamed Dad for not making me practice when I went round there. I don't like the flute, no one else plays it, so I have lessons on my own when the others are doing more fun things, but it's clear there is no way I am going to be allowed to give it up.

Francesca

I worry that Billy feels responsible for James, not the other way round. It is not right. Billy has told me that he thinks James is lonely and that his Dad seems very unhappy. He knows that James's mood lifts a bit when he is round there and I think that is why he says he would be happy with a 50/50 arrangement but I don't think it is really what he, Billy, wants, I think it is just because he is worried about James. Billy is a kind soul. He wants to help James.

What can I do? James is a grown man and I think it is almost like blackmail the way he shows Billy how unhappy he is. It's his choice, if he got up off his backside and wasn't so lazy perhaps he would be less unhappy and less lonely. It makes me angry the way he plays on Billy's good nature.

James

I do think Francesca is bad for Billy – he needs toughening up. I know she is more help to him with his education but there are more things to life. Surely we can find a way of sharing him and giving him a more rounded life. I know he likes spending time with me. He has a real sense of justice and I believe he thinks we should have a 50/50 arrangement, I am sure he does.

Billy

I know Mum is dead against this 50/50 idea which Dad wants, but perhaps it is the only way to get some peace. I would prefer to just spend time with each of them when I felt like it or when it made sense – Dad's house is just round the corner from school so I wouldn't have to get up as early but Mum is really helpful with my homework in the evenings and I do want to do well and go to university eventually. When I am 18 and do go that will sort everything out for everyone. I do like both my parents and I know that really they both love me but it will be easier for everyone when I can leave home and they see I am not choosing either of them.

I hate this packing my bag every day and forgetting what place I am supposed to go to at the end of school. Perhaps it would be easier, for me at least, if I spend one week with Mum and then the next with Dad.

I think they should act like grown-ups. Nothing they can do will really work for me. I would like us all to live together in one house but I know that will never happen. I worry about Dad and think he would be devastated if I chose to live with Mum and never stay with him. I don't know what he would do. I think he would be very depressed. I can't see Mum agreeing with me living with Dad and to be honest, although he is easier to get on with than Mum I think I would get lazy if I lived with him. I know eventually I want to go to university and get away from here and that means I need to study. Mum helps me to do that. She is strict . . . too strict, but I do need someone to care about how I am doing at school and to get stuff I need for me. I love both of them and when I am worried I can really talk to Mum and she will listen. I wouldn't tell Dad if I was worried about anything because I think that would just make him more sad and I can't imagine him knowing what to do to help.

Francesca

I know Billy thinks he should spend more time with his Dad but I think it is for the wrong reasons. He wants to look after James, to make him less miserable, and I don't think it's fair for him to take that responsibility on himself.

It would be hard for him to spend equal time with us both; our lifestyles are so different. I am scared that he might choose James over me. I can be quite strict and I know that James doesn't make him do anything. They play games together, have a kick around on the park – things I have no interest in. James doesn't put any pressure on him to do his homework or music practice and as Billy becomes a teenager that laid back approach is likely to be more attractive to him, I understand that. I am afraid that he may want to be with James all the time and that he thinks life would be easier there. It probably would be, but Billy is very intelligent and can have a really bright future. If he spent much time at James's I fear he would fall behind in his academic work and get into trouble like lots of teenage boys.

Reflections on the mediation

I have a long history of working professionally with young people but initially I was cautious about agreeing to mediate with a young person of 11. It seemed essential that Billy was an active part of the mediation process, as at least on the surface, he seemed to be at the centre of the dispute. Both parents were keen that he should be involved. Within the boundaries of the code of ethics it was important that I held his discussions with me as being in confidence, in the same way I would with any participant in mediation.

Both Francesca and James considered Billy to be mature and intelligent and, on meeting him, I agreed. I made my decision to fully involve Billy after considering his capacity in line with the Gillick Competency and Fraser Guidelines (see glossary).

Although they may have seen each other very differently, in my experience of them, I found both parents, Francesca and James, to be very strong characters and both were convinced that they knew what was in Billy's best interests. Unfortunately, their beliefs about what was best for Billy were very different. Their ways of expressing those beliefs and their presenting personalities also differed.

It was clear that initially both had verbally agreed that James would not have any special paternal relationship with their child. Francesca had been considering sperm donation using an unknown donor but was concerned about her child inheriting 'genetic problems or difficult personality traits'. She preferred to turn to someone she knew and liked to be the father of her child.

Although their sexual relationship had ended some time before, they had remained friends and when Francesca spoke to James about her desire for a child he agreed to help her achieve that by having sex with her on the days she was most likely to conceive. He didn't really think about the implications. He was clear, at that time, that he did not want to be a 'father' and wished to be free to go wherever he wanted in the future and to pursue his career wherever that may take him. He agreed and in fact, initially insisted, that he should not be named on Billy's birth certificate. Both agreed that they shared the understanding of this agreement although it was never committed to writing.

When Francesca became pregnant at the first attempt they were both very surprised. James felt that if it hadn't been successful he probably would have changed his mind about the agreement as he had begun to reflect on the potential problems. During the pregnancy James took a keen interest in Francesca's health and the development of the baby and attended the scans. At this stage he began to feel some 'macho' pride at his ability to father a child and still considered that his attentiveness during the pregnancy was primarily curiosity, increased by his belief that he would not have any children in the future.

However, Francesca was disconcerted by the interest James was showing and was already beginning to feel that she had made a mistake in
having a child with someone she knew. She wanted the pregnancy and
the child to be hers, not shared with anyone else, and felt that James
was 'pushing in and trying to take over'. Her anxiety continued throughout the pregnancy although James continually reassured her that 'nothing was further from his mind than changing nappies and pushing
prams'. James believed that to be the case. He saw his interest as 'scien-
tific and objective' and was shocked by the feelings he experienced at
Billy's birth, where he felt overwhelmed with love for his son. Even
then, he felt it was the emotion of the birth process and that the feelings
would go away with the reality of dealing with a small baby.

James tried to stay away from Francesca and Billy in the early
months of his son's life and indeed, Francesca and Billy went to stay
with one of her sisters for two months when Billy was four months old.
When they returned things seemed to have calmed down a little and
James would occasionally babysit for Francesca. However, as Billy
started to crawl, walk, and talk, James's feelings for him grew and he
knew he could not just be one of a network of babysitters. He wanted to
be a father to his son.

For the next ten years Francesca and James fought over how much
time Billy should spend with his father. Billy grew to be a very intelligent boy who felt both love and responsibility for both his parents. He
wanted to make them both equally happy by spending time with both of
them separately. His ideal would have been for them all to live together
but he knew this would not work and accepted that he would have to
go back and forth between both houses (a ten minute walk).

Billy was particularly worried about James, whom he believed to be
depressed. He felt he was the only person in the world who could cheer
up his Dad. He had hopes that James might meet another woman and
develop a new relationship which would take some of the responsibility
for James's happiness off his shoulders. In my time with James I found
him to be a cynical man with a dry sense of humour which could easily
be mistaken for depression by his young son. During the mediation,
when Billy was able to tell James that he worried about him, James was
shocked and was able to reassure Billy that he 'quite liked being miserable' and that he really was OK. He acknowledged to Billy that he had
probably spoken too openly to him about how he felt about negative
things at work and about how angry and frustrated he was with Francesca who he believed 'made him beg for every minute' he had with
Billy. He began to understand that this was too much emotional information to ask Billy to live with. He had not appreciated that Billy was

worried about him and made a commitment not to continue to burden Billy with his own worries.

Billy considered his mother to be much stronger than his father and therefore better able to cope without him. In some ways he found his mother overbearing and too strict, yet at the same time he valued some of her structure and discipline. Billy was very clear that eventually he wanted to go to university and to live a life away from both his parents. For him to achieve his ambitions he needed the support of his mother to keep him focused on his academic work. At the same time he felt he needed his father to do 'boy things' with and to get away from all the expectations and pressures he felt his mother placed on him. As we talked he recognised that both parents burdened him – his mother with her need for him to succeed and be well behaved and his father's need to use him for emotional support. We talked about this quite a lot and Billy began to think that both his parents were quite emotionally needy and looked to him to fulfil those needs. He was also clear that although he might feel guilty if he didn't make both parents happy, that was their problem not his. He believed that the moral solution was for him to alternate between his parents, spending one week with his father and then one week with his mother. This was different to the current relationship where they argued over whose house he should stay at, resulting in him feeling he didn't have a home and lived out of his rucksack.

Billy was able to speak to both his parents about his 'wants'. He wanted some consistency, thus allowing him to be able to unpack his bag and stay put at one place for a week at a time. He explained that this was something that would work better for him, it was not about choosing between the two of them, although it did mean that he would be spending more time at his father's than he currently did. He told both parents what he valued in each of them and in the other parent and asked whether they could work towards some shared values and beliefs about what was acceptable behaviours regarding school and leisure time. As it was he felt he had to live by two very different sets of rules which he found confusing and frustrating. Francesca and James were shocked and upset to hear Billy speak so clearly about how difficult life was for him. James was more ready to agree to change, promising to make sure Billy did homework and not to burden him with his own adult concerns. For Francesca things were much harder.

In private session Francesca became very emotional and spoke of her concerns that James would not follow through on his promises. She felt that by letting Billy spend more time with his father she was endangering his academic success and placing Billy in the difficult predicament of having to deal with his father's negativity and emotional blackmail. She was pleased that Billy had been able to express these same concerns to James and she did feel that James had heard and been affected by what Billy said, yet she did not feel James had the strength of character to follow through on commitments even if he wanted to.

She had found it difficult listening to Billy's perception of her as a strict and pushy mother but acknowledged that there was some truth in what he said. She became very upset when expressing her fear that Billy would opt for the easier life at James's house and choose to spend more and more time away from her, especially when he entered his teenage years. This seemed a very strongly held and deep fear. We discussed the reality that life was uncertain and that no guarantee could be given as to how Billy would feel in the future. She considered ways in which she could give Billy more freedom without endangering his schoolwork and ways in which she could be more welcoming to his school friends instead of seeing them as obstacles to his success. She decided that her first step would be to ask a couple of Billy's school friends to accompany them on their next camping trip and to give the boys some unstructured time without her during the holiday.

Returning to a joint session Francesca made it clear that she had heard and understood Billy's 'wants' and that to some degree she agreed with them. She promised Billy that she would allow him more freedom as long as she saw no deterioration in his school grades. Billy was anxious to reassure his Mum that he too wanted to achieve academically and that he valued the time she put in to helping him with homework and school projects. He made it very clear to both his parents that he wanted to succeed and to go to a good university and that he understood that this would require hard work. This gave Francesca some reassurance in the area. Billy was delighted at the prospect of taking two of his friends camping and immediately started a discussion about who he should ask, when they might go, etc.

Having discussed Billy's 'wants', Francesca moved on to discussing Billy's 'needs'. She was clear that if James wanted more time with his son he needed to take more responsibility. As things stood she felt she was solely responsible for buying Billy's clothes and what he needed for school or music and sports clubs. If Billy were to spend a full week at James's then Francesca wanted James to take responsibility for ensuring that Billy had what he needed during that week, that James would liaise with whoever needed to be kept informed if Billy were ill or couldn't attend school, music or German lessons that week and that James would not ring her up and report what needed buying or doing but would get on and do what was necessary himself. Together, all three of them drew up a list of what Billy's needs and wants were and how between them they would seek to address them. This list was revised a number of times before all three of them agreed it as the basis for a signed agreement which also covered arrangements for holidays and an agreement about special circumstances which may mean altering the pattern of alternating weeks.

By the end of the mediation, James and Billy were pleased with what had been achieved. Francesca had valued the process, and felt it had provided a much needed opportunity for the three of them to speak honestly together without it descending into an argument, but she was still worried about whether James would hold to what had been agreed. She asked whether as part of the agreement they could build in a review session when we would all reconvene to see how things were going. James was very happy to agree to this and so it was decided to build into the agreement a meeting at six months and another at 12 months.

At the six-month review I spent time with each of them separately before we all met up for a joint session. Billy was very pleased with how things had gone. He reported that although his father still moaned a lot 'about life, the world, the universe and everything', by spending time with him Billy could see that that was 'just how he was' and Billy was no longer afraid to leave him as he no longer saw him as 'depressed' but as 'a miserable old so and so' who chose to be that way. He expressed his wish for James to be a bit more involved in the homework he did when he was there but acknowledged that following the mediation James had bought him a desk and had put up bookshelves in his room, making it easier for him to work there. He also made sure that Billy had done all his homework before any computer games were played, although Billy pointed out that as James took little notice of what homework he had it would have been easy for him to say he had done it even if he hadn't! Billy also reported that although his Mum was still strict she had 'lightened up a bit'. She didn't seem to have a go at his Dad quite so often, although there had been two major rows during the six months. He spoke very warmly about the camping trip he had been on with his Mum and two of his friends. He had been afraid that she would 'lay the law down and his friends would rib him about it' but she had been 'quite cool'.

James also felt it had been a good six months. He felt that Francesca was taking more of a back seat and letting him form a better relationship with Billy. He was proud of having bought Billy the desk and felt he was encouraging him to do school work. He acknowledged that he had found it quite a shift taking on day-to-day responsibility for things like dental appointments and getting Billy to and from private lessons and social activities. He described how he and Francesca had rowed when he forgot about Billy's music lesson and although he thought the way she had shouted and 'caused a scene' was over the top he knew that he had failed to do what he had promised and he regretted that. Their other big row had been when Billy had left his football boots at his when he went to Francesca's and James had gone away for the week leaving them with no access to his house. Francesca had bought Billy new boots and posted the receipt through James's door with a demand that he reimburse her the money. Having at first refused to do so he had decided to give Francesca the money as an attempt to retain the better relationship which had developed. They had decided that one pair of boots would remain at Francesca's house and one at James's so that it wouldn't happen again. Having achieved what he thought was a fairer access arrangement, James no longer minded if Billy suggested that he spent the odd night at his mother's in a week allocated to James, and during his exam week Billy had spent three nights at Francesca's with James's blessing when he was due to be at James's.

Francesca had been the most dubious about the mediation agreement but she too was pleased with how things had gone so far. She felt more relaxed about Billy spending time with his father. Billy's school results had been excellent, although she continued to doubt that James spent much time encouraging him or helping him with homework in the way she did and which she believed was essential to Billy's future success. Francesca had been particularly relieved that Billy had shown no desire to spend any extra time with his father and she noted that 'now James had got his 50/50 arrangement he seemed more relaxed and wasn't pressing for his pound of flesh'. She had been pleased that when Billy was doing his exams he asked to be at her house because he felt he would get more support with his revision and she had been surprised and pleased that James had understood and encouraged that. It also transpired that the only week Billy's friends were free to go camping with him was a week when he was due to go to James. Despite this James had agreed to the trip and asked instead that Billy accompany him to a football match on a weekend which was allocated to Francesca – she had been happy to agree to this.

The arrangements regarding access seemed to be going well but Francesca was less impressed with the way James handled Billy's everyday needs, citing the missed music lesson and football boots incident. She did point out that as a result of the problem over the boots they had all got together and come up with a list of things which it may be useful to have duplicates of so that whichever house Billy was at he would have easy access to them. Although James had paid for the second pair of football boots, he was currently refusing to buy a second flute to keep at his house!

Overall the mediation had been a success and the 12-month review was equally positive.

15 Love and hate

A workplace relationship mediation

Mary

I don't know what has come over Tom. Something is very wrong with him. He isn't safe to be with.

Tom

I have known and worked with Mary for seven years. If it wasn't for me she wouldn't be in paid employment or have gone on to get her recent promotion. I have mentored her and worked hard to recommend her to others, despite her hot headedness.

Now what does she do? She tries to claim I am some sort of violent abuser who she is too scared to be in the same room with. What the hell is going on?

I don't feel I have abused her, she is tough but I feel abused myself by the accusations she is throwing around.

Mary

He really terrified me. He shouted at me, calling me a revolutionary and an anarchist and when I tried to get away he barred the door. He just stood there, wouldn't let me out and continued to rant and rave.

It takes a lot to scare me but in that moment I was terrified. You should have seen him, he was red in the face and waving his arms around. He was shouting so everyone could hear, 'You stupid little fool ... who do you think you are? Do you think you are above the rest of us that you don't have to abide by rules? I have spent years trying to get things into your stupid head and now you behave like this!' He has lost the plot, he is violent and I can't work with him anymore. In fact I can't bear to be in the same room as him. I don't know what he is going to do next. I don't know why I have turned up for this mediation; I really won't go into the same room with him. My last memory of him is of him standing between the door and me, and just yelling at me. It's not on, it's too much, I don't have to tolerate that behaviour. If a young person behaved like that he would be down on them like a ton of bricks!

Tom

Mary knows the rules. It is against the organisation's policy to take young people home with you. There is no need for it. We have good relationships with the night shelters and they will always take people in if we ask them, but that's not good enough for Mary ... she wants to be Mother Theresa. She thinks she is better than the rest of us – that she cares more than anyone else does – that only she knows the right thing to do. She is on a huge ego trip!

She is very lucky nothing awful happened to her. That young man could have been out of his head on alcohol or drugs, he could have attacked her or raped her. Even if he didn't do anything he could have accused her of doing something to him and she would have had no defence, no witnesses ... She was risking her job, her health, possibly her life. She thinks she is invincible, that she is some kind of super-woman and that no one would ever harm her. I hope she is right but it isn't something I think she should gamble on, if she is proved to be wrong then she could have to pay a heavy price.

Mary

I don't know what he is getting so worked up about. No one with any heart could have left that young lad there on the street. He was cold and exhausted. I know the dangers but I have been doing this work long enough to read people and to make solid professional assessments. I don't need policies and all that stuff to tell me how to be with young people. Those things are just there to cover the organisation's back. They don't care about the young people whereas for me they are all that matters.

I never thought twice about getting him into my car and taking him to my home. He needed a place for the night and I had a place I could offer. It was a no brainer. It was late there wasn't anything else I could do at that time of night.

He did hassle me a bit when we were on our own in my flat but, as I told you, I can handle myself. He was a bit difficult to get rid of in the morning, wanting to hang around the flat until I got back from work and he has turned up on my doorstep a couple of times since but I can handle it ...

I came into this work to help young people and that's what I am going to do. Tom and the organisation aren't going to stop me. Who does he think he is, telling me off, shouting and cursing like he did? Blocking my way! He should support me, not side with the bureaucracy of the organisation. He seems to have lost his political stance and I am wondering why he is still working here and whether he really has any true interest in the welfare of young people. He is getting too old, that's his problem. The spark has gone.

Anyway, regardless of all that, he was completely out of order in the way he spoke to me. I'm not putting up with it, it is bullying. I won't continue to work with him, even if it means me resigning, although I feel I have more to offer young people than he does, so I think it would be better for him to leave.

Tom

You know I really admired her at first. She is like a whirlwind. Such commitment. If she sees something needs doing she is on to it, she doesn't hang around and assess things. When she was new and I was her mentor I found that refreshing. I could do the reflection and analysing for her. I was in awe of her energy. I could hold the boundaries for her – keep her safe, both emotionally and physically. Over time I thought she would learn how do to this for herself but it seems that hasn't happened.

She is still such a risk taker. It worries me. I am worried for Mary and worried about the reputation of the organisation. I know that Mary hasn't got any time for 'the organisation'. She thinks it means well but that all the rules and regulations get in the way of doing what is really needed. She can't see the reason for boundaries, or so she says, although I do wonder if it is really all about her. She thinks she is better than everyone else, that she knows the right thing to do and the rest of us are in the wrong.

I know she thinks I should challenge the organisation more but I have a better understanding of reality. The organisation has to protect its workers and itself. It's a charity, it relies on the funding it can draw in. If people feel it is just a wild organisation which doesn't follow the necessary employment policies and risks something awful going wrong, then they aren't going to continue to fundraise and where will that leave us all – it will leave everyone (including Mary) with no job and it will leave the young people we currently work with unsupported. I wish Mary would stop and think of the implications before she acts. Confidence is good but over-confidence is stupid. Besides, if she is willing to collect a monthly salary from them she has to play by their rules. You are either inside or outside, you can't straddle the two.

Mary

Something has happened to Tom. He hasn't always had such a short fuse. He was great when I first started working with him. I have known him for over seven years. He encouraged me to make youth work my career. I started by working with him as a volunteer on one of his projects. Tom took me under his wing. He inspired me to do the work I do now. He was my mentor and was really supportive and encouraging when I first started. I made lots of mistakes but he never shouted then, he just pointed out what I should have done and why.

I have never liked rules. They just get in the way. I think that resonates with the young people we work with. They can see that there is not a lot different between me and them. When I first started the work I knew I had to keep to the rules or risk getting booted out of the project. That seems less the case now. I know the organisation rate me, they have given me promotion ... perhaps that's the problem ... perhaps Tom feels threatened ... thinks I am after his job. He can relax there, there is too much paperwork and kowtowing at his level. I need my freedom to do things my way; I have no interest in a post where I would be expected to keep other workers in line by stultifying their creativity.

Tom

She behaves like a revolutionary anarchist, not a professional youth worker with responsibilities. She thinks she is always right and will ignore rules if they prevent her doing what she wants. It wasn't too bad when she was a volunteer but once she signs a contract and is willing for the organisation to deliver a salary into her account then she has to play by the rules. The rules weren't drawn up to make things difficult. They are there to keep us, the youth workers, and the young people safe. Mary just doesn't seem to get that, or if she does she doesn't think the rules apply to her because she is so special ... God's gift to young people! She has got arrogant, I don't like who she is becoming. She doesn't have any time for me now. Before she would always come to me, her mentor, to discuss concerns and plan interventions. Now she just goes ahead and does whatever she feels she should.

Taking that boy home was the last straw. It was a dangerous thing to do, and OK, I lost it. I was so frustrated with her and worried about what she might do next. It can be dangerous working on the streets at night. She is meant to always work with another colleague and keep him informed of where she is but does she ever do that? – no. He has been to see me a number of times to say he is worried, he doesn't know where she is or what she is doing. We both know she won't be skipping off work or anything like that but she could be on her own, down an alley with some heroin addict trying to befriend him. It's a disaster waiting to happen. I need to get that over to her – that I am worried sick that something is going to happen to her. That was what I was trying to get across to her that day. I was out of line in how I did it, I know that, I shouldn't have shouted and I certainly shouldn't have blocked the door but she was just standing there saying, 'Whose side are you on, bureaucracy or young people?' I have given my life to working with young people ... too much of it according to my wife, and Mary accuses me of not caring!

Mary

I really think something has happened to Tom. He wasn't always uncaring. In many ways he has been a great mentor. It was Tom that brought me into this work. I was going off the rails a bit when I met Tom. He was a youth worker then and really helped me. It was what got me interested in working with young people. I wanted to be as important to someone else as he had been for me. He turned my life around and I wanted to do that for other young people.

I have always been impressed how hard he works. When I became his colleague I was surprised to learn that he had a wife and child. I don't know how he found time for them, he was always there to advise me when I needed him and he was always there for the young people too. Even then he did stick by the rules, never giving a young person a lift in his car when he was alone, never taking anyone home, always being clear whether he was working or not if I bumped into him somewhere. He was a bit of a hero for me in those days. I really admired him and found him inspirational.

He isn't the same, he seems very anxious about something. I can't believe it is just about me breaking a stupid rule. I have always done that sort of thing and he has always told me off about it but never lost his cool like he did this time. I know he is concerned that now I have a paid role and have been promoted I will need to play by the rules or they could get rid of me ... perhaps that is what made him so mad. He has put a lot of work into supporting and training me. I would be pissed off if I had done that for someone else and they risked it all. I can see now that he was probably really exasperated with me. He has told me loads of times not to give lifts, never to take people home and told me terrible stories of workers being attacked, robbed, sexually assaulted or the young person accusing the worker of sexually harassing or assaulting them. I know he has always stuck to the rules and strangely I have always admired the fact that I couldn't push him around. Before I worked here I would endless try to guilt trip him into giving me lifts but he never would. He explained to me even then that he felt it was risky, but he really needn't worry about me. I very quickly build good relationships with young people, they aren't going to do anything to me.

I know he isn't really a violent man, although he really did scare me that day − it was like I was in the room with someone I didn't know, it wasn't the Tom I have worked with all these years, he was out of control, he wasn't himself. I was scared because this was someone I thought I knew acting like he had completely lost the plot.

Tom

As I was saying, my wife, Trisha, is very critical of the amount of time I spend working and how much attention I give to Mary. She has even accused me of having an affair with Mary. Mary would die laughing if she knew that! Trisha really thought something was going on. I can see why, even though there is nothing in it. Mary and I are often phoning and texting one another over work issues and we meet up regularly, usually over a pint to debrief. As Mary works evening shifts it does mean that I can get home quite late on some evenings. In fact things got so bad with Tricia and her suspicions and accusations that we had a huge row about it the evening before I met with Mary about that incident.

I do admire Mary, she is an amazing woman and I am scared she will come to no good. She will either get hurt or lose her job through breaking the rules or doing something stupid. When I think about it, I guess I went into that meeting angry with Mary for causing trouble in my marriage ... although of course she hasn't done anything − it's between my wife and I. Our relationship is under a lot of strain, it isn't just my long hours but our lad, Ben, is going off the rails a bit. He was suspended from school for smoking cannabis in the school grounds. My wife was hysterical. I didn't see it as such a big deal and said I would speak to him when I got a chance but that just sent Trisha into orbit.

'You care more about those kids on the street than your own son. You are too busy hanging out with that Mary and putting the world to right than spending time with me and Ben'.

Mary has no idea of the pressure I have been under from Trisha the past three months. I like Mary. I may even have a little crush on her but that is something I would never act on. Although Trisha wouldn't believe it she and Ben are the most important things in my life and recently I have been considering finding another job ... something less demanding ... more regular hours. It would hurt to give this job up; I believe in what we do but if it's job or family, family comes first.

Mary

I am sure something strange must have happened to change Tom. Recently I have felt he has been trying to avoid me. We often used to meet up for a drink when I finished work just to check how things had gone. He doesn't do that anymore. Perhaps it's because of my promotion, perhaps he feels I should stand on my own feet, but I miss chewing things over with him. He seems angry with me all the time now, if I text or phone him for some advice he just says that we should discuss that in our next supervision meeting. I know he is angry about me taking that boy home but even before that he seemed angry with me. Things had already changed. He seemed to want to avoid me. I don't like all this formality – waiting for supervision meetings, all that stuff. In fact I was so angry with him about him not answering my texts that I didn't go to the last two supervision meetings. In theory that's a disciplinary offence but he didn't say anything about it.

Tom

I really am sorry I went off the handle and shouted at Mary. Please tell her that. I don't believe she is really scared of me – she is a tough cookie. We have worked together for years, she knows what I am really like. She has never seen me like that before ... and she won't again, I promise. I want us to work together again. She is good with young people but she does need to be more disciplined in her approach or she puts herself at risk.

Please tell her I am sorry. I was under a lot of pressure. Tell her I admire her and don't want her to give up working with young people ... they need people like her. I am worried that if she keeps refusing to toe the line and work inside the rules something bad will happen – she will get sacked or even worse she will get hurt.

In fact, I don't mind you telling her about Trisha. She will probably be amused but I think she will understand that I wasn't myself that day.

Mary

I have been thinking while you have been talking to Tom. I haven't told Tom but I did have trouble getting rid of that kid I took home. I am embarrassed about it. He keeps turning up at my place and asking me to take him in for the night. I haven't but I can see that makes no sense to him as I let him stay there that night, so why not now. He has also been difficult, wanting to kiss me, suggesting 'a quick shag', that sort of thing. It doesn't scare me, I can give as good as I get but it's a nuisance and horrible when he brings mates with him. I don't know what he has told them about what happened – and nothing did – but you know young guys, they brag, even when there is nothing to brag about.

In the past Tom would have been the first person I spoke to about all this . . .

Oh God, I am embarrassed by it all. Tom was right, it was a mistake and not one I will make again but he still shouldn't have lost it with me. It is not on that he blocked my way and wouldn't let me leave. He was aggressive. He should apologise, go to anger management classes or do something to sort himself out.

We are quite a good team really.

Reflections on the mediation

On first meeting Mary, I was struck by her formidable appearance. She had a very strong 'don't mess with me' air about her. Yet, when the mediation was first mooted, and I had spoken to her on the phone, Mary was very reluctant to attend and refused to be in the same room as Tom as she felt 'scared to be near him'.

It is not unusual in mediations for one or both parties to say that they are not willing to be in the same room as the other disputant. Although it is usual practice, in the Harvard Model, to start with a joint session with all parties in the room together, if one or more persons refuses to do so it does not mean that the mediation must be abandoned. I believe there is a lot of value in the first joint meeting. There have been mediations I have been involved in where the sight of the other party, often after a considerable period of not meeting or communication, is enough in itself to break down barriers. In other cases it is very clear that there would be no constructive way to bring the two parties together and the mediation has been successfully concluded without the parties ever meeting face to face. In each case, the mediator has to sensitively find a way to proceed which doesn't make any party feel uncomfortable.

In this case I did not try to persuade Mary to go into the same room as Tom, even though I did not think that she looked particularly scared. Instead I took Mary at her word and didn't start with a joint session but started with a private session with Mary, followed by one with Tom. To challenge or try to push any party at this early stage of the mediation when there has been no time to build trust between the parties and the mediator, is likely to make the mediation harder. As a mediator, it may also be necessary to consider how you will convey to one party the other's reluctance to be in the same room with them without breaking confidentiality. In this case, Mary had already indicated to Tom by email that although she was willing to attend the mediation she was scared and therefore unwilling to be in the same room with him.

Tom raised this in the first conversation I had with him. He was very anxious to let me know that he was not a violent man and that he couldn't really bring himself to believe that Mary was truly afraid of him. He felt she was posturing but couldn't understand why. He presented as very confused and contrite but also as being angry with Mary and feeling betrayed by her. He wondered if her current 'dramatic behaviour' was an attempt to undermine him in the eyes of their employers. He saw her recent promotion as having changed her and made her ambitious and 'determined that no one would stand in her way of her becoming the boss'.

In listening to both Mary and Tom it became very clear that for several years they had succeeded in working well together despite their different temperaments. Indeed, it was because of Mary's admiration of Tom that she had embarked on her career as a youth worker. She was grateful to him for the way in which he had helped her when she was going through a difficult time as a teenager and how he had helped her develop a belief in herself and her abilities.

When Mary started working for the same organisation as Tom as a volunteer and then paid worker, their close working relationship was obviously so good that Tom's wife, Tricia, suspected Tom of having an affair with Mary. Even if that were not true, Tricia felt passionately that she and Tom's son was not getting as much attention as Mary and his work and so there was a deep seated frustration and feelings of jealousy regarding what Tom chose to prioritise. This was putting considerable strain on Tom's marriage and he believed that, on the day he and Mary had rowed, he was feeling particularly stressed, having argued with Tricia the previous evening. At the start of the mediation Mary was unaware of Tom's tensions at home and of Tricia's suspicions regarding her relationship with Tom.

It was important in the mediation to let both parties express their emotional reaction to what had happened and not to challenge it. For Mary her primary expressed emotion was fear focused around Tom's behaviour in shouting at her and barring her exit but I also experienced anger. For Tom his primary expressed emotion was anger at being accused of being a violent bully. At the same time I experienced considerable sorrow and confusion in what Tom was expressing.

Both parties shared strong values regarding respect, fairness, equality, and compassion. These were expressed mainly in relationship to their work with young people which they both passionately wished to continue. This commonality of goal and purpose is a gift to any mediator as it indicates that the parties ideally need to find a resolution which would allow them both to continue working for the organisation in the future. At the start of the mediation, Mary was saying that she could not work with Tom and would resign her post but her evident commitment to the work and pleasure and pride in her recent promotion challenged the reality of any desire to resign.

Their shared values also gave me material to explore and work with. In the later part of the mediation, having fed back these emotions to them both in their private sessions, it was possible to explore how they played out in relation not just to young people but also to the two parties.

Mary had been brought into the profession through her respect of Tom and his work, although she felt this respect had been lost due to his angry outburst. In considering this Mary began to have a growing awareness that this 'angry Tom' was quite new and she expressed concerns that something must have happened to change him. This shift in thinking also marked a move towards the compassionate side of Mary, with her expressing a wish to understand what had changed and to rediscover the Tom she admired. In turn, Tom admired Mary's commitment and free spirit but was also concerned that this may cause problems for Mary in her chosen profession – if she broke the rules she could lose her job or she could come to some harm.

As the mediation progressed, Mary became less angry and more intrigued about what had caused the perceived change in Tom. She moved from a position of experiencing Tom as frightening, to acknowledging that on the day of the outburst she had actually felt more shocked than scared and couldn't believe what was happening as it was so out of character for Tom. When she had later discussed the incident with some female friends she had become upset and they had all described it as 'scary' or 'terrifying' and had expressed their concerns about whether Tom was a safe person to be with. On reflection Mary felt that it was only at this stage that she began to feel afraid of Tom. Her friends seemed to have projected their fears onto her and she had come to experience them as her own. In the private sessions she told me that she was not really afraid of Tom, even when the outburst happened, although she believed others would have been if he behaved as he had on that day. She expressed concerns that something had happened recently which meant that Tom seemed less in control and that this may result in him being angry with young people.

As the mediator it was interesting for me to note that both Tom and Mary had expressed concerns about each other's behaviours, potentially leading to them losing their jobs. I was able to explore why each thought this would be a bad thing and they both expressed admiration of the other's work and what a loss it would be to young people if either of them stopped their current work. This marked a change into a position where both wanted to find a way in which they could continue to work together, whilst seeking understanding and reassurances. Tom wanted Mary to understand that he had acted out of personal concern for her safety and because he felt she was an excellent youth worker who was putting her career in jeopardy by continually breaking the rules or attempting to push the boundaries. Mary felt she needed to know what had changed for Tom so that he now seemed so 'edgy and angry'. She asked that he seek some anger management training so that the behaviour wasn't repeated with others, particularly young people.

At this point Mary said she was willing to meet with Tom in the same room and seek answers to some of her questions. Tom readily agreed. In an emotional joint session Tom was able to tell her about the tensions at home. Mary was very moved to hear about what he had been coping with and acknowledged that this would have made it stressful for him and no doubt made him feel angry for her for taking up such a lot of his time and causing Tricia to be suspicious and jealous. She apologised to him for being difficult and demanding and recognised that in taking the young man back to her house she was breaking the rules and taking unnecessary person risks. In confidence she told Tom that she had taken the boy home because it was easier than taking him all the way across town to the hostel and competing all the necessary 'bureaucratic form filling'.

Tom was keen to praise Mary's work and commitment and spoke about his fears that if she didn't stick to the rules the young people could lose her, as she risked losing her job. He apologised for losing his temper and shouting at her and recognised that by blocking her exit he 'had behaved appallingly and was completely out of order' and that it must have been scary seeing him behave in a way in which he appeared out of control. Mary dropped her demand that Tom attend anger management training and instead suggested that Tom approached the HR department to request some counselling sessions while he sorted things out with Tricia. She also offered to cover some of Tom's work sessions for him if he wanted to 'take Tricia out somewhere nice'.

The mediation ended with them both hugging one another and going off for a coffee together.

16 Hyperventilating

A school based work mediation

George

This is really difficult for us. All of us on the governing body liked Debbie – I mean Ms Fraser. We found that we could always discuss things with her, we knew her plans and we all thought she was doing a good job. The children seemed happy anyway and that's important to most people.

Ms Fraser was also well liked by the parents and made sure that the school reflected the communities the pupils come from. We had some splendid cultural fairs and that sort of thing. She was very popular but it seems the school's results weren't too good and after the last OFSTED inspection we were put in 'special measures,' which has really upset the Local Authority. I don't really understand what they are looking for, we have happy children, satisfied parents ... we are a primary school when all is said and done ... children should be children; they should enjoy being young.

Anyway, when we got the results of the OFSTED inspection they were all in here like a swarm of flies. Local Authority officers we had never seen or heard from before were suddenly everywhere, whereas before that we could never get hold of them. Anyway, before we knew it Debbie was out and Mrs Creybell was in. Of course, we do realise it's important to improve the performance of the school in the OFSTED eyes and we know that the Local Authority think Mrs Creybell is the woman to do that but we aren't at all sure that she is going about it the right way. Everyone is upset. How can that help the children's performance?

Mrs Creybell has made herself very unpopular with all the staff but especially with the Teaching Assistants. Almost as soon as she arrived she decided that she just wanted to discipline all the Teaching Assistants and use that as a way to get rid of them. She doesn't believe that they are up to the job. That is news to us. There haven't been complaints before. They are all parents of children in the school, so imagine how that would go down with other parents. They are all members of local communities – ethnic minorities, so we could have a major incident on our hands if people start shouting about racism. The school has 87% of children for whom English is not their mother tongue. It is important that these children see good role models from within their own communities. Debbie was very keen on that. She encouraged parents to volunteer in the school and to apply for suitable posts if they came up. She would encourage them to go on training courses and she organised lots of in-house after school training for them too. She did that in her own time. She was very committed to helping the pupils in every possible way, not just academically. We do miss her.

Anyway, that's water under the bridge. Now we have this problem and we need to sort it before it gets out of hand. As I said, Mrs Creybell wants to go down the disciplinary route and performance manage people. We want to avoid this if possible and so have asked that they try mediation first. I know none of them are too keen. The TAs (Teaching Assistants) are scared of Mrs Creybell but see her as clever and think the mediators will side with her. Mrs Creybell thinks it's a waste of time but understands that it would look good if she were seen as giving it a go. The Unions in a way have to support it but they are keen to press for grievance procedures to be taken out against Mrs Creybell for bullying and racial harassment!

None of the governors will be attending the mediation. We prefer that it is just sorted out privately between Aysha and Mrs Creybell but we have agreed the budget for the mediation. If it doesn't work things are going to be impossible, we may even have a strike on our hands.

It's a mess. Good luck ... you will need it!

Aysha

I don't think I can go through with this ... I will just have to resign ... I ... I ... I ... oh I can't breathe ....

Mrs Creybell

I don't believe for one minute that she is stressed. She just can't cope so has gone off sick. I am fed up with it all. I have been brought in to turn this school around and that's what I am going to do. Aysha says she is sick ... well I am well and truly sick – sick to the back teeth with the lot of them.

When I arrived the place was in a mess. Ms Fraser, the previous head teacher had been weak, and not addressed everything that was going wrong. She had promoted the Teaching Assistants to the top grade when really I don't even think they should have even been employed – they aren't up to the job. There are more HLTAs (Higher Level Teaching Assistants) here than any school I have worked in! I think she was scared of them, worried in case she wasn't being PC enough. I think she tried to win favour with the parents because she knew that academically the school was poor. I know she was popular, but in my mind, it was for all the wrong reasons. She bought popularity by giving jobs to people in the community even if they weren't up to it.

It is difficult being white in this area. Being white is being the minority here. I believe that after she had appointed all the Teaching Assistants she was afraid to challenge them because they all come from local Asian and Afro-Caribbean communities. She failed to do her job. In my view she should have set competency procedures in place a long time ago and got rid of all of them. Instead it was all left for me to do as soon as I got here and so I become the wicked witch. Well, I can cope with not being liked. My priority is the children and getting this school through its next OFSTED with an improved rating. I want to get this school out of 'special measures' and on its way to being outstanding. That is what I have been brought in to do and I am determined to succeed.

Sandra

As a trade unionist, I am in favour of mediation but I can't see it working here. Mediation requires a willingness to listen and Brenda [Mrs Creybell] won't listen to anyone. She thinks she is right and that what she says goes. For her it is as simple as that.

Don't get me wrong, we appreciate that things do need to change in the school following the OFSTED report but there are ways and means of achieving this. We believe that Brenda has come in here wanting to make a name for herself, to be one of those super heads who turns a school round in no time. We wish her luck with improving the standing of the school but we don't agree with her methods. Indeed we believe that she has bullied staff and harassed them, causing stress and illness. We are considering whether her behaviour has a racial element to it. All the Teaching Assistants who she has bullied are from either an Asian or Afro-Caribbean background, so you can see why I say that.

All of the Teaching Assistants are preparing separate grievances against Mrs Creybell but are holding off for now while they see what happens in the mediation. Aysha didn't want to take a grievance procedure out. She is a gentle soul; she is afraid of the head teacher but also feels that it is somehow negative to go down a formal route which may end up with Mrs Creybell being disciplined. She is very worried about the mediation but wants to give it a go and hopes that some miracle will happen and alter how Mrs Creybell treats them all.

This would never have happened with Debbie. Mrs Creybell ignores the trade union whereas when Debbie was here we met her for coffee once a month to see if there were any concerns on either side. If there were, we tried to address them informally. Although that is our preferred way of going about things, Mrs Creybell needs to know that we will not take this lying down. We are not weak and we can't abide bullies.

If this mediation doesn't succeed we will consider our options.

Aysha

I am so sorry about that. It is so shameful and embarrassing but I can't seem to be able to do anything about it. I am under the doctor but I don't want to take anti-depressants and anti-anxiety tablets. I know I am anxious and depressed and these panic attacks are really scary. When they happen I can't breathe. I was getting them a lot before I went off sick. I still get them, even when I am at home, if someone mentions the school or Mrs Creybell. Thank you for talking me through the last one.

Sandra has asked me to represent all the Teaching Assistants at the mediation but I think I will have to get someone else to do it, even though I know Sandra will be there to support me. I don't think I can stand the stress. I don't want to have a panic attack in front of Mrs Creybell. She already thinks I am useless and weak. If I have an attack in front of her she will use that against me, say it proves I can't cope. I can cope with the work. I did really well under the previous head teacher. Debbie was always praising what I did and encouraging me to take further training.

I have never had a paid job before this one. I'm proud of what I have achieved. When my children first came to the school I was very shy and found it difficult to talk to people. Ms Fraser really made an effort to make me feel welcome and encouraged me to start helping out as a volunteer in the nursery. I found I really enjoyed the work and I began to read all about teaching as a profession. It improved my confidence in every way. I made more friends and felt better about myself.

When a vacancy came up for a Teaching Assistant Ms Fraser encouraged me to apply and I was amazed and pleased when I was offered the post. She arranged for me to attend a course at the local college. When she first suggested it I was terrified but I went and really enjoyed it. My plan had been to train as a teacher once all my children were through school but since Debbie left, things have changed. Mrs Creybell is always criticising me and the other Teaching Assistants, saying we don't know what we are doing. That's not right. We don't know everything but we are all willing to learn and anyway Mrs Creybell doesn't know everything, but she can't accept that.

I really annoyed her when I refused to take 35 children from the school to the local swimming baths on my own. It is a fifteen minute walk and includes crossing some main roads. Four of the pupils have ADHD and one has a disability which makes it very hard for him to walk as quickly as the others. It wasn't sensible or safe to ask just one person to take all the pupils, on her own. It's a requirement in the school's Health and Safety policy that there should be one member of staff or volunteer to every six pupils for that kind of outing. I tried to tell Mrs Creybell but she just accused me of being lazy, not wanting to walk and refusing to do as she instructed. It wasn't like that, I was afraid there would be an accident and I would be blamed and I knew that it went against Health and Safety but she just wouldn't listen when I tried to point that out to her. She told me to do my job or get out. That's when I had my worst panic attack. I couldn't breathe, I had pains in my chest, I was shaking and everything was blurred. I thought I was having a heart attack. I managed to get out of her office and into the playground where I sat on the floor until I felt a bit better. I then went home and have been off sick since then. It's about six weeks now and Mrs Creybell hasn't even been in touch to see how I am.

I don't want to take out a grievance against Mrs Creybell even though I know that is what all the others would prefer. I want this mediation to work. I want to go back to work. But I am very scared.

Mrs Creybell

I think I am being set up. All I am trying to do is do my job. The TAs know they aren't up to it, they know they have been getting money ... good money ... for nothing. It can't go on. If the school is to be turned round I need a clean start. I need all those who aren't up to their jobs to leave so I can get some good staff in to replace them and start rebuilding this place. I want people who know what they are doing and are committed to change.

I can't understand why I haven't got the backing of the governors. They seem very cowardly, not wanting to upset people. They don't seem to appreciate the implications for the school if things don't change, or God forbid, get any worse.

Sandra

If this mediation doesn't work there will be five grievances taken against Mrs Creybell and we will consider calling a strike. I believe we have the backing of all the staff, although some are too scared to do anything. I'm amazed Aysha is standing firm. She suffers terrible panic attacks. I think she believes that mediation will be less stressful than taking out a grievance. I hope it is, for her sake. I think she thought the others would be part of the mediation but Mrs Creybell says she is not willing to 'go up against all of them at once'. I think she feels she can pick them off one at a time.

We were warned about her before she arrived. She already had a reputation as a bully. She never stays long in any school. She just swans in and sweeps through whatever is already there without a thought, changing everything in her path. Usually several of the staff leave after her first term in charge. 'Leave' isn't really the right word – she pushes them out – makes life so stressful and unbearable that they have to go. Many of them leave the teaching profession for good; it's such a horrible experience. She brings with her 'mates' from other schools and gives them senior positions. I can find no evidence that she ever advertised the posts either internally or externally. It is disgusting, she ignores equal opportunities policies and employment law – she thinks she is above all that and so far she seems to have got away with it. Both the new teachers she has appointed are white and middle class, I believe she just wants to appoint people like her; white careerists, only interested in their own progression not the pupils' and to get rid of all the staff who are from diverse racial backgrounds and communities. To me it is racist behaviour. As a union we have taken it up with the Local Authority but they don't want to know. They are terrified that the school won't get out of 'special measures' and that will reflect really badly on them. Mrs Creybell doesn't hang around to see the consequences of her actions. People are usually very impressed with her energy and enthusiasm at first but she doesn't care about people and God help anyone who gets in her way.

Aysha

My husband is worried about me being involved in this mediation. He thinks it makes me look like a troublemaker. He doesn't want me to become 'known' in the community as someone who causes problems. At the same time he knows how unpopular Mrs Creybell is and how almost everyone would like Debbie back. He wasn't keen on me becoming a TA in the first place but the hours are the same as the children's school day so it doesn't interfere with me being a good mother. In fact I think it makes me a better mother as I get to know much more about their schoolwork and can help them with it.

Since I started the work his opinion has changed because he sees what a positive difference it has made to me. As I said I am a much more confident person than I have ever been, or I was until the change in head teacher. I don't want to go back to how I was before. At the moment it is even worse than that, I hardly go out because I am afraid of panicking and looking stupid. I am even nervous when the phone rings in case it is something to do with the school. My husband has to be here to answer the phone or I just let it ring.

I never had panic attacks before Mrs Creybell arrived. I was shy and nervous but that was all. My whole family is worried about me now. It is horrible for my children and husband to see me so afraid – unable to breath and shaking. My husband has learnt how to help me when it happens and fortunately it doesn't happen that often – only when I have to think or talk about the school. I have really cut down on what I do, it isn't just that I am not working but I am avoiding going out or having people round to my home in case they mention something which will start an attack. I am really worried it will happen during the mediation.

My doctor has given me a prescription for anti-anxiety drugs but I don't want to take them. You hear about people becoming addicted to them and I don't want that to happen to me. I don't like to think about myself as the kind of person who can't cope without drugs. I want to be strong, I want to work but at the moment I feel a mess. Something has to happen. I can't go on as I am. I need to be brave and get back to work although I am terrified of seeing Mrs Creybell.

I know Mrs Creybell doesn't even believe there is anything wrong with me. She should see me ... I am really struggling. I can't bear the thought of her getting angry during the mediation or mocking me if I have an attack – although she will probably just think I am acting.

Although my husband isn't keen on the mediation he knows that if I can be part of getting the school back to being a happier place everyone will be pleased. I am realistic – I know that we can't turn the clock back – Debbie has gone, she has left the area and has a new post but perhaps if the mediation makes Mrs Creybell less aggressive and scary we will all feel less stressed and be able to do our jobs better. That's the best I can hope for.

I know Sandra will be at the mediation to support me. She has been really helpful over the past few months. She has explained to me how a head teacher should behave and what isn't acceptable – what counts as bullying and harassment. I have checked with her about some of the things Mrs Creybell has asked me to do and Sandra has shown me the documents showing that what she has asked goes against school policies. I always thought head teachers, and people like that, were always right, that they knew what they were doing but it isn't true of Mrs Creybell. She just does what she wants regardless. I don't think she cares about people at all. Staff members are always coming out of her office in tears but it doesn't seem to bother her. Sandra says she probably enjoys it because it shows she is powerful.

Mrs Creybell

I do understand that the TAs are not used to having their work criticised. It is clear that they had nothing but praise from Ms Fraser. Indeed, somehow or other she managed to get several of them on the highest possible grade for a TA. It isn't right and has given them a false impression of their abilities. It must be confusing when I arrive and start asking them to change the way they do things or to do things they haven't done before. I don't have anything against any of them personally. I don't really know them. Although I do think Aysha is playing a fast one here. I am surprised that she seems to be such a little activist; she always seemed so shy and quiet until one day when she refused to take a group of children swimming. I saw another side to her then, arguing with me and refusing to do what I asked of her but I still wouldn't have suspected that she would be the one to ask for a mediation ... well, I know it was the union and the governors who requested it ... but Aysha is fronting it. Bit weird isn't it? She is off sick because 'she is too afraid to work with me and suffering panic attacks', yet she is able to face me at a mediation. I think that speaks for itself – panic attacks, indeed!

In my eyes one of the main problems in this school is that the TAs have been allowed to get paid for doing little more than babysit. There is an awful lot to do to get this school back on track. I have managed to move out some of the old teachers who were frankly incompetent and outdated and now I need more from my TAs. Being a TA isn't a pastime for bored parents who want to earn some pin money, it is an important role, offering support to the teaching staff and to those pupils with special needs who can be very disruptive in the classroom setting.

They need to respond quickly to what I or the classroom teacher need and ask them to do, not argue the point with us. They can't win, or blackmail me through going off sick or taking out grievance procedures. The Local Authority supports me and knows that the school requires a radical overhaul to get it through the next OFSTED inspection. I am surprised and disappointed that I am not getting much support from the governing body, as they must know what a mess the school was left in. They have seen the OFSTED reports and have had Local Authority officers take them through it explaining what needs to change. I am fully aware that because of the diversity in the school catchment area there is a great deal of sensitivity about race and culture. I understand that and know that a school has to have good relationships with parents and local communities but it's the academic achievement that is the top priority. These pupils are already disadvantaged because of their backgrounds. Many speak no English when they arrive at the school. Having pupils who are fluent in written and verbal English is more important to their future prospects then each child knowing and celebrating all the religions of the world. If they are going to do well in life they need to have the academic tools to compete against those from more privileged backgrounds. I want to see pupils form my school excelling when they go on to secondary school. I want parents to be proud that their children attend my school and to be confident that in doing so they will fulfil their potential.

I am not a bad person, as I said, I just want to do the best for this school and its pupils. I am very determined and won't let anything stand in my way but I do know that change is difficult. If I thought the TAs wanted to change and were willing to work with me I would be delighted and support them in every way I can but I think all these pending grievances show the true picture; they want to get things back to how the school was before. That isn't possible and by not working with me they put the future of the school in jeopardy.

Reflections on the mediation

The request for the mediation came from George, the chairman of the school governors. He was very concerned about the situation, particularly the morale of the staff team and the impact of the situation on the parents and the community. He didn't hold out much hope for a successful outcome from the mediation and was very worried about the possibility of grievances, employment tribunals, and other procedures which he had never had to deal with before.

In speaking with him it was clear that he was extremely committed to the school and its pupils but had been very shaken by the recent OFSTED inspection which had resulted in the school being put in 'special measures', and pressure being put on Ms Fraser, the head teacher, resulting in her resignation. Ms Fraser, Debbie, had been much loved by pupils, parents, and the local communities as well as the governing body. It seemed that everyone had been upset that she had left and been replaced by Mrs Creybell who was a very different character. George was a local businessman with no real knowledge of the educational world or OFSTED criteria. He had raised a lot of money for the school through his business networks and believed strongly that primary education was an important step in developing social skills, and that it needed to be enjoyable, so that a love of learning was developed in the pupils. He understood that OFSTED judgements and league tables were important but they weren't his chief priority. He wanted a happy school and believed if that happened then academic success would follow. He found it hard to form a good working relationship with the new head teacher who he felt did not value non-academics and saw the school governors as an irritation she would prefer she didn't have to deal with.

From the perspective of the school governors, as soon as she arrived Mrs Creybell had begun to implement changes in school procedures and was very openly critical of the previous head teacher. The whole staff team became unsettled and nervous about the pace of change. Many spoke to George about their increasing unhappiness with what was happening. Within a few months a number of members of the teaching staff had handed in their notice and Mrs Creybell had made new appointments, included two teachers who had worked with her in her previous school.

She was particularly critical of the Teaching Assistants. The majority were local mothers with children at the school. Ms Fraser had valued them highly as she saw them as providing very positive links to the local Afro-Caribbean and Asian communities from which they were drawn. In addition, she felt that they offered good role models to her pupils. Ms Fraser saw herself as having a broad educative role for the whole community and encouraged adult education classes on the campus at evenings and weekends. She also encouraged all her TAs to take up training and in addition offered in-house training sessions on issues such as health and safety and aspects of the curriculum. George was concerned that all the good work with the local communities would be undone.

My first interaction with Aysha, one of the Teaching Assistants, was by phone. Her husband answered and passed the phone across to her. She only managed to get a few words out before she started hyperventilating. While she struggled with her breathing I helped count her breaths and to slowly help her bring her breathing back to normal. I tried to normalise what had happened by reassuring her that it wasn't unusual and that I was not fazed by the panic attack. She was very tearful and we scheduled another call for the next day.

The following day Aysha was calmer but still very tearful. By nature she was quiet and quite retiring and what had happened with Mrs Creybell had shocked her. She was shocked that she had challenged the head teacher over incidents where she felt the pupils' health and safely was being jeopardised. She had never challenged anyone in authority before. She felt that Mrs Creybell had refused to listen to her concerns and angrily focused on the fact that Aysha was challenging her decisions. The head teacher's anger and shouting had resulted in Aysha suffering her first full panic attack. Following the incident she had been unable to continue working and was off sick.

Our second call increased the trust that Aysha had in me and in the mediation process. Ironically, the fact that she had experienced a panic attack whilst speaking to me and I had been able to talk her through it was the main reason she felt she could trust me; even so, she remained very concerned about the possibility of having an attack during the mediation. I did not try to convince her that this wouldn't happen as I thought it very likely that she would be very stressed during the mediation day. Instead I reassured her that should this happen I would do the same as I had on the phone and that the attack would pass. I also felt that no one seeing her have an attack could continue to believe that she was faking her level of stress and so that even though it may feel very embarrassing and frightening for her it could potentially be positive. At this point Aysha felt that she would like to meet me in person.

At our meeting Aysha appeared very nervous and spoke very quietly but did not suffer a panic attack. She took me through several incidents which had concerned her and which had led up to the incident where she had refused to take a large group of pupils to the swimming pool. After her confrontation with Mrs Creybell, Aysha had turned to Sandra, the union representative, for help and learnt that several staff members were proposing to take grievances out against the head teacher on the grounds of bullying and racial harassment. Aysha felt very uncomfortable about this, particularly the racial element as she envisaged it causing problems in the local community and she wanted to find a different way of addressing the conflict. Sandra and Aysha had discussed their concerns with the chairman of the governing body who was keen to avoid the situation escalating and suggested mediation.

Aysha remained very frightened of attending the mediation day but wanted to find the courage to see it through. She had valued her TA role highly and desperately wanted to return to the work. The role had benefited her on a personal level, increasing her confidence and allowing her to consider a future career in teaching. She was grateful to Debbie, the previous head teacher, for giving her an opportunity which had changed how she felt about herself and her own potential. Aysha also thought it was important to her children that they saw her outside the home, in a position in which she was respected. She hoped her two daughters would be encouraged to consider futures beyond that of wife and mother, although she continued to see her own role of mother as being the most important thing in her life. She saw one of her most important tasks as a mother as being to help her children fulfil their potential and was keen that they did well academically as she saw this as a way of opening doors to gaining successful careers in the future.

One of the most hurtful things about what had happened was her belief that that she had in some way let her children down by not earning the respect of the new head teacher and not standing up to the 'bullying'. She hoped that her children would be proud of having a mother who worked in the school and she felt that by going off sick she was showing weakness and was not helping her children to 'have self respect, feel equal to everyone else and stand up to bullies'. This thought was very distressing to her. She hoped that by going through with the mediation she would be seen as brave and not someone who would submit to bullying.

When I met Mrs Creybell I was struck by her energy and determination. She had taken on a difficult task and was committed to seeing it through and getting the school out of 'special measures'. It was clear that she valued academic achievement above most things and that she wanted all the pupils in the school to achieve their full academic potential. In common with Aysha she believed that if children achieved academically it would increase their chances of career success in the future. In enabling that to happen she was very aware of the benefits for her own career and wanted to fulfil her own career potential. Indeed, she believed everyone should test themselves to the full, and embrace challenge.

When arriving at the school she had been shocked at the amount of the budget being paid to unqualified TAs, many of who were designated HLTAs. She believed that the individuals in post had not been appointed because they were the best candidates but because they reflected the diverse racial mix of the school catchment area. She was critical of the previous head teacher's 'desire to be PC [politically correct] rather than academically excellent'. She 'understood that the diversity of the school calls for sensitivity and good relationships with the local communities but not at the expense of the pupils' academic achievements'. She was keen to 'turn the school round as quickly as humanly possible' and she believed the way to do this was to replace many of the current staff, who she considered to be lacking in knowledge and experience and wishing to keep the status quo, by experienced staff who enjoyed challenge and change.

She did not believe that Aysha was suffering from stress. By being off sick she felt Aysha was confirming that she was not up to the job and merely couldn't cope. She believed that the TAs had experienced an easy time of it before she arrived and she wanted a greater professionalism and commitment from them. Commitment seemed to equal an unquestioning adherence to her wishes.

She was not used to being challenged and on the few occasions it had happened in the past she felt she could rely on the school governors to support her in disciplining her challengers. She had been surprised that the governors here had not reacted in that way and instead they had suggested mediation. She didn't really see why she should go ahead with the mediation but did not want to totally lose the support of the governors. She believed that the mediation would validate her actions and gain her support to follow through on her plans.

As the trade union representative Sandra's role in the mediation was to support and protect her member, Aysha. She expressed concern about Aysha's vulnerability and the possibility of her suffering a panic attack during the mediation. Like almost everyone involved in the mediation, Sandra held out little hope that it would be successful. For Sandra it was the first step in removing Mrs Creybell, who she believed to be a racist bully. If the mediation did not work then she was ready to support other TAs in taking grievances out against the head teacher. In my pre-meeting with her she drew my attention to a number of school policies and employment policies which she believed Mrs Creybell was flouting. Sandra did not feel that Mrs Creybell had followed employment law in appointing two members of staff who had previously worked for her in another school. Sandra could find no evidence that the posts had been advertised either internally or externally. Both new teachers were white and Sandra felt this reflected the head teacher's racism and her desire to replace all the old staff who were 90% non-white with 'people like her; white careerists, only interested in their own progression not the pupils'.

On the day of the mediation Aysha was very concerned that she would not be able to be in the same room as Mrs Creybell but with

Sandra's encouragement she managed to come into the first joint session. Throughout the session, whilst Mrs Creybell described in some detail how she saw the TAs as lazy, not well qualified and standing in the way of progress, Aysha sat either with her head in her hands or looking down at the table. At times we could all hear her struggling for breath and quietly sobbing.

When it came Aysha's turn to speak, Sandra laid out the position for her. She expressed the view that Mrs Creybell's behaviour constituted bullying and that she thought it came from a racist position. At this Mrs Creybell became very angry and loudly defended her view that 'they' were ganging up on her because she was white and that if they had done their jobs properly there would never have been a problem. During this heightened dialogue Aysha began to experience the beginnings of a panic attack, she was deathly pale, shaking, struggling to breath, and trying hard not to hyperventilate. I helped her to get her breathing back under control by counting her through it as we had agreed I would do at the pre-mediation.

As soon Mrs Creybell saw Aysha's reaction she stopped shouting and became very concerned. It was clear to her that Aysha was not acting. For the first time she had to accept that Aysha was genuinely afraid of her and under real stress. It was evident to all in the room that Mrs Creybell was frightened and was genuinely concerned for Aysha. Once Aysha's breathing returned to normal Mrs Creybell began to very quietly cry. She apologised to Aysha and Sandra and expressed her belief that Aysha's stress was genuine and that she was right to be taking time off from work and needed support to recover.

This seemed a good point to move to private sessions. As Mrs Creybell seemed to have undergone a real change in her perception of the situation, I decided to start with her. This also allowed some time for Aysha to settle and for Sandra to support her.

Immediately Mrs Creybell began to tell me how upset she felt to see Aysha 'in that state', stating that it was 'clear that she is genuinely upset and frightened and really having panic attacks'. Mrs Creybell had never seen someone have a panic attack before and had feared that Aysha was having a heart attack and might die. She felt 'mortified' that she might have been the cause of Aysha's distress.

She also felt caught in a dilemma. She didn't want to cause that level of distress to Aysha and the other TAs but she was committed to 'turning the school round and getting it back on a successful path' and she still did not believe that the TAs were sufficiently skilled to help her in that task. She did not know how to reconcile these two desires. She asked me to explain the dilemma to Aysha and Sandra and to make sure they knew how badly she felt about Aysha's distress. I discussed with her whether she felt that she might be able to talk to Aysha and Sandra herself. At first she was very concerned that to be back in the same room with Aysha would cause her further suffering and possibly set off another panic attack. She asked that I convey her desire to apologise to Aysha, saying that she was willing to do that face to face if Aysha agreed but that if Aysha 'couldn't bear to be in the same room' she would willingly write an apology. She also felt she would like the opportunity to describe to Aysha and Sandra her concerns about the school and the actions she felt were necessary to make the school successful.

When I talked to Aysha and Sandra about Mrs Creybell's wish to apologise. Aysha burst into tears and was keen to accept it. Sandra was more cynical, not believing it was a genuine apology but a 'ploy' on Mrs Creybell's behalf to make her look 'more human' and 'get her out of trouble'. Initially Aysha decided that she wanted to see Mrs Creybell without Sandra and to accept the apology but having thought a bit more she felt it was important that Sandra should hear it and decide for herself whether she would accept it as genuine.

When Mrs Creybell entered the room to meet Sandra and Aysha she was in tears. For once Aysha was the stronger one and listened quietly to what Mrs Creybell had to say. Mrs Creybell told Aysha how sorry she was that she had caused her such distress and confessed that it was only when she saw her having the panic attack that she really understood how awful things had been for her. At this point Aysha too started to shed tears and accepted the head teacher's apology. Throughout this exchange Sandra remained silent. Mrs Creybell then asked very respectfully whether she could talk to Aysha and Sandra about the problems she was having in ensuring that the school did not fail another OFSTED inspection. All agreed that another failed inspection would be negative for all of them.

Mrs Creybell spoke honestly and openly about her concerns and the three parties began to discuss what they could all do to help the situation. Sandra needed the head teacher to list the specific areas in which she believed the TAs were not competent. Once this was done, they considered ways in which these concerns would be addressed and together devised an action plan of mentoring and training. Mrs Creybell felt that she could get the Local Authority to fund these developmental requirements, as they were very concerned about the negative impact of the OFSTED report on them. Failing financial support from the Local Authority she committed to finding alternative funding. She accepted that out of her own panic and the short time she had to turn things around she had not always done things the right way and had 'cut some corners' with regard to reading up on the latest health and safety requirements and on employment law. Sandra was able to put her in touch with some educational HR specialists who could give her some support in these areas. Sandra was also clear that this support for the head teacher should come from the Local Authority and that they should be approached over this.

By the end of the mediation all three were working on a detailed action plan which started with a meeting between all the TAs and Mrs Creybell. The head teacher offered to listen to all their concerns about her, which were currently outlined in the proposed grievances, and to share with them her needs to get things in the school functioning better and what she could offer them to help develop their skills further. Everyone hoped that they could move forward as a team.

17 Warring cousins

Global family business mediation

Jeremy

I have had enough of Vernon not pulling his weight in this business. He is lazy, careless and leaves everything for me to do. I am expected to be the sensible one whilst he socialises with his celebrity mates. The number of times I have had to rescue him from committing money to projects which would never have worked, but he just doesn't learn. The latest enterprise is him lending an old school friend of his £9 million. That's the last we will see of that money.

I have had enough. I want to terminate the partnership. I want out of this business and I want him out of my life. It is going to be complicated. It's a global business, we employ lots of people in several countries but I want out. Neither of us need the kind of money we are making, we have enough to last us for the rest of our lives, so why should I suffer this pain and anxiety when I don't have to. I would rather just call it a day and spend more time with my wife and our animals.

I'm not sure why Vernon has suggested mediation, we both know this is the end, it just can't continue like this. We have both been through mediations and court cases before, although not against each other, and I haven't relished the experiences. There isn't any point in this because I have made up my mind, but I will go through with the mediation – I don't want him painting me as the evil one who didn't want to try to resolve things. However, nothing will resolve this – he is who he is and I can't stand him anymore and I want out. Unless mediation magically changes people there really is no point.

Vernon

I don't understand what is happening. Jeremy and I are family; we aren't just business partners. We are more like brothers than cousins. Jeremy's mother died when he was quite young so he spent lots of his time at our home, he came on holidays with us, I thought of him as a brother. We are both only children so I have always felt close to him while we were growing up. We went to the same school, we flat shared whilst at university and we set this business up together six years ago. We never thought it would go so well, it has all been quite a shock really . . . a good shock . . . we have terrific lives. I live here, Jeremy lives in Zurich but I thought we were very close. I love him, like a brother loves a brother. I had envisaged the business continuing to go from strength to strength and us both benefiting from it for years to come and now he wants to just throw that all away. It just doesn't make sense.

I know I am not the best administrator ever, but then that's not my role. My job is to find the clients, wine and dine them and get them to buy into our business, and I have been hugely successful at that. Jeremy is absolutely brilliant at the more administrative things. He is a details man – he knows everything about everything within the business, he is never without his laptop . . . always checking on things, he works morning to night. I know that but I think he works too hard and that it is taking its toll on him. I am worried about him; he looks pale, thin and tired. Having said that it is hard to imagine what he would do if he didn't work so hard. I know he loves his animals but there are only so many hours you can give to walking the dogs. I guess he would be in his gym all the time.

I can't understand what feels like a sudden decision on his part to sell the business. It's tough work but I thought we both enjoyed it. I know he has had a little go at me a few times about not pulling my weight but I never thought that he was angry enough with me to want to close the business. There must be more to it. If he is unwell and wants a rest I would support that but he seems to be blaming me for his decision.

Jeremy

I think our task in this mediation is to sort out all the shares and to try to act ethically in relation to our staff, most of whom will regrettably lose their jobs, unless any buyer wants to keep them on. I don't see that there is any other way forward. The only thing wrong with this business is Vernon and I can't see any possibility of change there. He is happy with how he is and to hell with the business and with me. I don't believe he gives a damn.

I can't really believe how Vernon has changed into the lazy, fat man he now is. We grew up together. My mother died when I was six and Vernon's mother, my mother's sister, has been a mother to me ever since. We were very close growing up and that makes it worse seeing him behave like an idiot and putting the business at risk. When I go into our head office I get complaints about him all the time. He doesn't answer emails, he is rude and he doesn't fill in his diary so nobody knows where he is. I think he has lost all interest in the business. He just wants to be out and about with his celebrity girl-friend or photographed with his entire *Hello* magazine friends, while I do all the boring, bureaucratic work which keeps the whole ship afloat. It is not on. I have had enough and I am not going to do it any longer. If that means it is the end of the company then so be it. I want to enjoy life again.

He hasn't always been so selfish and lazy. When we were at school he was my hero. He is slightly younger than me but I have always been very slightly built and serious whilst Vernon has always been the life and soul of the party and quite sporty. I was picked on quite badly and Vernon would sort out the bullies for me. I felt he was always there for me. He would look out for me. We were partners. Now we are business partners and I feel he abandons me to deal with all the shit. I have to do all the paperwork because he can't be trusted with it. I have to make sure things are OK with the staff, he never bothers calling into the offices to see how they are doing. I make sure we give people gifts on their birthdays. He hardly remembers their names. If there is a problem I have to sort it. Any court cases it is me who is out there representing the company. We are poles apart and I no longer enjoy what we are doing or the man he has become.

We had fun when we started the business. It was a fluke it took off like it did. We were very lucky and we continue to do well. Slowly though we have just drifted apart. We used to meet up regularly, taking regular holidays together and discuss how to move the business forward, what to invest in, all that kind of thing, but now we hardly see one another. I know I don't live in London, for tax reasons, and because of that I am limited in the number of days I can spend here, but even so he could come out and see me at my home. Who would say no to a few days in Zurich? Well Vernon would, he is always too busy, so most of our business meetings are now over Skype. I feel that I am running this whole thing on my own and it is no longer any fun, it just causes me immense stress. That is all down to Vernon. If I walked away the business would fold, Vernon wouldn't even have a clue what needed doing, never mind have the ability or commitment to do it.

Vernon

I feel very upset about this. I know I have irritated Jeremy. I understand that he feels he is doing more than his fair share in the business. Perhaps he is right there but I don't think there is a huge difference, perhaps 60/40. I have always believed that we worked to our strengths and that's what lay behind our success. It is what we agreed. Jeremy is very clever, he thinks clearly and strategically, he is good with words – talking and writing and he has always known what direction to take the company in. I have always been happy to follow him because he has always been right. I thought he was happy with that. It gives him the power to dictate the direction of the company. I really believe that once he sets the direction I do everything possible to help to implement his vision. We fell into this success, we were lucky, honestly I haven't got a lot of interest in 'strategic planning' and all that sort of stuff and Jeremy is really good at all that. I do have most of the ideas though. That's how it works – I dream and Jeremy turns them into reality or brings me down to earth explaining why that particular idea would never work. I am really fussy about what we do. I want our names to be linked to quality and excellence. I am around, in London, and can see the little details, I can visit our sites easily, I can check things and if things aren't just so, then I am not happy. I understand that when things are wrong I can be a bit sharp with staff but I want to feel proud of what we offer. We are so lucky the way the company just grew and grew. I want us to continue enjoying our success.

Jeremy is quite shy and hates social functions but our business requires rich and prestigious clients for the business to survive and develop. It is my role to bring those clients on board. I know from the outside that it just looks as though I spend all my time on 'jollies'. I have to wine and dine people, take them out on one of the yachts or invite them to stay at one of our houses. The reality is I wake up most mornings with a hangover and have to get down the gym at 5am to work off all the extra calories I have put on from having to entertain people at breakfast, lunch and dinner. I know a few hours in the gym are a luxury to Jeremy but I hate every minute of it. When your business is focused on luxury goods, prospective buyers expect to sample some of that luxury. It's hard on my partner too, she has to come and act out the perfect hostess. She would much prefer that we just spent time together at home but she is a real asset, the clients like meeting her because she is well known. Most of the people I have to take out are very boring; I don't enjoy it but I do a good job – I get the sales. I never have any personal time. I thought Jeremy appreciated that. He would hate the whole thing. Even at family gatherings with people he feels comfortable with and knows very well he doesn't enjoy socialising, he slopes away as soon as he gets the chance. I am very shocked by what he has been saying. It sounds like he hates me. I don't get it. I thought we loved one another. I know that because we are so busy these days there isn't much time to do things together – social things, and I guess I never get round to thank him for all the time and energy he puts into the business. I thought he appreciated me and that he knew I appreciated him. Seems I was mistaken. He just thinks I'm a lazy sod who relies on him to do all the work.

Look, I want to put this right, put things back to how they were. What does he want me to do? I value him. I value our business. This is ridiculous. I am sure we can sort it out. Surely, whatever I am supposed to have done or not done, it isn't worth throwing away our history together. My mother keeps ringing and asking what on earth I have done to upset Jeremy and telling me I must put it right.

Jeremy

It has gone beyond anger now. I have tried to talk to him about it, told him he needs to pull his finger out and do more but he doesn't take any notice. Most of the time I am talking to him he is texting or emailing and he is often rushing out mid-sentence because he has some social function or other to attend.

Clearly he has no interest in me. He hardly gives me the time of day. He can't wait to see his girlfriend or a mate. He never seems to consider that I might value having some time with him outside work. It is not just me he acts badly towards. When did he last go and visit Irene, his mother? I bet he hasn't been there in months. I don't live in the same country and yet I see her every month, either here or I arrange to meet her in France or she spends time with us in Zurich. He needs to treat her better. He has no time for any of his family.

I really did used to admire him. I would say I loved him once but now I have no love for him at all. I would be happy never to see him again. I want us to cut our losses and go our own ways.

Vernon

This is having a terrible effect on my mother. She practically brought Jeremy up after his mother died. She can't believe what is happening. I found out this morning that he had written to her, saying he was sorry that it had come to this but he had no option but to leave the company and he knows I can't run the company without him. He blamed me, called me lazy and selfish. He gave her a long list of what I do badly or don't do at all. My mother is distraught and rang to tell me about the letter and ask me to explain myself – what had I been doing to make Jeremy feel so bad? It feels like he wants to turn my mother against me. That's awful. I really don't understand what it is I am supposed to have done. I love the guy and I am finding all of this difficult to bear.

I can survive financially if the company closes. I'm not short of money, probably got enough to last a lifetime really and wouldn't have to work again but I have enjoyed working with Jeremy. I admire his hard work and his brilliant memory. I think we make a good team; I don't want to lose that. My mother has always been really proud of the way we work together and what we have achieved; she often says how proud it would have made Jeremy's mother too. She has raised Jeremy as her son and I always think of him as my brother. I don't want to lose all that, it's very important. At the end of the day this isn't just about the business, it's about family and I have always felt really good about my family and how we all look after one another. Closing the partnership would feel like splitting the family. Speaking about my mother reminds me I really must find the time to pay her a visit. I hadn't realised how long it has been since I was down there. We are in touch all the time by phone but she does need a visit. It is quite isolated where she lives. I wish she would move into the city. Things would be so much easier. You only have to take a look at my diary to see how ridiculous things are but business is risky and you have to strike while the iron is hot. If we weren't busy we would be worried or bored or both!

Look, tell him that I don't want things to be like this. We are good together. I agree that from the outside it may not look as though we do an equal share of the work but I don't really think that's true. It's important for the business that I have a high profile in certain social circles and that I get my picture in magazines. It helps sell the brand. I don't like it but that's the reality of it. What does he think it is like to have to see yourself growing older, looking fat or tired in all the magazine photos? My girlfriend hates it. They comment on how she looks, what she wears, we can't ever just relax. She is often in tears about what she reads about us.

I will do whatever it takes. Just get him to tell you what I need to do and I will do it. I don't want things to end. I will do some management or business course or get some coaching if that is what he wants – whatever it takes. Just tell him.

Jeremy

Since he got to hang around with all these celebrities he doesn't want to know me ... he has no time for me but will jump if any of them ring him. It is clear where his priorities lie and it isn't with the business. If he cared he would put more time, energy and care into his work. I wouldn't have to keep redoing his paperwork or getting him out of some hole he has dug for himself. It seems I'm the rescuer now, following him around, ready to cover for any of his mistakes. I am tired of it. I don't want to do it anymore. What happened to the great guy he used to be when he looked out for me? He is just a selfish arrogant person now, chasing the limelight.

How does he think the business keeps going? Who does he think answers all the emails – certainly not him. He has to step up or ship out. All this partying has got to stop, he has to grow up, take life seriously, buckle down to some hard work.

I think it is too late for him to change. He would really have to put some time and effort into things – starting with learning everyone's name and not being rude to people. He needs anger management training. He is always rushing around so if people want or need to talk to him he gets impatient and rude. I then have to go and smooth things over. I don't think he even knows he has upset someone, I don't think he would care even if he knew. He is above all that now with his fancy friends, some of whom he buys with nice handouts and gifts. I doubt that he even really knows how to use any of our software systems – people are lucky if he even replies to emails. Would he really want to put the time into getting up to speed? I doubt it. It would mean he wouldn't have as much time for his famous friends.

Vernon

I understand he has a problem with my work. I will do something about it. Even so, I think there is more to it than that.

He is a serious guy; you don't often see him laugh. He seems to resent that I'm quite happy – I enjoy my life. I know I am quite a simple guy. I enjoy good company, good food and wine and being with my friends. I know that a lot ... probably all ... of what I enjoy is down to how well Jeremy and I have worked together, the success we have had, the money we have made – I wouldn't have such a good life if it hadn't been for him. I understand that and I am grateful to him for that ... Perhaps I need to tell him that and not take it that he knows how grateful I am.

We have always been different. He has always been quiet and studious even when we were at school and university. I got by academically by the seat of my pants ... and quite a lot of help from Jeremy. Sometimes he even did my homework for me! I was the sporty one and Jeremy the geek – he helped me with work and I got him lots of invites to things.

I have always been more interested in people and partying. I don't see anything wrong with that, I enjoy it and it has helped the business. I have amazing business networks which have helped us succeed. I know that sometimes my friendships have clouded my judgement and I have been more generous with some people than was wise but there has been no real harm done. Jeremy was horrified when I lent an old friend quite a bit of money for a business venture recently and he lost the lot. Jeremy was right there and I have acknowledged that it was a mistake but quite honestly I can live with that loss. It came from my own money. It has hurt that I have lost a friend in the process. He is ashamed he can't repay the money and is avoiding me. I really value my friends. I am still friendly with people I knew in primary school and often meet up with old university friends. Jeremy has probably got a better idea about people, he is more cynical – I can be naïve. I have learnt that lesson.

Although we are very different I thought we were both enjoying life and the benefits that the work brings. I know Jeremy values his privacy and likes the quiet life. His favourite thing is to walk his dogs along a sunny beach. The money we have earned means he has a fabulous yacht which allows him to travel, with his dogs, all over the world and I know he values being able to do that. When I had more time I would often go with him, although I'm not a fan of dogs and work commitments have meant I haven't been able to go with him at all this year. That's a shame. Perhaps we should try to arrange a trip together – wishful thinking – he can't even bear to be in the same room as me at the moment.

When I think about it, things seemed to come to a head with Jeremy when I started going out with my current girlfriend. I don't know if he doesn't like her. I am serious about this relationship. I want it to work. Jeremy has a wife and a home, a place where he can relax and just be himself. I envy him that.

I can't believe that he doesn't like Joy. She is terrific and really easy to get along with. She is well known but doesn't have any airs or graces or think she is better than anyone else. She has tried to be friendly with Jeremy and invited him to some great social events but he never wants to come. She has really pressed that I work hard to make this mediation

214 Studies in conflict and resolution

work. She thinks it would be tragic if Jeremy and I stopped being so close. Her family is so important to her and she always says we can't afford to ignore our family relationships.

My work takes up a lot of time so it is hard to prioritise everyone I should. If you are committed to be available to clients for breakfast, lunch and dinner it's a long day, starting in the gym at 5am and often going on beyond 2am, with lots of jetlag from flying all over the place. I am shattered most of the time. It is tiring being nice to people if you don't particularly like them or enjoy their company but that's my job. What time I have left I want to spend with my girlfriend, just relaxing at home. Past relationships have suffered because I haven't given them time. I don't want this relationship to fail. It is important to me.

Sounds like I want everything, I know – a good relationship, great job, good partnership with Jeremy ... well, I do want everything and I am lucky enough to have it and can't see why Jeremy wants to let all that go. No doubt he will just add greedy to my list of faults.

Jeremy

I don't hold out any hope that we could get things back to how they were when I could trust Vernon and believe that the business and me were important to him. If I could believe that is possible I would want that but I really can't see it. Things have got worse and worse since he took up with his latest girlfriend ... OK, this one does seem to be lasting longer than his previous relationships, they must have been together for nearly a year now, but he doesn't seem to have time for anything but her and their showbiz friends. We used to have holidays together but not anymore. Growing up we were hardly ever apart. He keeps mentioning that it would be nice for us to take some time out with each other, perhaps a short vacation where we could just enjoy one another's company and not talk about the business, but he never does anything to make that happen. He just doesn't prioritise it. He doesn't see me or appreciate the work I do. Some thanks and recognition wouldn't go amiss.

My wife finds it hard seeing the two of them in the press all the time, all glammed up and there being very little mention of all my work. Sometimes it seems as though people have forgotten that the two of us set up and run this business.

Reflections on the mediation

When this mediation was first proposed it appeared to be focused on helping two business partners dissolve a successful and complex global business partnership in the most fair and least aggressive way. Due to the nature of their business, heavy diary commitments and limited access to the UK for one of the participants it was agreed that the mediation would be spread over a number of four-hour sessions, each a week apart. The weekly sessions were to include the potential for both individual and joint sessions.

As the mediation developed the whole focus of the mediation shifted from the practicalities of dissolving the business partnership to the relationship between the two cousins and their different perceptions. The work shifted from a process of dissolution to one of rebuilding.

As well as having different perceptions, the two cousins looked very different. Jeremy was very slim and athletic looking, although his movements were somewhat stiff and formal. He rarely smiled and had a very serious demeanour. He was extremely angry with Vernon and saw no possibility of a reconciliation, personally or professionally. In his manner he portrayed himself as hard, and it was easy to see how he had been so successful in his business dealing. Even in his most casual clothes he portrayed a buttoned up sharpness – formal jackets or blazers, ironed jeans, etc. Perhaps somewhat paradoxically, even in the pre-mediation session he explained how he had a deep-seated interest in psychology and meditation and was in therapy to try to deal with his emotions around Vernon which focused deep feelings of anger, hurt, and rejection. However, he expressed a strong view that Vernon was the party really needing therapy.

Vernon, in contrast, although not overweight, clearly struggled to keep in shape. Although his clothes were expensive it was clear from the casual way in which he wore them that, although always fashionably dressed, fashion was not of much interest to him personally and most of the time he seemed to be about to spill out of his clothes. Vernon had a happy disposition and conveyed the air of an eternal optimist. Yet, he was deeply hurt, confused, and upset by the conflict between him and Jeremy and was distressed and shocked by the hard manner his cousin showed towards him. He was desperate to continue the professional relationship with Jeremy and to repair the personal relationship they had previously enjoyed and which he valued highly. He expressed a degree of scepticism about therapy and mediation generally but told me he would try anything to recover his relationship with Jeremy.

In the early sessions Jeremy portrayed Vernon as a lazy character, only interested in socialising and enjoying the fruits of their shared labour. He was very angry that in his view Vernon did little for the business other than socialise with clients. He felt he was left to do the more mundane tasks but also the most important tasks, without which the business would collapse. He worked extremely long hours, never considering himself to be off duty. Indeed in all our meetings he found it necessary to keep his phone and iPad on and to address any business matters which came up. He blamed Vernon for his long working hours, believing that if Vernon 'did his share' it would free up a lot of his time. He saw himself as doing 75% of the work, whilst believing Vernon did 25% 'at the most', and 'that would be on a good day'.

Early in the mediation, in both individual and joint sessions, Vernon made it clear that he was deeply hurt by the breakdown of his personal relationship with Jeremy. He thought of Jeremy as his brother and had believed that although they were very different characters they would always be there for each other. He reminisced about many happy times they had shared both as children and more recently as men.

Vernon also felt that they made a good business partnership into which they brought different skills. He valued what Jeremy did and considered that he would not have been able to handle those parts of the business so well. At the same time he did not think that Jeremy really gave him credit for what he did do. He was very committed to the mediation process and wanted the partnership to continue.

In our private sessions Vernon would use me as a sounding board for his ideas to try to convince Jeremy he could really change and address the issues. He expressed a desire to improve his interpersonal skills, acknowledging that he often did not respond quickly or in the best way to staff. We talked about an individual's need to be heard and how when we are criticised many of us want to explain or give excuses for the actions which the other has found frustrating. This tends to intensify the conflict rather than diffuse it and turns into a table tennis match of insults being lobbed across the table. He recognised that this pattern existed between him and Jeremy. He acknowledged that he was often impatient with Jeremy's 'moans, fears, and criticisms' and tended to dismiss them, wanting to cut the conversation short. We looked at the advantages to just listening to, rather than challenging, concerns and ways in which he might show he was listening. This kind of discussion was very new to Vernon who operated instinctively and quickly in most of his actions. He was quite excited at the thought that he may be able to make changes in his behaviour whilst remaining true to himself and his priorities in life.

Most of the mediation took place in long joint sessions with both the cousins being together in the room with me, occasionally interspersed with shorter individual sessions. Jeremy often seemed as though he had rehearsed what he wanted to say and, regardless of any progress made in the previous meeting, would start the session with a diatribe of

Vernon's faults, shouting at Vernon and telling him he no longer respected or loved him. When this happened Vernon's eyes would fill with tears, but he always listened carefully to what Jeremy had to say, not interrupting or trying to defend himself and would try to take onboard all the complaints. He would acknowledge the truth in some of them and ask Jeremy what he should do to try to address them. At this point Jeremy would jump on that question as proof that Vernon could not take responsibility for his own actions and as usual was looking to him to tell him what he should do. Amazingly, Vernon would remain calm and ask for time and space to think about what he could do to address the issues and we would take a break.

A breakthrough occurred when Jeremy quite suddenly began talking about his sadness over how Vernon had changed from the boy who always supported him at school, who defended him against the bullies and made him feel better about himself, into the 'selfish bastard' he had become. Vernon did not react to the insult but told Jeremy that of course he still loved him and would always be in his corner but that these days he didn't see Jeremy as the vulnerable one. He saw Jeremy as having got his life together with a lovely wife and home, things he, Vernon, wanted for himself. He told Jeremy that he always saw him as the backbone of the company, the clever, strategic one, the one who had grown up whilst he had stayed a 'Peter Pan' – a situation he was determined to address by growing up himself and taking his share of the responsibilities. He also explained that he believed he still did the best he could to protect Jeremy by taking on all the public relations work for the company which most of the time meant wining and dining foreign clients. He knew Jeremy hated doing those kind of social things, not just because he was shy, but because he was committed to a healthy diet which excluded alcohol, dairy, and gluten, making it more difficult to dine out in places their clients would enjoy. He went on to tell Jeremy how much he admired his work and how, no matter how hard he tried he would not be able to match his capabilities, but that he would do his best to take on Jeremy's concerns and address them. At this point Jeremy asked for a private meeting. Vernon was aware of the request and happy for it to go ahead.

In the session Jeremy expressed how deeply Vernon's words had affected him. They were what he wanted and needed to hear. He loved his cousin and had felt abandoned by him. He had felt that Vernon was no longer interested in him and preferred his 'new friends' and this had been deeply painful. He had been shocked and pleased that Vernon saw him as the strong adult one but he also needed to have Vernon continue to be on his side. He agreed that he couldn't think of anything less attractive than the role Vernon carried for the company, with its requirement to look good and be sociable the whole time. He hadn't understood the stress the role took on Vernon's part and the impact on his personal life. He had been moved at the thought that Vernon may be taking this on to shield him rather than because Vernon saw it as an easy 'jolly' which he enjoyed and got paid for.

Although at this point he had moved from wanting to end the partnership and never see his cousin again, he was not yet ready to drop his anger. He felt it was important that Vernon 'did not get out of it that easily'. There were clearly a number of legitimate concerns about Vernon's work, particularly in relation to his impatient and sometimes rude interactions with colleagues and his tendency to bankroll 'daft ideas for projects' which his friends asked him to fund.

We considered how these concerns could be addressed and Jeremy drew up an 'action plan' for Vernon to consider. This contained ideas for training and coaching focused on improving his interpersonal communication and IT skills and also suggesting anger management training. In addition, Jeremy suggested that they agreed a figure which they could have per month from which they could fund any projects or charities they might wish in their own name and not that of the company. By doing this, any losses were only a problem for the individual. At this point I had hoped that Jeremy would go back into the joint session and convey his reactions to what Vernon had said and put across his proposals but he did not feel ready to do so, asking me to 'sound Vernon out first', giving me permission to convey his emotional response and practical suggestions to Vernon.

When I returned to Vernon he was confused and upset. He was surprised that Jeremy had seen him as his defender, as he had no memory of Jeremy having been bullied at school, but instead of disputing it he had held his tongue and just accepted Jeremy's perception of their history. He had hoped that Jeremy would respond well to what he had said and was disturbed when Jeremy had said nothing to him before asking for an individual session and leaving the room. I was able to tell him of Jeremy's emotional and positive response to what he had said. I then expressed Jeremy's ongoing concerns and laid out the suggestions Jeremy had offered to address them. Vernon was just keen to say yes to everything, get his cousin back in the same room, and give him a hug. I reflected that one of the things Jeremy seemed to be seeking reassurance on was Vernon's commitment to reflect and take authentic responsibility and this may provide an opportunity to demonstrate those things to Jeremy. Vernon then patiently went through all Jeremy's suggestions. On consideration Vernon was not happy with the suggestion of anger management training, which he thought 'laughable', and not something he needed. He decided to think about the best way to tell Jeremy this and decided to suggest that he would undertake some leadership coaching focused on 'interpersonal communication and addressing any anger issues'.

He also thought about some things he wished to ask of Jeremy. He wanted both of them to commit to meeting up somewhere nice at least twice a year, with their partners, merely to socialise together for a few days and to begin to get to know one another again outside of the business. He also wanted additional meetings as often as Jeremy's commitments would allow, for he and Jeremy to meet outside the office but to discuss business matters over a coffee ('or in Jeremy's case, water, as he doesn't take caffeine'). He hoped this would improve communication between the two of them and allow them to address any issues of concern quickly. He also hoped that he could share his concerns about his mother's physical isolation and his desire for her to move into the city and that Jeremy would support him in his plans to buy somewhere for her in London.

The final joint session started with Vernon acknowledging the truth of some of Jeremy's concerns and sharing his plans to address them. Jeremy received this very positively and did not raise the question of separate anger management classes, seeming satisfied that this would be addressed through the leadership coaching. He was very pleased that Vernon had also thought about how they could rebuild their personal relationship and immediately looked to get something in his diary for a short holiday for the two of them and to agree dates for regular informal meetings.

Over the following years both Vernon and Jeremy stayed in touch with me, sending the occasional email of their news. Their business continued to flourish and in Jeremy's words 'their relationship had never been better'. Vernon described their ongoing commitment to family holidays and regular business meetings, feeling very pleased that they had got back to the point where they could have 'fun' together.

Conclusion

People in dispute are still more likely to go to a lawyer rather than to a mediator. It is difficult to see why this remains the case, with on average 89% of mediations achieving a successful settlement and managing to do so without the high costs in time, money, and psychological stress which a court case would entail. Mediation also offers other benefits. When we compare litigation and mediation we find the following main differences:

Litigation	*Mediation*
Can take years	Quick (often one day)
Expensive	Inexpensive
Binding	Without prejudice
Formal	Informal
Public	Confidential
Confrontational	Collaborative
Destroys relationships	Preserves relationships
Last resort	Early resolution
Lose/lose	Win/win

So, why does litigation remain 'popular'? People use litigation for a number of different reasons. They may believe that it is the only place for their views to be heard, and that it presents them with a unique opportunity to 'have their day in court'. They may wish to demonstrate power over the other disputant, who may not have the time or funds to sustain a long-running and expensive court case. They may trust in what they believe to be the more traditional processes or they may feel that mediation is synonymous with compromise, when they want nothing less than to win. They may be looking to punish the other party and be seeking a judgement that places them in a position of righteousness. All of these factors may be involved in choosing litigation over mediation.

It is possible to find some of these things in litigation; however, even when litigation is seen to be a success, we need to look at what that success means. Usually the lawyers, rather than the disputants, define 'success'. I had a very powerful example of this when I took on a new therapy client. The woman, let us call her Jane, presented with depression. She was not in work and barely eating. Five years previously, Jane who was highly qualified in her field, had been in a very high powered, stressful, and well-paid position, which she had held for 18 years. She had achieved well at school and university despite being on the higher end of the autistic spectrum, which for her included difficulty in relating to other people. One day Jane made a mistake in her work, which did not cause harm to anyone emotionally or financially, but added to a long list of people finding her 'difficult' and reporting their unease to senior management. Even though people found Jane a hard person to like she was very successful in her job. However, the organisation for which she worked decided that they had received too many complaints from her colleagues over time and so used the opportunity to dismiss her. Jane pursued her employers for constructive dismissal through the tribunals and courts for four long years and finally received a six-figure pay out. Her barrister was thrilled with the result and cracked open the obligatory bottle of champagne.

Jane came into therapy a year later to deal with the depression which the whole experience had caused. Jane was still angry with her past employers and in no sense felt that the litigation had been a success despite the high financial pay out. Jane described the pay out as 'dirty money', which she did not feel she could touch. She described how she believed the whole experience had demeaned her and stolen any remnant of the self-esteem she had fought so hard to build throughout her life. Jane could not imagine ever working again in the future and her shame had caused her to become very reclusive.

Jane had found the court case very painful. She had listened to constant criticism of herself from her past employers, none of which had ever been raised with her whilst she was in post. Jane knew she could be perceived as difficult but her dismissal had been a terrible shock. She was devastated to hear the way in which she was described in court. She had never held a high opinion of herself, but this had been kept hidden behind a façade of confidence that her employers interpreted as 'rude arrogance'. At times they described her as 'bullying' fellow workers. They failed to acknowledge anything good about her work, although she had always been extremely efficient, well organised, and effective. Indeed, if difficult clients confronted the company Jane was usually the person asked to deal with them.

In the statistics Jane's case would be recorded as a successful one, but for her it was anything but. During the whole legal process nobody asked Jane what kind of outcome would help her. When I talked with her about this it quickly became very clear that what Jane had needed was some type of acknowledgement that although she did not behave well on one occasion she had done a good job for 17 years and had received praise from many of the organisation's most difficult clients. This could have been clarified, acknowledged, and addressed in mediation, thus enabling Jane to have a settlement that was meaningful for her and which allowed her to move on with her self-esteem still intact. It probably would also have saved the organisation a lot of time and money.

One problem with litigation is that humans are emotional beings, whilst the law likes to consider itself to be logical and rational. As I have pointed out, there is no dispute in which emotions do not play a central part. In the 'studies' I have shared with you, we can see that whatever the nature of the dispute, the key components and the elements that mattered most to the parties were emotional. In listening to the disputants' narratives, and through hearing and experiencing their emotional content, not just the facts are addressed, which when all is said and done cannot be changed, but we can discover what is important to the individual. We can explore the nature of a number of potential outcomes that may best address those needs, values, and beliefs which the person is communicating. Mediation, through the building of a trusting relationship between the mediator and all the parties in the dispute, allows all these elements to be at the core of the process.

There are a number of accredited courses which will teach the basic skills and processes to those wishing to train as a mediator. A few of these will include, or indeed focus on, psychological approaches, whilst others are more process led.

Once trained, a mediator needs to know how to find work. I have mentioned that this may be through networking, setting up a partnership or company with its own website, offering to give free presentations, or joining one of a number of mediation panels open for accredited mediators which aim to refer disputants to available mediators. Newly qualified mediators may be wary of starting out as solo mediators and may prefer to find a more experienced mediator to work with. Most panels will require new mediators to observe or co-mediate at least three mediations before they will offer them work. Finding opportunities to observe or co-mediate can be difficult. Trying to co-mediate with someone whose philosophical approach is different from one's own can also prove to be quite a disturbing experience. Successful co-mediators have a good understanding of each other's approach, strengths, and weaknesses. Often trainee mediators identify kindred spirits on their training course and the shared philosophy of the training may provide them with the perfect co-mediator.

Each mediation provides the mediator with new experiences and challenges and mediators continue to learn with each new case they take on. As few mediators work at mediation full-time, with the majority offering it within a portfolio of services, continuous professional development is recommended, and some panels may require it. I hope that the studies in this book may at least have given a feel of what it may be like to be present at a mediation, but they can never give the richness of the actual experience.

Mediation is challenging and rewarding and offers a more collaborative way of exploring differences and finding ways forward. I hope I have shown that, whatever the nature of the dispute or conflict, mediation is about how people perceive their experiences, and how they experience those others involved. It is therefore essentially relational and psychological and so calls for a psychologically informed response.

Appendix
Basic Pre-Mediation Contract

The Agreement:

The Parties described below hereby agree to submit their dispute to mediation in accordance with the Terms and Conditions set out here:

The Parties:

Party A: ....

Party B: ....

Party C: ....

Party D: ....

The Mediators:

The Parties hereby appoint .... and .... to act as Mediators.

Venue:

The Mediation will take place at: ....
.... on the .... 2020. The first mediation session will commence at ... am and will continue until ... pm or until such time prior to this at which the Parties agree a break or a resolution.

Terms and Conditions:

A. The Mediator

1. The Mediator shall throughout the mediation act as an independent and impartial neutral facilitator and will not seek to adjudicate, arbitrate, furnish advice or impose a decision or solution in respect of any issues between the parties.

2. The Mediator shall not be liable to any party for any act or omission with the conduct of the mediation, save for any wilful misconduct.

3. The Mediator shall not be called as a witness or an expert in any pending or subsequent litigation or arbitration relating to the dispute or subject matter of the mediation, save where the Mediators and all parties agree in writing.

4. The Mediator hereby confirms that all known financial and/or other interests, all social, business and professional relationships with any party and/or representatives, or any facts or circumstances which may create doubt as to the impartiality of the Mediator, have been disclosed to the Parties in writing. The Mediator shall immediately disclose any said interests, relationships or circumstances that become apparent hereafter.

5. The Mediator shall be entitled to conduct the mediation process at his/her discretion, including the structure of the process, the attendance of the participants, the agreeing of a timetable for the exchange of any relevant information or documentation, and the scheduling and re-scheduling of meetings with the Parties, both before and during the mediation, whether in private caucus or with the Parties jointly.

B. Representation

6. The Parties may choose to be represented or to remain unrepresented at the mediation and the legal advisors to the parties shall be entitled to participate in the mediation, save that:

   i) the manner and extent of their participation shall remain at the discretion of the Mediator insofar as such the participation may be appropriate or beneficial or otherwise conducive to the success of the mediation process, and

   ii) the Parties shall remain free at all times to consult with their legal advisors.

7. The Parties and/or their representatives hereby confirm that they have the full authority to settle the dispute.

C. Confidentiality

8. The entire mediation process shall be confidential and conducted upon and without prejudice basis. All offers, promises, statements, whether oral or in writing, in the course of the mediation shall not be disclosed to third parties and shall remain privileged and confidential, save that:

   i) any disclosure may be made that is or may be necessary for the implementation of any agreement reached in the mediation;
   ii) any evidence that would otherwise be admissible or disclosable shall not be rendered inadmissible or not disclosable by reason only of its use in the mediation;
   iii) where any information is given or received which relates or gives rise to a material risk of harm, injury or other risk to safety, the duty of the confidentiality shall terminate, save where appropriate as the Mediator shall seek the prior agreement from the Parties as to the manner and extent of any disclosure to be made; and
   iv) the Mediator's obligation of confidentiality shall cease if the Mediator is under any overriding obligation by law or by other public policy considerations to make disclosures, or may be subject to criminal proceedings if the disclosure is not made.

9. At the conclusion of the mediation, at the request of any of the Parties, any written materials or documentation furnished to the Mediator or to another party shall be returned without the Mediator or the Parties retaining a copy thereof.
10. There shall be no stenographic, audio or visual record made or kept of the mediation process without written agreement of the Mediator and all the Parties.

D. Termination:

11. The Mediation process may be terminated when:

    i) the Parties and the Mediator are in agreement that the mediation has been unsuccessful; or

    ii)   the Mediator is of the view that further steps in the mediation process are unlikely to achieve a settlement; or

    iii) one party withdraws from the mediation; or

    iv) the Mediator decides in their absolute discretion that he or she should withdraw from or terminate the mediation for any reason, and in which event the Mediator will be under no obligation to give any explanation for so withdrawing or terminating.

E. Settlement:

12. If agreement is reached between the parties, or if any issues are resolved, the parties or their representatives will execute Heads of Agreement for signature by or on behalf of all the parties to the agreement.

13. The agreement shall not be binding until it has been reduced to writing and signed by or on behalf of all the Parties to the agreement.

F. Fees and Costs:

14. All fees for professional services of the Mediators shall be borne by the Parties equally, unless otherwise agreed in writing.

15. The Mediators' joint fee for said mediation shall be £ ... per mediation, including pre-mediation phone calls and writing of the agreement if appropriate. In addition, the parties will pay any standard class travel required by the mediators and the venue costs as agreed prior to the mediation day.

16. This is to be paid in two instalments – 50% (£ ...) is due on the agreement to mediate as evidenced by the signing of this agreement. This is not refundable. The remaining 50% (£ ...) of the full amount shall be payable by the Parties at least 48 hours prior to the date of the mediation.

G. Interpretation

17. The term 'Mediator' shall include the masculine and the feminine, and the plural as well as the singular where the context permits.

18. The agreement shall be governed by English law and construed and applied in accordance with the rules and jurisdiction of the English courts.

DATED: the _____ day of _____ 2020

SIGNED: _____Party A
SIGNED: _____Party B
SIGNED: _____Party C
SIGNED: _____Party D

SIGNED: _____by the Co-Mediator
SIGNED: _____by the Co-Mediator

Glossary

Glossary of legal terms likely to be encountered by a mediator

Acknowledgement of Service   Formal document used by defendants to acknowledge receipt (service) of Claim Form from claimant.

Action   Term applied to all proceedings brought in the High Ancillary Relief Additional monetary claims attached to a divorce judicial separation, or nullity petition.

ADR   Alternative Dispute Resolution.

ATE   'After The Event' insurance, to cover legal and other costs/ expenses of bringing or defending a claim.

Brief   Instructions sent by a solicitor to a barrister (counsel) to attend at a court hearing, usually including brief outline of the case.

'Cab-Rank' Rule   Rule applied by the Barrister's Code of Conduct, which obliges a barrister to accept any brief, or instructions from a solicitor and prohibits refusal other than on specific professional grounds.

Case Management   Introduced by the CPR whereby the court takes an active role in monitoring the progress of an action.

Caveat   Notice given to registrar to prevent action by another party without prior notification.

CMC   Case Management Conference – a hearing conducted by the judge to monitor the progress of an action.

Chancery Division (Ch.D)   One of the three parts or 'divisions' of the High Court, dealing mainly with specialist civil work such as companies, patents, and probate.

Chancery Guide   'Rules' providing additional practical information and guidance on procedures in the Chancery Division.

Charging Order   Court Order, imposing a charge upon the property of a judgement debtor, in favour of a judgement creditor.

CPR Civil Procedure Rules – introduced under the 'Woolf Reforms' in 1998 – rules governing all civil procedure.

Claim Form Formal document initiating proceedings.

Committal Committal to prison for breach of a court order.

CFA Conditional Fee Agreement – agreement whereby fees will not be paid in full or in part if the case is lost, but may be paid with an uplift if the case is won.

Court of Protection Court set up to protect and administer the property and affairs of persons incapable of dealing with their own affairs as a result of mental disorder.

Defamation Includes libel – the publication of written defamatory words, and slander – spoken defamatory words.

Default Judgement Judgement awarded in the absence of the filing of a formal defence.

Detailed Assessment (of Costs) Detailed assessment of costs, where the bill of costs is subjected to the scrutiny of the court.

Directions Court orders prescribing the future conduct of an action.

Disbursements Payments which a solicitor is obliged to make, irrespective of whether they have been kept in funds.

Discontinuance Withdrawal by one party of the entire claim, rendering them liable to the whole of the costs of the other party.

Disclosure Stage in an action where parties are obliged to disclose all relevant documents upon which they seek to rely.

Disposal Hearing Short hearing (usually 30 mins) without oral evidence to decide the amount payable, if any, under a judgement.

Distraint Right (usually of landlord) under court order to seize goods for non-payment (usually of rent).

District Judge Lowest 'rank' of civil judge.

ECJ European Court of Justice.

EAT Employment Appeal Tribunal.

Fast Track 'Track' allocated for cases with a financial limit of £15,000 and likely to last for no longer than one day.

Filing Lodging papers or documents with the court.

Freezing Order An 'interim remedy' whereby assets, including property and monies in bank accounts, are 'frozen' or preserved Garnishee Order (now known as a 'Third Party Debt Order') – if A has a judgement against B, and C owes money to B, A can obtain an order directly against C to pay A the debt.

HRA Human Rights Act 1998.

IVA Individual Voluntary Arrangement – an agreement between debtor and creditor for the payment and discharge of all or part of the debt.

Injunction Court order requiring a party to do or to refrain from doing a particular act.

Interim Payment A payment on account of any damages or debt that a party is likely to have to pay.

Interlocutory Proceedings Steps taken in proceedings after the commencement of an action and before final judgement.

Interpleader A party (usually a stakeholder e.g. an estate agent or solicitor) who faces competing claims for property from two or more persons, can bring an action for the court to decide the rival claims.

Irregular Judgement Judgement wrongly entered, and required to be set aside.

Joint Expert Single expert appointed and instructed jointly by both claimant and defendant.

Joint and Several Liability Where two or more persons enter into an obligation and each shares a single liability for the whole amount (joint), whilst at the same time each is separately liable for the full amount (several).

Judicial Review Procedure for appealing or reviewing the decision of a public body, court, or tribunal, or the decision of any person or body performing a public duty or function.

Letters of Administration Authority from Probate Registry allowing a personal representative to administer the deceased's estate.

Lien The right (usually of a solicitor) to retain all property of a client or customer until costs or fees are paid.

Limitation Period The time limit within which a claim must be brought.

Liquidated Damages The fixed amount agreed between the parties to be paid as compensation in the event of a breach of contract.

Listing Allocating and giving a date and time for a case hearing.

Listing Questionnaire (Now 'Pre Trial Check List') – Court document sent to parties to ascertain whether case management directions have been complied with, and to set a trial date.

Litigation Friend Person appointed by the court or authorised to act on behalf of a child or 'patient'.

LSC Legal Services Commission – the body authorised to provide Legal Aid or funding to assist litigants.

Mareva Injunction See Freezing Order.

Master Lowest rank of 'judge' in the High Court.

Multi-Track 'Track' allocated for all cases with a financial limit of over £15,000 or are likely to last for longer than one day, or where there is more than one expert for each party.

Negotiable Instrument A document or paper (e.g. cheque, banknote) giving the holder a right to enforce the contract contained within it.

Official Receiver   Person or officer appointed to act as manager and 'receiver' of a bankrupt's estate and property.

Ogden Tables   Actuarial Tables for use in personal injury and fatal accident cases for calculating projected loss.

Overriding Objective   The first and foremost of the general principles of the CPR, whereby the court is obliged to deal justly, fairly, proportionately and expeditiously with all cases.

Part A   Section or chapter of the CPR e.g. Part 8 (below).

Part 8 Claims   Part 8 of the CPR (q.v.) provides rules for an alternative procedure for commencing proceedings, usually cases where a decision of the court is required on a question unlikely to involve a substantial issue of fact.

Part 20 Claims   Part 20 of the CPR governing counterclaims and claims against further parties not already party to the proceedings.

Part 36 Offers   Part 36 of the CPR whereby claimants and defendants are permitted to make formal open offers to settle the claim. If recipients of an offer reject it, they can be penalised in costs and interest if they subsequently fail to achieve a better result at trial.

Particulars of Claim   A formal document served by the claimant upon the defendant in which full details of the claim are set out.

Patients   Persons deemed incapable of managing their own affairs as a result of mental disorder, who thereby do not have capacity themselves to bring or defend a claim.

Payment into Court   Payment made into court to settle claims, with similar characteristics and consequences as a Part 36 Offer.

Personal Representatives   Either executors (those dealing with a deceased's will) or administrators (those dealing with the estate of a person who died without a will or without an executor).

Practice Direction   A set of 'rules' which supplement, explain, amplify, and complement the relevant 'Parts' of the CPR.

Practice Master   Master available daily to answer procedural questions on the practice of the QBD.

Pre Action Protocols   Set of 'rules' outlining the steps parties are expected to take prior to the issue of proceedings.

Pre Trial Review   A hearing to decide how the case is to be tried, the nature and extent of the evidence to be heard and to review any outstanding procedural matters.

Privilege   A right claimed (usually by lawyers on behalf of clients) to prevent disclosure of (usually confidential) information, or documents or other communications.

Proportionality   Concept introduced by the CPR whereby cases must be dealt with in a way 'proportionate to the value, importance and complexity of the case, and the financial position of the parties'.

Provisional Damages An award of damages where the claimant proves that they are likely in the future to suffer a deterioration of a physical or mental condition caused by the defendant, giving the right to seek a further award of damages.

Quantum The monetary value of a claim.

Queen's Bench Division (QBD) One of the three parts or 'divisions' of the High Court dealing with general civil matters other than those dealt with in the Chancery Division.

Relief against Forfeiture Where a breach of covenant in a lease would entitle the lessor to terminate (forfeit) the lease, the lessee may apply to the court for 'relief' – i.e. permission to retain the lease and possession of the property providing the breach is rectified or compensation is paid.

Reserved Judgement Judgement by the court after taking time to consider.

SCCO Supreme Court Costs Office.

Security for Costs A guarantee or 'security' provided by a claimant to 'guarantee' payment of the costs if unsuccessful.

Sequestration Means of enforcing a judgement/order whereby property is seized and kept pending payment or compliance.

Service Procedure for bringing documents to a party's attention.

Skeleton Skeleton Argument: written summary of legal submissions to be made to the Court.

Small Claims Track 'Track' allocated for cases with a financial limit of under £5,000, or £1,000 in Personal injury cases.

SIF Solicitors Indemnity Fund Ltd (Solicitors' 'insurers').

Split Trial Where issues of liability and quantum are dealt with separately, usually on separate occasions.

Specific Performance Where a party is compelled to perform their side of the bargain, which they specifically contracted to perform.

Standard Disclosure The obligation to disclose all relevant documents including those documents which adversely affect the case or support the opposing party's case.

Standard of Proof The degree of proof required: in civil cases it is 'on the balance of probabilities' and in criminal cases 'satisfied so as to be sure' (sometimes referred to as 'beyond reasonable doubt').

Statement of Case Formerly referred to as 'the Pleadings', the formal documents in proceedings including the Particulars of Claim, Defence, Reply, and Further Information.

Stay Suspension of proceedings, usually whilst or until a party performs a duty or complies with an order to do something, e.g. a stay pending ADR.

Structured Settlement   Means of paying damages by instalments for the rest of the claimant's life, agreed between the parties, and usually funded by some form of annuity.

Summary Assessment of costs   Assessment and award of costs carried out by the Judge immediately at the end of a trial or hearing (cf. Detailed Assessment).

Summary Judgement   Judgement delivered by the court when satisfied that there is no real prospect of a successful defence.

Taxation (of Costs)   (Now known as 'assessment' of costs): see Detailed and Summary Assessment.

Third Party Proceedings   (Now known as 'Part 20 proceedings'.)

Tomlin Order   Form of court order where proceedings are stayed (q. v.) upon terms specified in a Schedule to the Order.

Tort/Tortfeasor   A civil wrong giving rise to an action for damages; person who commits a tort.

Trial Bundles   'Bundles' of documents (usually lever arch files) prepared and paginated by the Claimant's lawyers for use by the Judge and all parties at trial.

Undertaking   Binding promise given to a solicitor or to the court, having the same effect as a court order.

Unless Order   Court order threatening a particular consequence if the order is not complied with.

Waiver   Abandonment or renunciation of a claim or a benefit to which a party would otherwise be entitled.

Wasted Costs Order   Order compelling a legal representative to meet the whole or part of any costs deemed as wasted.

Without Prejudice   'Without any adverse consequence' – i.e. cannot be cannot be used against a party at any later stage or in court.

Glossary for case studies

ADHD   Attention deficit hyperactivity disorder (ADHD) is a group of behavioural symptoms that include inattentiveness, hyperactivity, and impulsiveness.

Common symptoms of ADHD include: a short attention span or being easily distracted; restlessness, constant fidgeting, or over-activity; being impulsive.

ADHD can occur in people of any intellectual ability, although it is more common in people with learning difficulties. People with ADHD may also have additional problems, such as sleep and anxiety disorders.

Symptoms of ADHD tend to be first noticed at an early age, and may become more noticeable when a child's circumstances change, such as when they start school. Most cases are diagnosed in children between the ages of six and 12.

EAP (Employee Assistance Programmes) These are employee benefit programmes offered by many employers, which are intended to help employees deal with personal problems that might adversely impact their work performance, health, and well-being. Until recently their main offering has been counselling but some are now broadening their services to offer mediation.

Existentialism A philosophical theory or approach which emphasises the existence of the individual person as a free and responsible agent, determining their own development through acts of the will.

Gillick competency and Fraser guidelines Gillick competency and Fraser guidelines refer to a legal case which looked specifically at whether doctors should be able to give contraceptive advice or treatment to under 16-year-olds without parental consent. But since then, they have been more widely used to help assess whether a child has the maturity to make their own decisions and to understand the implications of those decisions. The case went to the High Court where Mr Justice Woolf dismissed Mrs Gillick's claims. The Court of Appeal reversed this decision, but in 1985 it went to the House of Lords and the Law Lords (Lord Scarman, Lord Fraser and Lord Bridge) ruled in favour of the original judgement delivered by Mr Justice Woolf:

... whether or not a child is capable of giving the necessary consent will depend on the child's maturity and understanding and the nature of the consent required. The child must be capable of making a reasonable assessment of the advantages and disadvantages of the treatment proposed, so the consent, if given, can be properly and fairly described as true consent.

Lord Scarman's comments in his judgement of the Gillick case in the House of Lords (1985) are often referred to as the test of 'Gillick competency':

... it is not enough that she should understand the nature of the advice which is being given: she must also have a sufficient maturity to understand what is involved.

He also commented more generally on parents' versus children's rights:

Parental right yields to the child's right to make his own decisions when he reaches a sufficient understanding and intelligence to be capable of making up his own mind on the matter requiring decision.

OFSTED   Ofsted is the Office for Standards in Education, Children's Services and Skills. It reports directly to Parliament and is deemed to be independent and impartial. It inspects and regulates services which care for children and young people, and those providing education and skills for learners of all ages.

PC/Politically Correct   Behaving in a way which conforms to a belief that language and practices which could offend political sensibilities (as in matters of sex or race) should be eliminated.

Phenomenology   The science of phenomena, as distinct from that of the nature of being. It is an approach that concentrates on the study of consciousness and the objects of direct experience. It calls for truthfulness and authenticity.

Restorative Justice (RJ)   Restorative processes bring those harmed by crime or conflict, and those responsible for the harm, into communication, enabling everyone affected by a particular incident to play a part in repairing the harm and finding a positive way forward. In criminal justice, restorative processes give victims the chance to tell offenders the real impact of their crime, to get answers to their questions, and an apology. Restorative justice holds offenders to account for what they have done, helps them understand the real impact of their actions, to take responsibility and make amends.

Special Measures   The Education Act 2005 states that a school requires special measures if it is failing to give its pupils an acceptable standard of education, and the persons responsible for leading, managing or governing the school are not demonstrating the capacity to secure the necessary improvement in the schools.

TAs   Teaching Assistants who support qualified teachers in and out of the classroom. They often provide support for pupils with special needs. Schools differ in the qualifications that they require for TAs. Training programmes are available offering Level 2 Award in Support Work in Schools and Level 3 Award in Supporting Teaching and Learning in Schools.

Salaries for full-time teaching assistants range from £12,000 to over £17,000 a year. Salaries for full-time HLTAs can be between £16,000 and £21,000 a year. This will vary depending on the Local Education Authority (LEA) and the responsibilities of individual jobs.

There is no national pay scale and wage rates are set by each LEA. Teaching assistants who work part-time, or are paid only for term-time, earn a proportion of full-time rates. This is known as pro rata payment.

Bibliography

ADR and Civil Justice. (2018, November), *CJC ADR Working Party Final Report*. www.judiciary.uk/wp-content/uploads/2018/12/CJC-ADRWG-Report-FINAL-Dec-2018.pdf (accessed 25 Jan 2020).

Altman, N. (2003), How White People Suffer from White Racism. *Psychotherapy & Politics International*, 1(2): 93–106.

Arts, H., & Ashdown, K. (2015), *Conflict Resolution for Musicians (And Other Cool People)*. Markham, ON: Fifth House Group.

Atwood, G. E., & Stolorow, R. D. (2016), Walking the Tightrope of Emotional Dwelling. *Psychoanalytic Dialogues*, 26(1): 103–108.

Bandura, A. (1977), *Social Learning Theory*. Upper Saddle River, NJ: Prentice Hall.

Baruch, R. A., Bush, B., & Folger, J. P. (1994), *The Promise of Mediation*. San Francisco, CA: Jossey-Bass.

Burton, J. (1990), *Conflict: Resolution and Prevention*. London: St Martin's Press.

Cobb, S. (1994), A Narrative Perspective on Mediation: Toward the Materialization of the Storytelling Metaphor. In J. P. Folger & T. S. Jones (Eds.), *New Directions in Mediation: Communication Research and Perspectives* (pp. 50–51). Thousand Oaks, CA: Sage Publications.

Conlon, D. E., & Jehn, K. A. (2010), Behind the Music: Conflict, Performance, Longevity, and Turnover in Punk and New Wave Rock Bands: Organizational Behavior, Performance and Effectiveness. In *Current Topics in Management* (Vol. 14, pp. 13–48).

Costantino, C. A., & Merchant, C. S. (1996), *Designing Conflict Management Systems: A Guide to Creating Productive and Healthy Organizations*. San Francisco, CA: Jossey-Bass.

de Beauvoir, S. (1947), *The Ethics of Ambiguity*. New York: Philosophical Library.

Deutsch, M. (1973), *The Resolution of Conflict: Constructive and Destructive Processes*. New Haven, CT: Yale University Press.

Deutsch, M., & Coleman, P. (Eds.). (2000), *The Handbook of Conflict Resolution: Theory and Practice*. San Francisco, CA: Jossey-Bass Publishers.

Fanon, F. (1986), *Black Skin, White Masks*. London: Pluto Press.

Feldman, M. W. (2002), *People from Distant Lands Have Strikingly Similar Genetic Traits*. www.sciencedaily.com/releases/2002/12/021220080005.htm.

Ferguson, H. (2002), In Search of Bandhood: Consultation with Original Music Groups. *Group: The Journal of the Eastern Group Psychotherapy Society*, 26(4): 267–282.

Foster-Harris, W. (1981), *Basic Patterns of Plot*. Norman, OK: University of Oklahoma Press.

Freud, S. (1909), Analysis of a Phobia of a Five Year Old Boy. In *Pelican Freud Library's Case Histories 1 'Dora' and 'Little Hans'* (pp. 149–287). London: Penguin Group.

Freud, S. (1930), *Civilisation and Its Discontents*. Penguin Freud Library. London: Penguin, 1985.

Glasl, F. (1999), *Confronting Conflict*. Bristol: Hawthorn Press.

Groce, S. B. (1989), Occupational Rhetoric and Ideology: A Comparison of Copy and Original Music Performers. *Qualitative Sociology*, 12(4): 391–410.

Groce, S. B., & Dowell, J. A. (1988), A Comparison of Group Structures and Processes in Two Local Level Rock N' Roll Bands. *Popular Music and Society*, 12(2): 21–35.

Hanaway, M. (2012), *Co-Mediation: Using a Psychological Paired Approach to Resolving Conflict* (1st ed.). Oxford: The CH Group.

Hanaway, M. (2014), *Tales of Conflict and the Role of Mediation*. Henley-on-Thames: The CH Group.

Hanaway, M. (2020), *An Existential Approach to Leadership Challenges*. Abingdon: Routledge.

Heidegger, M. (1962), *Being and Time*. Oxford: Blackwell Publishing.

Heraclitus. (2003), *Fragments*. London: Penguin Books.

Hicks, T. (1996–2000), *Seven Steps for Effective Problem-Solving in the Workplace*. www.conflict-resolution.net/articles/index.cfm edn.

Husserl, E. (1913), *Ideas Pertaining to a Pure Phenomenology and to a Phenomenological Philosophy – First Book: General Introduction to a Pure Phenomenology*, trans. F. Kersten. The Hague: Nijhoff, 1982.

Imperati, S. J. (1997), Mediator Practice Models: The Intersection of Ethics and Stylistic Practices in Mediation. *706 Willamette Law Review*, 33: 3.

Jensen-Campbell, L. A., Graziano, W. G., & Hair, E. C. (1996), Personality and Relationships as Moderators of Interpersonal Conflict in Adolescence. *Merrill-Palmer Quarterly*, 42: 148–164.

Kovel, J. (1995), On Racism and Psychoanalysis. In A. Elliot & S. Frosch (Eds.), *Psychoanalysis in Contexts* (pp. 205–223). London: Routledge.

Kramer, M., & Yahn, S. (2010), *And the Band Broke Up*. Los Gatos, CA: Smashwords.

Marshall, T. (1999), *Restorative Justice: An Overview*. London: Home Office.

McKimm-Vorderwinkler, J. (2014), Co-Mediation in Cross-Cultural Settings. In M. Hanaway (Ed.), *Co-Mediation: Using a Psychological Paired Approach to Resolving Conflict* (2nd ed., pp. 160–177). Oxford: The CH Group.

Mindell, A. (1995), *Sitting in the Fire: Large Group Transformation Using Conflict and Diversity*. San Francisco, CA: Harper Collins.

Mischel, W. (1993), *Introduction to Personality* (5th ed.). Fort Worth, TX: Harcourt Brace Jovanovich.

Mitchell, D. (2014), Is Co-Mediation Better for Parties and Mediators? In M. Hanaway (Ed.), *Co-Mediation: Using a Psychological Paired Approach to Resolving Conflict* (2nd ed., pp. 63–69). Oxford: The CH Group.

Monk, G. (1996), Guidance and Counseling. *Narrative Approaches to Therapy: The "Fourth Wave" in Family Therapy*, 11: 41–47. [On-Line] Abstract taken from Wilson Web Journal Database (1–10).

Morris, A. (2002), Critiquing the Critics: A Brief Response to Critics of Restorative Justice. *British Journal of Criminology*, 42(3): 596–615.

Murnighan, J. K., & Conlon, D. (1991), The Dynamics of Intense Work Groups: A Study of British String Quartets. *Administrative Science Quarterly*, 36: 165–186.

Newmark, C., & Monaghan, A. (2005), *Butterworth's Mediators in Mediation: Leading Mediator Perspectives on the Practice of Commercial Mediation*. Haywards Heath: Tottel Publishing.

O'Kennedy, M. L., & O'Hehir, P. (2012), Co-mediating with an Established Partner. In M. Hanaway (Ed.), *Co-Mediation: Using a Psychological Paired Approach to Resolving Conflict* (1st ed., pp. 128–147). Oxford: The CH Group.

Rand, A. (2000), *The Art of Fiction: A Guide for Writers and Readers*. London: Penguin.

Randolph, P. (2013, January), Compulsory Mediation, www.mediate.com/art icles/RandolphP1.cfm (accessed 25 Jan 2020).

Randolph, P. (2016), *The Psychology of Conflict*. London: Bloomsbury.

Reich, W. (1967), *Reich Speaks of Freud*. London: Condor.

Reich, W. (1973), *The Discovery of the Orgone* (Vol. 1). New York: Farrar, Straus and Giroux.

Riskin, L. L. (1994, September 1), Mediator Orientations, Strategies and Techniques. *Alternatives to the High Cost of Litigation*, 12: 111. SSRN: https://ssrn. com/abstract=1506704.

Rummel, R. J. (1970), *Understanding Conflict and War* (Vols. 1–4). Beverly Hills, CA: Sage Publications, 1975–1979.

Samuels, A. (1993), *The Political Psyche*. London: Routledge.

Sartre, J. P. (1958), *Being and Nothingness: An Essay in Phenomenological Ontology*, trans. H. Barnes. London: Routledge.

Sartre, J. P. (1962), *Sketch for a Theory of Emotions*. London: Routledge.

Scheff, T., & Retzinger, S. (1991), *Emotions and Violence*. Lexington, MA: Lexington.

Sgubini, A. (2006), *Mediation and Culture: How Different Cultural Backgrounds Can Affect the Way People Negotiate and Resolve Disputes*. www.mediate.com/articles/sugbini March 2006.

Shantz, C. U. (1987), Conflicts between Children. *Child Development*, 58: 283–305.

Strasser, F., & Randolph, P. (2004), *Mediation – A Psychological Insight into Conflict Resolution*. London: Continuum.

Sun Tzu. (2009), *The Art of War*. London: Pax Librorum.

Suttie, I. (1936), *The Origins of Love and Hate*. Harmondsworth: Penguin.

Tantam, D. (2002), *Psychotherapy and Counselling in Practice – A Narrative Framework*. Cambridge: Cambridge University Press.

Taylor, A. (2002), *The Handbook of Family Dispute Resolution: Mediation Theory and Practice*. San Francisco, CA: Jossey-Bass.

Thomas, R. (2011), *Precarious Colloborations: A Study of Interpersonal Conflict and Resolution Strategies in Local Rock Bands*. Lincoln, NE: University of Nebraska–Lincoln.

Totton, N. (2006), *The Politics of Psychotherapy*. Maidenhead: Open University Press.

van Deurzen-Smith, E. (1984) Existential Therapy. In Dryden, W. (Ed.) *Individual Therapy in Britain* (pp. 152–172). London: Harper and Row.

Vuchinich, S. (1990), The Sequential Organization of Closing in Verbal Family Conflict. In A. D. Grimshaw (Ed.), *Conflict Talk: Sociolinguistic Investigations of Arguments in Conversations* (pp. 118–138). New York: Cambridge Univ. Press.

Weixel-Dixon, K. (2016), *An Existential Psychotherapeutic and Practical Model*. Abingdon: Routledge.

White, M., & Epston, D. (1989), *Literate Means to Therapeutic Ends*. Adelaide: Dulwich Centre Publications.

White, M., & Epston, D. (1992), *Experience, Contradiction, Narrative and Imagination: Selected Papers of David Epston & Michael White, 1989–1991*. Adelaide, South Australia: Dulwich Centre Publications.

Winslade, J., & Monk, G. (2001), *Narrative Mediation*. San Francisco, CA: Jossey-Bass.

Yarn, D. H. (Ed.). (1999), *Dictionary of Conflict Resolution*. San Francisco, CA: Jossey-Bass.

YJB (Youth Justice Board for England and Wales). (2004), *National Evaluation of the Restorative Justice in Schools Programme*.

Zizek, S. (1989), *The Sublime Object of Ideology*. London: Verso.

Zizek, S. (1993), *Tarrying with the Negative: Kant, Hegel and the Critique of Ideology*. Durham, NC: Duke University Press.

Index

actions 102–103
active listening 56, 84
affairs 70, 73–74, 152, 153–154, 160
aggression 4–5, 66, 103–104, 119, 129
Altman, N. 101
ambivalence 56, 59, 60, 104
anger 53, 54; family mediation
    84–87, 215, 218–219; workplace
    mediation 97, 98, 119,
    184, 187, 188
anxiety: dissolution of self 124;
    emotions 53; existential approach
    43, 50, 51, 121; meaning 49;
    workplace mediation 127, 129,
    193, 196
apologies 184, 188–189, 204
Arb-Med 16–17
archetypes 99, 103
assistants 27, 39
assumptions 59, 65; bracketing 50, 54,
    105; marital mediation 156;
    workplace mediation 106
attitudes 8, 41
Atwood, G. E. 15
authenticity 34, 42, 45–46, 50, 61, 129
awards 16–17

band conflict 131–147
Baruch, R. A. 15, 42
behaviour change 33
beliefs 4, 41, 47–48, 49, 55, 222;
    bracketing 58; child access
    mediation 171, 173; emotions 52;
    existential approach 42, 121;
    mediator's own 31; rigid 43; spiritual

dimension 124; tuning in 122;
    workplace mediation 106
bias 35
body language 58
bracketing 50, 54, 58, 65, 105
breaks 29, 34
bullying 180, 191, 195, 197, 200–201,
    203, 222
Burton, J. 4
Bush, B. 15, 42
business mediation 206–219

'catastrophic what if' challenge 60
caucuses 25, 37
Centre of Effective Dispute Resolution
    (CEDR) 9
challenging 59–60
change 106, 199
child access 161–177
choice 6, 51, 59–60
Civil Justice Council (CJC) 13
Civil Procedure Rules 13–14
class 98, 123
co-mediation 27–39, 223; advantages
    of 28–35; de-briefing 67; definition
    of 27; tensions and challenges
    35–39
coaching 116, 120
coalitions 103
Cobb, S. 18
collaboration 9–10, 30–31, 32, 44
commonalities 32, 43, 44, 55; band
    conflict 140, 146–147; workplace
    mediation 97, 106, 107, 117,
    129, 187

communication: authentic 45–46; band
conflict 141; co-mediation 38; family
mediation 218; meaning 49;
modelling 32; pre-mediation 21;
transformative mediation 15;
unconscious 57; workplace
mediation 119
compromise 97, 99
compulsory mediation 13–14
confidentiality 9, 23, 186; co-mediation
29, 37; e-mediation 17; family
mediation 85; pre-mediation
21, 28, 85; sample pre-mediation
contract 226; workplace
mediation 90
conflict: authenticity 45–46; band
131–147; co-mediation 28;
definitions of 3–4; emotions 7,
51–54; existential approach 43;
freedom and responsibility 51;
meaning 49; as part of human
nature 5; plots 6–7; psychological
nature of 40, 42–43; realistic conflict
theory 99; relatedness 43–45; steps
to resolution 97; time and
temporality 46–47; uncertainty
49–51; values and beliefs 47–48
connectedness 31–32, 37, 107
continuing professional development
35, 127, 223
contracts 22, 28, 46, 224–228
coping strategies 55, 58–59, 122
Costantino, C. A. 4
costs 13–14, 33–34, 39, 227
court-mandated mediation 13–14
criticism 36, 142, 216
culture 31; otherness 98; power
dynamics 45; school based work
mediation 198; shame 105

de Beauvoir, Simone 45
de-briefing 34, 35, 67
debate 102
depression 80, 82, 138, 144, 172,
193, 221
diamond of divergence 25
difference 32, 33, 44, 98, 146–147; *see
also* otherness
dignity 7
disputes 4

divorce 155, 160
Dowell, J. A. 141

e-mediation 17
ego 33, 38–39, 140
Eigenwelt 123–124, 126
emotional dwelling 15
emotional support 30
emotions 5–6, 7, 40, 43, 51–54, 66;
band conflict 141; bracketing 58;
centrality of 222; co-mediation 29;
existential approach 121; family
mediation 215; lawyers 10; marital
mediation 154–155, 156, 158;
values and beliefs 48, 52, 122;
workplace mediation 104, 106,
107, 187
empathy 65; band conflict 140;
transformative mediation 15;
workplace mediation 97–98, 101
Employee Assistance Programmes
(EAPs) 67
empowerment 12, 15, 19, 41–42, 60
energy 29, 34
Epston, David 17
evaluative mediation 12, 14–15, 42
existential approach 41, 42–43, 62,
121–122; authenticity 45; band
conflict 146; emotions 51; freedom
and responsibility 51, 103; narrative
mediation 18; relatedness 43–44, 61;
time and temporality 46; tuning out
59; uncertainty 50, 51
expectations 146

face 103–104
facilitative mediation 12–13, 41–42
facts 7–8, 40, 41, 47, 50, 122
fairness 14, 42, 105; band conflict 140;
workplace mediation 97, 126,
127, 187
family background: band conflict 132,
136–137, 143, 144; child access
mediation 163, 166; family business
mediation 207–208
family mediation: business mediation
206–219; child access 161–177;
mother-daughters relationship 68–88
Fanon, F. 98–99, 103
fees 33–34, 39, 227

Feldman, Marcus 32
Folger, J. P. 15, 42
forgiveness 83–84, 105
Foster-Harris, W. 6
Fraser Guidelines 171
free will 6
freedom 51, 127–128
Freud, Sigmund 5, 15, 57
funnel model 55–56

gangs 104
gender 6–7, 11; coalitions 103;
    otherness 98; power dynamics 45;
    workplace mediation 105, 106
Gillick Competency 171
Glasl, Friedrich 102–103, 104
goals 146, 187
Graziano, W. G. 99
Groce, S. B. 141
group mediation 141
guilt 80, 81, 84, 153

Hair, E. C. 99
Hanaway, M. 41
hardening 102
Harvard model 22, 24–25, 30, 37,
    85, 185
hate 5, 123
Heraclitus 57
Hicks, T. 106
hierarchy 143
humiliation 97
Husserl, E. 57

identity 4, 43, 99; band conflict 143;
    marital mediation 156; psychological
    dimension 123, 124; workplace
    mediation 118, 126
images 103
impartiality 35, 37, 105, 225
Imperati, S. J. 42
industrial disputes 22
intentionality 52, 57–58, 122

Jensen-Campbell, L. A. 99
joint sessions 22–23, 26; co-mediation
    29, 38; family mediation 85, 87,
    216–217, 218; school based work
    mediation 202–203; workplace
    mediation 185–186, 188

Jung, Carl 99
justice 105, 117–118

Klein, Melanie 5
Kovel, J. 101

language: existential approach 42;
    power dynamics 45; workplace
    mediation 98, 106
lawyers 10, 14, 220–221
leadership 141, 143
'likeness' 31
listening 44–45; active 56, 84;
    authentic 46; band conflict 144, 147;
    co-mediation 32; empathic 15;
    existential approach 121; family
    mediation 216; non-judgemental 66;
    pre-mediation 21–22; respectful
    21–22, 60, 62; tuning in 57–58;
    workplace mediation 117
litigation 10, 13–14, 220–222
logic 7, 40, 222
love 5, 123, 150, 157
loyalty 116, 117, 126, 127

manipulation 37, 46
marital discord 183–184, 186–187,
    188–189
marital mediation 148–160
Marshall, T. 19
masculinity 105
meaning 42, 49, 50, 124
Med-Arb 16
mediation: business mediation
    206–219; child access 161–177;
    co-mediation 27–39; competition
    and challenge 108–130; concept of
    9–11; emotions 222; fear and
    difference 89–107; finding work
    66–67, 222–223; funnel model
    55–56; litigation compared with
    220; marital 148–160; meaningful
    resolution 8; mother-daughters
    relationship 68–88; musical
    131–147; process of 21–26;
    school based 190–205; styles
    12–20; tuning in 55, 56, 57–59;
    tuning out 55, 56, 59–62; youth
    workers 178–189
mediation panels 67, 222–223

244   *Index*

Merchant, C. S. 4
Mindell, A. 5, 45
'miraculous what if' challenge 60–61
Mitchell, D. 34
Mitwelt 123, 125–126
modelling 32–33
Morris, A. 19
musical mediation 131–147

narrative mediation 17–19
nature 6
negotiation 104
neutrality 27, 34, 61, 65
noema and noesis 57–58, 122
non-verbal skills 32, 56

online dispute resolution (ODR) 17
opening statements 22–23, 24
oppression 18
otherness 32, 44, 52; band conflict 147;
    workplace mediation 98, 104, 105;
    see also difference

panels 67, 222–223
panic attacks 193–194, 195, 196, 197,
    199–200, 203–204
parenting 161–177
perception 3, 8, 40–41
phenomenological approach 18, 41,
    50, 52, 57–58, 62
Phillips, Lord 13
philosophy 41
physical dimension (Umwelt) 122, 123,
    124–125
polemics 102
power dynamics 23, 36, 45, 105–106
powerlessness 61
pre-mediation 21–22; co-mediation 28,
    37; family mediation 84–85; sample
    contract 224–228; workplace
    mediation 95–96, 106
prejudice 99
projection 30, 99, 188
projective identification 99
promotion 91, 109, 113–114, 117–118,
    127, 181, 186
psychological dimension (Eigenwelt)
    123–124, 126
punishment 84, 86, 221
purpose 50, 124, 187

race: otherness 98; power dynamics 45;
    school based work mediation 192,
    198, 201–202; social dimension 123;
    workplace mediation 91, 92–93, 95,
    98–99, 101, 103, 105–106
racial harassment 191, 200
racism 102, 103, 191, 195, 202, 203
Rand, Ayn 6
Randolph, Paul 4, 10, 13, 43, 46,
    52, 104
realistic conflict theory 99
recognition 4, 16, 43, 145, 214
Reich, W. 5
relatedness 21, 42, 43–45, 52, 61
relationality 6, 40, 223
respect 33, 118, 126, 129, 187
responsibility 41–42, 50, 51, 103;
    child access mediation 174,
    175–176; family mediation 218;
    marital mediation 152; workplace
    mediation 128
restorative justice 19, 105
Retzinger, S. 52, 104
reviews 175
Richbell, D. 27
rules 180–181, 182–183, 188
Rummel, R. J. 99

safety 11, 45, 60, 88
Samuels, A. 5
Sartre, Jean-Paul 45
Scheff, T. 52, 104
school based work mediation 190–205
security 4, 19, 43, 122
self-awareness 53
self-defence 4–5
self-esteem 4, 7, 43, 61–62, 222;
    authentic communication 46; band
    conflict 140, 141, 143, 145;
    bracketing 58; co-mediation 36;
    coping strategies 58–59; emotions
    52; litigation 221; low 66; modelling
    33; need for 8; transformative
    mediation 15; workplace mediation
    105, 116, 118
self-harm 75, 77
self-respect 19
separation 155, 159–160
sexism 102, 103
sexual harassment 94, 97, 101

Sgubini, A. 98
shame 52, 97, 104–105, 221
Shantz, C. U. 3
shuttle diplomacy 14, 30
social dimension (Mitwelt) 123,
    125–126
social media 67
spiritual dimension (Uberwelt) 123,
    124, 126–127
standoff 97, 99
status 118, 127, 144
stereotypes 95, 98–99, 101, 103,
    105, 106
Stolorow, R. D. 15
Strasser, F. 4, 43, 52, 104
stress 191, 200, 202, 203
'stuckness' 41
submission 97, 99
Sun Tzu 40
supervision 34–35
Suttie, I. 5

Tantam, D. 106
teaching assistants (TAs) 190–205
technology 17
termination of mediation 226–227
third-party intervention 97, 99
Thomas, R. 141, 142
threats 104
'thrownness' 51, 128
time/temporality 42, 46–47, 50,
    60, 121
Totton, N. 4, 5
training: mediators 36, 65, 222;
    workplace 113, 114, 116, 120, 130
transference 30
transformative mediation 12, 15–16,
    41–42
triggers 30
trust 11, 23, 61; co-mediation 33, 35,
    36; family mediation 88; funnel
    model 56; loss of 47; school
    based work mediation 200;
    tuning out 59
truth 7–8
tuning in 55, 56, 57–59, 122

tuning out 55, 56, 59–62

Uberwelt 123, 124, 126–127
Umwelt 122, 123, 124–125
uncertainty 43, 48, 49–51, 127,
    128, 129
unconscious communication 57

value for money 33–34
values 10–11, 41, 47–48, 49, 50, 222;
    band conflict 146; bracketing 58;
    child access mediation 173; co-
    mediation 36; emotions 52;
    existential approach 42, 121;
    mediator's own 65; psychological
    approach 4, 8; spiritual dimension
    124; tuning in 55, 122; workplace
    mediation 106, 117, 129, 187
verbal skills 32, 56
video-conferencing 17
Vuchinich, S. 97
vulnerability 66; band conflict 144;
    marital mediation 156, 158;
    workplace mediation 100–101, 103,
    105–106, 107, 114, 120

Weixel-Dixon, K. 44
White, Michael 17
withdrawal 97, 99
working alliance 15, 61; co-mediation
    31, 36; funnel model 55–56; tuning
    in 55; workplace mediation 106–107
workplace mediation: competition and
    challenge 108–130; fear and
    difference 89–107; school based
    190–205; youth workers 178–189
worldview: spiritual dimension 124
worldviews 4, 11, 45, 49, 55, 65;
    bracketing 58; existential approach
    42; workplace mediation 99, 100,
    106, 121
written agreements 16, 23, 29, 50, 175

Yarn, D. H. 4

Zizek, S. 101

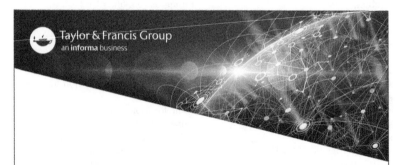

.

For Product Safety Concerns and Information please contact our EU
representative GPSR@taylorandfrancis.com Taylor & Francis Verlag GmbH,
Kaufingerstraße 24, 80331 München, Germany

Printed and bound by CPI Group (UK) Ltd, Croydon, CR0 4YY
08/06/2025
01897001-0004